CW01498128

SPIRITUAL LIVES

General Editor
Timothy Larsen

SPIRITUAL LIVES

General Editor
Timothy Larsen

The *Spiritual Lives* series features biographies of prominent men and women whose eminence is not primarily based on a specifically religious contribution. Each volume provides a general account of the figure's life and thought, while giving special attention to his or her religious contexts, convictions, doubts, objections, ideas, and actions. Many leading politicians, writers, musicians, philosophers, and scientists have engaged deeply with religion in significant and resonant ways that have often been overlooked or underexplored. Some of the volumes will even focus on men and women who were lifelong unbelievers, attending to how they navigated and resisted religious questions, assumptions, and settings. The books in this series will therefore recast important figures in fresh and thought-provoking ways.

Titles in the series include

Arthur Sullivan
A Life of Divine Emollient
Ian Bradley

Queen Victoria
This Thorny Crown
Michael Ledger-Lomas

W. T. Stead
Nonconformist and Newspaper Prophet
Stewart J. Brown

John Stuart Mill
A Secular Life
Timothy Larsen

Christina Rossetti
Poetry, Ecology, Faith
Emma Mason

Ebenezer Howard

Inventor of the Garden City

FRANCES KNIGHT

To Ian,
Happy Birthday!

Frances Knight

OXFORD
UNIVERSITY PRESS

OXFORD
UNIVERSITY PRESS

Great Clarendon Street, Oxford, OX2 6DP,
United Kingdom

Oxford University Press is a department of the University of Oxford.
It furthers the University's objective of excellence in research, scholarship,
and education by publishing worldwide. Oxford is a registered trade mark of
Oxford University Press in the UK and in certain other countries

Published in the United States of America by Oxford University Press
198 Madison Avenue, New York, NY 10016, United States of America

British Library Cataloguing in Publication Data

Data available

Library of Congress Control Number: 2022951044

ISBN 978–0–19–879081–5

DOI: 10.1093/oso/9780198790815.001.0001

Printed and bound by
CPI Group (UK) Ltd, Croydon, CR0 4YY

For David M. Thompson

Contents

Abbreviations   ix

Introduction: Ebenezer Howard – the Man and
the Message   1

1. The Early Years of Exploration 1850–1876   10
    The City childhood   10
    The minister's secretary   15
    The American adventurer   24

2. Laying the Foundations 1876–1889   33
    Early married life   33
    Spiritualism   42
    The turn to the social gospel and the housing and
    land questions   49

3. The Days before *To-morrow* 1890–1898   60
    Early drafts and speeches   60
    The Howard family in the 1890s   68
    To-morrow: A Peaceful Path to Real Reform   71

4. The Path to the First Garden City 1899–1904   80
    The Garden City Association   80
    The final years of Lizzie Howard   94
    Opening the Letchworth estate   101

5. Howard in Letchworth 1905–1914   109
    Moving to the Garden City   109
    Building Letchworth   113
    Cooperative housekeeping   123
    The growing industrial town   131
    The 'founder and Garden City pioneer'   134

6. The Spiritual Life of the First Garden City 1904–1918   141
   A blank canvas?   141
   The evangelical free churches   143
   Non-evangelical free churches, and esoteric and
   free-thought traditions   154
   The Garden City Adult School   161
   Adrian Fortescue and Roman Catholicism   168
   Letchworth and the War   173

7. Howard and Welwyn – the Second Garden City
   1919–1928   177
   The Garden City relaunched   177
   Welwyn's development   186
   Howard's final years   190

   Conclusion: Ebenezer Howard – A Spiritual Life   198

Select Bibliography   207
Index   215

Abbreviations

BL	British Library
GCA	Garden City Association
GCC	Garden City Collection at Letchworth Heritage Foundation
GCTPA	Garden Cities and Town Planning Association
HALS	Hertfordshire Archives and Local Studies
IFTCPGC	International Federation of Town and Country Planning and Garden Cities
LCC	London County Council
LGC	Letchworth Garden City
LNS	Land Nationalization Society
NCASU	National Council of Adult School Unions
ODNB	*Oxford Dictionary of National Biography*
RPAA	Regional Planning Association of America
WGC	Welwyn Garden City

Introduction

Ebenezer Howard: the Man and the Message

Ebenezer Howard was forty-eight years old when he published his famous book, *To-morrow: A Peaceful Path to Real Reform*, in 1898. It was to be his only significant publication, and an example of a first book that had an unexpectedly large and lasting impact. The book described a plan for creating a new form of social and economic life by building a network of new cities in the countryside. Howard had been living quietly in London with his family, but he was not completely unknown, and it is possible to exaggerate the extent of his obscurity. He was known to the Remington typewriter company, as an inventor who appeared periodically with prototypes for typewriters that would produce text with variable spacing. He was known in the vicinity of the Palace of Westminster and at the London County Council, where he made his living recording debates and committee proceedings in lightning-fast Pitman shorthand. He was known in the circles of London Spiritualism, and had a long-standing friendship with the famous American spiritualist, Cora Richmond, who had given him introductions to various other notable individuals. He was known at the Holborn Literary and Debating Society (the Zetetical Society) and as a result of friendships established there was well acquainted with George Bernard Shaw and Sidney Webb. And he was known in the flourishing world of North London Congregationalism, where politics, progressive thought, and Nonconformist faith cross-fertilized to produce a culture of positivity and optimism. In this world, people not only believed that tomorrow could be better than today but were planning to make it happen.

Ebenezer Howard: Inventor of the Garden City. Frances Knight, Oxford University Press.
© Frances Knight 2023. DOI: 10.1093/oso/9780198790815.003.0001

During the next thirty years, Howard's name became known throughout the world. *To-morrow: A Peaceful Path to Real Reform*, republished as *Garden Cities of To-morrow* in 1902 was 'destined to become the most influential and important book in the entire history of twentieth-century city planning'.[1] In response to the twin crises of urban overcrowding and rural decline, Howard advocated the building of self-contained and sustainable new communities, which would be based on the idea of a 'marriage' between town and country, and would create the most perfect environment for people of all classes to live and work together in harmony and good health. He illustrated the book with a series of intriguing and frequently reproduced diagrams, which undoubtedly contributed to the rapid spread of his ideas by making them visually memorable.

Howard was not simply another *fin de siècle* utopian visionary; his ideas produced the twentieth-century's first environmental movement, and directly informed the creation of the world's first Garden Cities, at Letchworth, from 1904, and at Welwyn from 1919. From there, the 'gospel of the garden city' as he termed it, spread rapidly throughout the world. The first German Garden City, at Hellerau, near Dresden began construction in 1909, and in the same year, Howard's ideas were being insisted upon when a competition was launched to design Canberra as a new capital city for Australia. The Garden City movement, with Howard as its chief publicist and spokesman, had become international by 1914, with Garden City associations in eleven countries, under the umbrella of the International Garden Cities Association. David Bebbington pointed out that 'the garden city tradition, with its long-term influence over government new towns policy and town and country planning worldwide, is the greatest single fruit of the schemes of Nonconformists at the turn of the twentieth century for remedying the problems of industrial Britain'.[2] Howard's ideas, mediated by an influential group of disciples, including Lewis Mumford in the United States,

---

[1] Peter Hall and Colin Ward, *Sociable Cities: the 21st Century Reinvention of the Garden City* 2nd edition (London and New York, 2014) p. ix.

[2] D.W. Bebbington, *The Nonconformist Conscience: Chapel and Politics 1870–1914* (London, 1982) p. 57.

and Frederic Osborn, Patrick Abercrombie and Raymond Unwin in Britain, influenced twentieth-century town planning in many parts of the world.[3] They filtered into the New Towns Act of 1946, which led to the construction of twenty-eight new towns. Howard is therefore a bridging figure connecting *fin de siècle* radical London and Nonconformity with the worlds of twentieth-century professionalized town planning and housing reform, and the design of well-functioning and affordable new communities for large populations.

In the Spring of 1928, Howard lay dying in his home in Welwyn Garden City. He was visited frequently by his neighbour Frederic Osborn, who had worked with him since 1912 and had become his close friend. Howard hoped that Osborn would become his biographer, and he must have known that Osborn had been collecting material and interviews for this purpose since at least 1918.[4] Howard naturally wanted the biography to give full weight to the matters that he considered most important, and he gave Osborn specific instructions, urging him to remember that the 'spiritual dimension' had been central to his life and work. He was concerned that Osborn, an agnostic who later joined the British Humanist Association, would downplay this aspect of his life. Osborn recollected the conversation in notes he made in 1969: 'On his death bed, knowing I disagreed with him on this, he urged me very strongly to remember this in writing his life-story.' In another note written in the 1960s, Osborn commented that 'EH is always thinking about religion; it is his third obsession (along with the Garden City idea & mechanical inventions).'[5]

[3] Michael R. Hughes, (ed.), *The Letters of Lewis Mumford and Frederic J. Osborn: A Transatlantic Dialogue 1938–70* (Bath, 1971). This edition illustrates effectively the ways in which Howard's ideas were promoted in the years after his death, as does Hall and Ward, *Sociable Cities*.

[4] There was debate within the family during the last weeks of Howard's life about who the biographer should be. The candidates were Osborn, Egerton St John Pettifor Catchpool, George Bernard Shaw, and James Burns, the local Free Church minister. This is discussed more fully in chapter 7. HALS DE/Ho/F27/3; HALS DE/Ho/F/27/2/11 and HALS DE/Ho/F/27/2/12.

[5] HALS DE/FJO/I1/2 Notes made for a lecture in 1963. See also F.J. Osborn, 'Sir Ebenezer Howard: the evolution of his ideas' *Town Planning Review* 21, 3 (October 1950) p. 226.

Osborn died in 1978 without having written the biography, although he did publish a useful article to mark the centenary of Howard's birth in 1950.[6] He had made copious notes and collected all the papers that were not destroyed by Howard's widow. These materials, now in the care of Hertfordshire Archives and Local Studies in Hertford, form the main body of primary sources on which this study has drawn. In the late 1960s, and presumably aware that the biography was beyond him, Osborn bequeathed the project to Stanley Buder, a young American historian who intended to write a history of the Garden City movement, and was particularly interested in Howard's early influences. He spent a year researching in Welwyn Garden City under Osborn's guidance. But after Buder returned to America, relations with Osborn became strained when Osborn criticized a draft article. He suggested that Buder had misunderstood Howard by wanting to cast him as a 'visionary' and a 'utopian', and by claiming that he was anti-urban: 'he was no more anti-urban than a man who disliked bad apples could be described as anti-fruit.'[7] Osborn was further annoyed by Buder's decision to put off writing his book on the Garden Cities in order to concentrate on a more prestigious project on the history of the American city.[8] Buder proceeded very slowly, and his book, *Visionaries and Planners: The Garden City Movement and the Modern Community* finally appeared in 1990. In the meantime, Robert Beevers, a founding member of the Open University, had published *The Garden City Utopia: A Critical Biography of Ebenezer Howard* (1988). This book remains useful and replaced the sketchy and

[6] Osborn, 'Howard' pp. 221–35.

[7] HALS CDE/FJO/2/25. The article in question was Stanley Buder, 'Ebenezer Howard: The Genesis of a Town Planning Movement' *Journal of the American Institute of Planners* 35,6 (1969) 390–8. This article provided one of the earliest scholarly accounts of Howard and the Garden City movement. It still provides a useful introduction and was more balanced than Osborn implied. Another early scholar, Robert Fishman, also suggested that Howard hated cities. Robert Fishman, *Urban Utopias in the Twentieth Century: Ebenezer Howard, Frank Lloyd Wright and Le Corbusier* (New York, 1977) p. 12.

[8] Osborn described his anger at this in a letter to Lewis Mumford on 19 February 1970. Despite a year of work in Welwyn and with Osborn's unstinting help and that of the librarian, Michael Hughes, Buder had only 'got up to about 1893 in his study of Howard'. Hughes, *Letters of Mumford and Osborn* p. 468.

unreliable early memoir that had been produced by Dugald MacFadyen, *Sir Ebenezer Howard and the Town Planning Movement* (1933, reprinted 1970) which, although it had usefully captured some of the memories of the Garden City pioneers, had been little more than a stopgap while people awaited Osborn's definitive biography. Beevers's book was a significant advance on John Moss-Eccardt's *Ebenezer Howard: An Illustrated Life of Sir Ebenezer Howard 1850–1928* (1973) which benefited from pictures but lacked references.

Other scholars have written about Ebenezer Howard, and they have emphasized, reasonably enough, his enormous significance in the town planning movements of the twentieth century. Robert Fishman's *Urban Utopias in the Twentieth Century: Ebenezer Howard, Frank Lloyd Wright, and Le Corbusier* (1977) was an early contributor to the field, and although useful in parts, suffered from various inaccuracies, and an attempt to cast Howard in the same mould as Wright and Le Corbusier. Standish Meacham's *Regaining Paradise: Englishness and the Early Garden City Movement* (1999) compared Letchworth with Bournville, Port Sunlight, and Hampstead Garden Suburb. A critical edition of *To-morrow: A Peaceful Path to Real Reform* was produced by Peter Hall, Dennis Hardy, and Colin Ward in 2009. All three authors have produced other works in which Howard has featured significantly, including Hardy's *From Garden Cities to New Towns: Campaigning for town and country planning, 1899–1946* (1991) and Hall and Ward's *Sociable Cities: The Legacy of Ebenezer Howard.* This book was first published in 1998, with a second edition, *Sociable Cities: The 21ˢᵗ-Century Reinvention of the Garden City* published in 2014. Also in 2014, the Wolfson Economics Prize set the question 'How would you deliver a new Garden City which is visionary, economically viable and popular?' and this created a new surge of interest in the topic.[9] A search for journal articles citing Ebenezer Howard that were published in just the first eight weeks of 2022 yielded seventeen results.[10] It showed that Howard's ideas remain significant for a wide range of theorists, and also artists.

---

[9] The competition attracted 279 entries, and the prize, worth £250,000 was won by David Rudlin.

[10] This was done using the University of Nottingham library catalogue on 2 March 2022.

The search revealed work from those who wanted to adapt Garden City ideas in the light of the climate emergency,[11] public health specialists,[12] planning historians,[13] exponents of 'half earth socialism', and the artists Lukas Eigler-Harding and Ariel Noltimier-Strauss, whose 2021 work 'To-Marrow: A Peas-ful Path to Real Reform' had a pro-vegan message.[14]

Ebenezer Howard's religious background and interests, although touched upon in some of the existing works, have never been fully explored, and there has not been a proper attempt to explain the context of his religious ideas. This study will show that Howard was in many respects quite typical of the progressive Free Church people of his age. Indeed, he has been described by Clyde Binfield as a 'proto-type Free Churchman'.[15] This book will throw some new light on an influential seam of late nineteenth- and early twentieth-century British culture. Born in 1850, and brought up in Congregational Noncon-formity, Howard remained at home in the Free Church world throughout his life and was deeply concerned by religious questions. He learned his radicalism in part by drinking deeply at the wells of the English Dissenting tradition. With a sound elementary schooling but no formal education after the age of fifteen, he was, like many of his generation, largely self-educated through private reading, public lec-tures, and conversation. He collected ideas from a diverse range of sources and put what he considered to be the best aspects of them together, sometimes in ways which more sophisticated thinkers

[11] Anastasia Nikologianni and Peter J. Larkham, 'The Urban Future: Relating Garden City Ideas to the Climate Emergency' *Land* 11, 147 (2022) pp. 1–18.

[12] Julian Bolleter, Nicole Edwards, Robert Cameron, et al, 'Implications of the Covid-19 Pandemic: Canvassing Opinion from Planning Professionals' *Planning Practice & Research* 37,1 (2022) pp. 13–34.

[13] Andrea Gimeno-Sánchez, 'Urbanism of zines: the potential of environmen-talist zines as sources for planning history' *Planning Perspectives* published online 7 February 2022.

[14] Troy Vettesse, Drew Prendergrass and Filip Mesko, 'Town, Country and Wilderness: Planning the Half-Earth' *Architectural Design* 92,1 pp. 112–19 (2022). The 'To-marrow' artwork is reproduced in this article.

[15] Clyde Binfield, 'Garden City Religion: The Free Churches of Letchworth and Welwyn' *The Chapels Society Journal* 2, 2016, p. 64. Binfield also noted that Howard was however 'never in the mould of organized Edwardian Free Church-manship, Free Church Council style' a view that I would also endorse.

dismissed as naïve, or obsessive. His instincts were always practical – he was deeply interested in new inventions, new ideas, and new theories for making sense of the world – and his instincts were also always humanitarian. He cared deeply about improving people's living conditions and promoting what he called 'the social spirit'.[16]

After a serious religious upbringing which included Sunday worship at the City of London's Poultry Chapel, and a period in the employment of the famous Congregational minister Joseph Parker, Howard spent most of his twenties as a free-thinking agnostic, triggered in part by the experience of living in Chicago. He became intensely interested in the perceived conflicts between religion and science, and, in common with many others, alighted on Spiritualism as the means through which religion and science could be reconciled. He experienced a period of religious doubt, followed by an intensification of faith, which he linked to his belief that God had raised him up, from nothing, to deliver a new message to the world. It appears that his sense of himself as the prophet of the 'New Jerusalem' – literally interpreted as a command to build new communities – was what drove much of his intense activity. It was natural that Howard's religious beliefs, which were so essential to his nature, should give him an active interest in developing the spiritual lives of the early residents of Letchworth. He assumed that everyone's religious needs should be met, and that the Garden City would be a place of theological and spiritual exploration. He himself took full advantage of the religious freedom of Letchworth. Although he retained his links with the Letchworth Free Church (an early ecumenical enterprise) he spent many Sundays attending devotional meetings at the Howard Hall and blended his progressive Nonconformity with Spiritualism and an interest in Theosophy.

This book seeks to combine a critical approach to Howard, with an unsensational, properly contextualized, analysis of his religious views. Howard was well over halfway through his life when he became famous as the author of *To-morrow*, and he would live for a further thirty years, becoming progressively more famous. The significance which other scholars have placed on his impact and legacy has meant that much less attention has been paid to the first half-century of his

---

[16] Osborn, 'Howard' p. 234.

life. This study will redress this imbalance, as it was in his earlier years that the multiple religious influences that shaped him and his ideas were most keenly expressed. As it is thirty-five years since the publication of Beevers's biography, it is hoped that this book will also appeal to readers in search of a concise and up-to-date appraisal of Ebenezer Howard's life and significance.

This book has been a pleasure to research and write. As a native of Hertfordshire, Howard has always been somewhere on my horizon: at school we were taught that St Alban was the first British Christian martyr, and Ebenezer Howard founded the Garden Cities – a sort of secular saint for the twentieth century. My parents, who were Londoners in search of land in Hertfordshire on which to build a house, considered both Letchworth and Welwyn before alighting on a plot in Harpenden. Having built the house, my father spent the next thirty years commuting to London (Howard would not really have approved of this, although he too was a regular commuter) and gardening energetically every weekend. Welwyn Garden City, just eight miles away, was where my mother and I went for 'special shopping' in the Welwyn Department Store, a retail facility that Howard had insisted upon, in order to avoid the less coherent retail offering that had taken hold in early Letchworth.[17]

It is many years since I left Hertfordshire, and it has been interesting to return to research this book. The staff at Hertfordshire Archives and Local Studies have been unfailingly helpful, and the location of their office next to the ceremonies room in County Hall meant that I was sometimes able to combine my interest in Ebenezer Howard with my interest in rites of passage, by observing people getting married. My other port of call was the Garden City Collection, which is part of Letchworth Heritage Foundation, and contains an extraordinary collection of artefacts, as well as documentary sources. Some of this material can be viewed on-line, which proved invaluable during the lengthy period of pandemic closure. Readers may like to follow up points of interest by going to http://www.gardencitycollection.com/home and typing footnote references to photos, which mostly (but not

[17] The original Welwyn Stores was founded in 1921, and the current building was constructed as Welwyn Department Store in 1939. It was taken over by John Lewis in 1983.

always) begin 'LBM', into the search box. The large number of photographs in the GCC have led to the decision not to include pictures in this text. Howard's Garden City diagrams, which he used to illustrate his lectures and book, are also widely available on-line.

Sophie Walter, formerly of the Garden City Collection, was particularly helpful during my visits to various Letchworth Heritage Foundation sites, and Josh Tidy has answered my enquiries subsequently. Financial assistance for this project came from the Faculty of Arts at the University of Nottingham, and I am especially grateful to two successive Heads of the School of Humanities, Judith Mossman and Mark Pearce, who supported my applications for small grants, and then an additional semester of research leave. I have continued to make good use of Nottingham's Hallward Library, and its invaluable electronic resources. The fact that the books on Ebenezer Howard were periodically recalled was an indication that I was not alone in my interest, which, even if it irritated at the time, I was pleased to see confirmed. The National Library of Wales in Aberystwyth has proved invaluable for sourcing some of the otherwise difficult to obtain works on Nonconformity.

Earlier versions of some of the material were tried out on audiences in Nottingham, Durham, Cambridge, and Manchester, and I am grateful for the invitations and the discussion. Sustained interest in and enthusiasm for this project has come from David Bebbington, Clyde Binfield, Timothy Larsen, Tom O'Loughlin, and Stewart J. Brown, who 'led the way' with his own study of W.T. Stead for the *Spiritual Lives* series. Helen McLoughlin and Elizabeth Booth, friends who are also former residents of Hertfordshire, have provided, as always, their friendly support. Bill Jacob, once again, read the whole of the manuscript, and made helpful suggestions. This is my first book-length foray into English Nonconformity, and I am dedicating it to one of English Nonconformity's foremost historians, David Thompson of the University of Cambridge. I had the good fortune to have David as my doctoral supervisor, and I have appreciated his friendship, and admired his fine and wise scholarly mind ever since. I hope that he will enjoy reading it.

Easter 2022

1
The Early Years of Exploration
1850–1876

The City childhood

For someone who became famous for planning alternatives to life in existing cities, it is striking that Ebenezer Howard had loved London. Around 1910, he remembered an intense experience of revelation and physical delight that he had had back in 1874, when home on a visit from the United States:

> One of my greatest delights on this visit was to mount an omnibus and to ride through the crowded streets of London – the city where I was born – the city of which I was so proud. A strangely ecstatic feeling at such times often possessed me. There flowed through every nerve of my body from head to foot as it were streams of electricity, giving intense and long continued physical pleasure, the like of which I have never before or since experienced. The crowded streets – the signs of wealth and prosperity – the bustle – the very confusion and disorder appealed to me, and I was filled with delight.[1]

But he admitted that at that time he was still innocent and had no knowledge of the great social problem of grinding poverty amid abounding wealth that afflicted London. Howard had been born in the heart of the City of London, exactly halfway through the nineteenth century. His parents, like hundreds of thousands of others, had been drawn into London from elsewhere. His father, also called Ebenezer, had moved from Harwich, where his father had been a tailor, and his mother, Ann Tow, came from Colsterworth in Lincolnshire, where her

---

[1] HALS DE/Ho/F10/6/3–4.

Ebenezer Howard: Inventor of the Garden City. Frances Knight, Oxford University Press.
© Frances Knight 2023. DOI: 10.1093/oso/9780198790815.003.0002

father had been a road surveyor. Both his parents had been born in 1818, and at the time of their marriage in 1845, Ann was living in Battersea, and Ebenezer in the parish of St Giles' Cripplegate, where he owned and ran a bakery. It was in the flat above the bakery, at 62 Fore Street, that the younger Ebenezer was born on 29 January 1850.

Official records describe Ebenezer senior as a 'baker', a 'biscuit baker', and a 'pastry cook'.[2] Howard himself maintained that his father was a master confectioner; the baker-to-confectioner progression was quite common at this time, and the term suggests that he thought of him as a specialist sweet maker, offering a product superior to that of the industrializing Cadburys, Rowntrees, and Frys, who were becoming the mass-production confectioners of the late nineteenth century. The shop served hot drinks and steak-and-kidney pies at a long counter with high stools. Stale pastries were sold at half price next morning, and there were queues of children for the ha'penny buns. The Howards opened a restaurant nearby at London Wall which was managed by Ann Howard. The move into the restaurant business was common among baker-confectioners. It was busy in the week but on Sundays, the family enjoyed the deserted City of London, with its churches, music, and historic buildings. A particular annual highlight was the Lord Mayor's Show, which passed down Fore Street.[3] By 1861, the family had moved the short distance to London Wall, presumably to be closer to the restaurant. Ebenezer senior worked long hours in one or other of the underground bakehouses, and Ann was always busy in one of the shops. Ebenezer senior had a reputation for humanity and kindliness, on one occasion refusing to press for compensation from a man who in fog had run his horse and hansom cab through the plate-glass window, and on another, refusing money from a man who admitted that he had regularly eaten at the restaurant without paying.[4] Business prospered, with the number of

[2] Marriage record for Ebenezer Howard and Ann Tow, St Mary's Wandsworth, 1845; Census records for 1851, 1861, and 1871.

[3] HALS DE/FJO/I3/2 This was an account provided for the *Welwyn Times* 15 November 1957, by Howard's daughter, Editha Berry, which was presumably drawing on family memories.

[4] Dugald MacFadyen, *Sir Ebenezer Howard and the Town Planning Movement* (Manchester, 1933) pp. 5–6.

staff employed rising from one man and three boys in 1861, to two men, three boys, and two women, in 1871.[5] By 1881, the Howards had moved out of the City and were residing in Lambeth, with Ebenezer senior still working in the business and employing staff, although now none of them lived in with the family. By 1891, Ebenezer and Ann were enjoying their retirement, living with various members of their extended family in a spacious house in Evering Road, Stoke Newington, which was a strongly Nonconformist district of North London. The business in Fore Street was being managed by their daughter-in-law Clara Howard, and her sister Emma Bills.[6]

The young Ebenezer, always known as Ben within his family, had early memories of his mother in tears, whenever he and his two sisters were put in a cab for Shoreditch station, in order to catch a train for school. He was just four-and-a-half when he was first sent away to school, and his sisters only slightly older. In later life, he viewed this early separation as having been 'necessary, and indeed wise', in view of his parents' work commitments.[7] There were perhaps other reasons why sending the children away would have seemed a good idea. London's public health crisis was particularly acute in the 1850s, with a cholera epidemic across London in 1854, the year that Ben was sent to school in Suffolk. Cholera, coupled with the other diseases which festered in the capital city – smallpox, typhoid, scarlet fever – were particularly dangerous for children, and Ben's younger brother Harry was nursed through smallpox at 62 Fore Street.[8] Of the nine children that Ann Howard bore, four died in childhood. London contained other dangers for a small child. As a six-year-old, Ben was nearly run over by a fire engine, while crossing the road on the way back from an errand.[9]

The children were brought up in the Congregational faith of their father, and perhaps his desire to avoid having them educated at a local Church of England parish school was a further factor in sending them away. Although Ann and Ebenezer had been married in the Church

[5] Information derived from the census.
[6] HALS DE/FJO/I34.
[7] HALS DE/Ho/F17/7/1.
[8] HALS DE/FJO/I34.
[9] HALS DE/Ho/F17/7/4.

of England, there is no record of any of their children being baptized in the Church of England, and according to their daughter Elizabeth, the parents 'had different religions' and did not discuss religion in the home.[10] Elizabeth recalled that she and her siblings were not sent to Sunday school, because there was not one for them to attend, but that they read the Bible during the week at school.

Congregationalism was one of the major Protestant Nonconformist denominations in nineteenth-century Britain, with its roots in the 'old dissent' of the seventeenth century. Congregationalists were broadly Calvinist in theology, although their Calvinism was diminishing, and they were becoming open to newer modes of thinking, which led inevitably to some tensions between those of a more conservative and those of a more progressive outlook. They valued a learned ministry, and invested heavily in training their ministers, expecting them to be persuasive preachers of the gospel, and to show the hallmarks of evangelical faith. They believed in the primacy of the local gathering of believers, and although there were county unions and a Congregational Union of England and Wales, they did not see themselves as a 'church' but rather as a local gathering of like-minded believers. In parts of London and some other urban centres, they had particular support among the middle class, but this was far less true in the countryside. Partly because non-Anglicans were more-or-less excluded from the ancient English universities until the 1850s, they had a tradition of making their living in business. Although strongly committed to hard work and sturdily independent, they also created supportive social networks, and as the century went on, some upper-middle-class congregations increasingly took a lead in promoting art and culture,[11] and social reform projects, as well as missionary activities at home and overseas. It should not be surprising that the

[10] HALS DE/FJO/I32 Interview with Mrs Harrison by F.J. Osborn. Elizabeth Harrison née Howard was two years older than her brother, and this interview was conducted shortly after his death, when she was about eighty. Osborn claimed that Ann Howard was a 'Calvinist', and Ebenezer senior a 'Congregationalist and a Liberal'. F.J. Osborn, 'Sir Ebenezer Howard: the evolution of his ideas' Town Planning Review 21, 3 (October 1950) 224.

[11] See for example P.T. Forsyth, Religion in Recent Art: Being Expository Lectures on Rosetti, Burne Jones, Watts, Holman Hunt and Wagner (Manchester and London, 1889).

founder of the Garden City movement should emerge from within Congregationalism.

The Howard children were sent first to a school in Sudbury, Suffolk, where one of their cousins also boarded. The school was kept by two sisters, Miss Foster and Miss Emma Foster, who were strict disciplinarians, beating the infant Ben for scattering flower petals. They were extremely well taught in reading and writing, and all of the Howard children acquired beautiful handwriting, and the ability to write at speed.[12] At the age of nine, Ben was moved to 'Mr Duke's school' in Cheshunt, Hertfordshire, where the work was less demanding than it had been in Sudbury. Cheshunt was also the location of a prominent Dissenting academy, which had become strongly Congregational in focus.[13] Whether there was any sort of link between the school and the Congregational College is not clear, but as a place of higher learning for those who were destined for the Congregational ministry, Cheshunt may have seemed a particularly suitable place to send the boy. At the age of twelve, Ben returned to Suffolk, to what would be his final school, at Stoke Hall, near Ipswich. He remembered sitting with a group of boys and having the uncanny premonition that he knew exactly what one of them was about to say. Around the same time, now aged fourteen, he read an article in a boys' paper about automatic writing that could be performed by people placing their hands on a planchet. The idea was that their hands would be guided by a spirit communicating with them from the spirit world. At the time, he dismissed this as 'humbug', but a few years later, at the house of his friends the Harrisons in Aldersgate Street, he experimented with automatic writing generated through a planchet.

> I became convinced that a new force, not yet recognized by Science, was clearly manifested. I found that it was quite possible to manipulate the Planchet that it would write what one wished, on the other hand, when simply willing a word or two and not pushing the table it would still write, and I felt rather impatient that scientific men had paid so

[12] HALS DE/Ho/F17/7/1.

[13] Stephen Orchard, 'Cheshunt College (1792–1967)', *Dissenting Academies Online: Database and Encyclopaedia*, Dr Williams's Centre for Dissenting Studies, July 2011.

little attention to this mysterious force which in some way emanated from human bodies.[14]

Howard's interest in the supernatural developed early and would remain prominent throughout his life.

With his formal education officially complete, Ebenezer Howard left school at the age of fifteen, in 1865, and returned to the family home at London Wall. Work as a City clerk was the obvious next step for someone of his background, connections, and level of education. He duly went to work for a firm of stockbrokers, copying letters into a book with a quill pen, in the neat, round hand he had learned at school. Over the next few years, he was employed by a merchant, and at a firm of solicitors. And that might have been the whole of the future of Ebenezer Howard – whiling away the years as a clerk in a London office, copying endless letters and documents for an employer, while practising automatic writing, and attending Congregational worship, at the weekend. But Howard wanted to develop his skills in order to take on more interesting and lucrative employment. Initially he did this by improving his shorthand,[15] and later by developing what would become his lifelong obsession with typewriters. With his father, and his sister Elizabeth, he was a regular attender at the City of London's oldest Congregational place of worship, the Poultry Chapel. An obvious, and at this date quite popular, way of honing shorthand skills was to take a notebook and pencil to chapel, and to record and then transcribe the sermon.

The minister's secretary

In late nineteenth-century Britain, sermons remained what they had always been: an important means of conveying ideas to a regularly assembled congregation. From the 1850s, London had witnessed a new phenomenon: the rise of the celebrity preacher, whose sermons

[14]   HALS DE/Ho/F17/8/3–4.

[15]   Shorthand is a writing system which abbreviates speech into symbols, allowing the writer to capture speech at rapid speed. Howard first taught himself 'O'Dell's system' of shorthand at school at Stoke Hall, but very soon he switched to Pitman. HALS DE/Ho/F17/19/4.

were reckoned to be of such interest as to merit immediate publication. The most famous of the celebrity preachers was the Baptist, Charles Haddon Spurgeon, and others included the Congregationalist Newman Hall. Celebrity sermons were transcribed by shorthand reporters as they were preached, with the resulting texts published in newspapers, or printed as free-standing publications. At St Paul's Cathedral from 1870, Henry Parry Liddon rapidly established his reputation as one of London's most popular Anglican preachers, and his sermons sold for a penny each. Liddon complained, however, of the unreliability of reporters. 'People write to me and ask what I mean by particular expressions which I have never used, and which convey ideas more or less erroneous. I can only reply that I cannot help being more or less paraphrased by reporters . . .'[16] It was clearly a serious hazard for preachers. Eventually, Liddon gave up his earlier custom of speaking from notes, and resorted to writing a full text, which had the advantage that it could be passed to the printers immediately without transcription errors creeping in.[17]

While Liddon was preaching at St Paul's, just a few hundred yards away another celebrity preacher was beginning to attract a large crowd. The Congregational minister Joseph Parker, who had developed a reputation as a popular preacher in Manchester, had arrived at the Poultry Chapel in Cheapside in September 1869. He was there until June 1872, when the chapel closed so that the congregation could prepare to move to bigger premises at the City Temple in Holborn, which was being built, and would become Congregationalism's late nineteenth-century flagship. Because of its convenient location, it seems likely that the Poultry had been Ebenezer Howard senior's place of worship from the time that he had opened the first bakery in Fore Street. It was, however, rather forlorn at the time that Parker received the call to minister there. It had become

> An obscure place in the midst of warehouses, offices, shops, and other places of business. On week days, it, with neighbouring streets, was thronged with people hurrying to and fro, jostling each other as they

[16] J.O. Johnson, *Life and Letters of Henry Parry Liddon* (London, 1904) p. 192.

[17] Michael Chandler, *The Life and Work of Henry Parry Liddon* (Leominster, 2000) p. 111.

sped on their several ways, but on Sundays it was utterly deserted, presenting the appearance of a city from which all the inmates had fled. The few who still found their homes in this locality were mostly composed of caretakers, with here and there young men and women who occupied apartments in connection with the business places in which they were engaged. Congregations had dwindled, churches which once flourished had become empty, and the general opinion prevailed that it was next to impossible to obtain anything like a respectable gathering within a mile of that neighbourhood.[18]

During the course of his first Sunday, Parker announced that he intended to begin a one-hour service for City workers at noon each Thursday. This was seen as a novel and bold development.[19] He told the congregation that he 'believed in printing', and that it was his intention to publish 'on Thursday, a revised report of what proceeds here on Sunday morning . . . for one penny'.[20] At some point shortly thereafter, Ebenezer Howard sent Parker a full transcription of his Sunday sermon, with the offer to do this for him every Sunday 'for the good of the church'.[21] Parker was an extempore preacher,[22] and the presence of a willing and reliable young stenographer in his congregation must have been particularly welcome. Howard was immediately summoned for an interview with Parker and his wife, which took place in the dining room of their home in Highbury Park. Why, Parker asked Howard, had he reported the sermon, but not the prayer? He made a characteristically egotistical analogy with the Psalms of David: the 'Prayers of Dr Parker', Parker suggested, were just as worthy of reporting as the Psalms of David.[23] Howard, presumably attracted by the prospect of working for the charismatic Parker, and by the fact that the post provided 'a good deal of spare time', was appointed his personal secretary, at a salary of about £80

[18] William Adamson, *The Life of Joseph Parker, DD* (Glasgow, 1902) pp. 87–8.

[19] G. Holden Pike, *Dr Parker and His Friends* (London, 1904) p. 86.

[20] Joseph Parker, *The City Temple: Sermons preached in the Poultry Chapel, London, 1869–70* (London, 1870) p. 11.

[21] HALS DE/Ho/F17/10/3.

[22] Holden Pike, *Parker* p. 88.

[23] Alan Argent describes Parker as 'an egotist, a popular and histrionic preacher, reigning supreme . . . from his pulpit throne'. Alan Argent, *The Transformation of Congregationalism 1900–2000* (Nottingham, 2013) p. 2.

a year.[24] Parker's methods of recording his sermons were unusual. Rather than requiring Howard to take shorthand during a 'live' sermon preached at a service, he would deliver his sermon a second time in his library, to an audience of Howard only.[25] But despite this duplication, it seemed that Parker could not make use of a full-time secretary, and the employment lasted little more than three months.[26] Years later, Howard claimed, perhaps somewhat implausibly, that the arrangement broke down because Parker tired of paying his wages. But as the officeholders at the Poultry Chapel had had to work hard to persuade Parker to move from Manchester, it seems unlikely that they would not have provided him with finance for adequate clerical support.[27] Howard later decided that he had been intolerant in his attitude towards Parker. In a religious address on 'Tolerance' that Howard delivered in 1912, he lamented the fact that he had deliberately broken away from Parker as a result of his own intolerance, and commended the tolerance manifest in the theological views of Parker (specifically in relation to Roman Catholics, as expressed in his book *Ecce Deus*).[28]

Howard seems to have become uncomfortable with Parker, and in 1912 implied that the break was something that he had initiated. Parker was twenty years older than himself, and a man of powerfully expressed views; Howard may have felt that he was being pressurized by Parker to take up the preaching ministry which Parker considered a calling higher than any other.[29] Howard recounted on several occasions a curious incident which is the fullest anecdote that survives of the relationship between them:

> I well remember that Dr Parker once said to me when I was in his study, 'Mr Howard' – he always called me Mr Howard, though I was only a boy of 19 – 'Mr Howard, I don't believe in phrenology as some people do, thinking they can read every bump and pimple on a man's head, but in its broad features I think there is something in it and

[24] HALS DE/Ho/F17/10/3.

[25] HALS DE/Ho/F17/19/4.

[26] HALS DE/Ho/F17/10/4.

[27] Adamson, *Parker* p. 81.

[28] HALS DE/Ho/F10/26 Howard Hall Sunday evening 14 April 1912. Paper read by Ebenezer Howard on 'Tolerance'.

[29] Adamson, *Parker* p. 90.

I should like to feel your head.' I then stood up while he moved his hands over the ups and downs of my cranium and presently he said, 'Mr Howard, I will say to you what many young men have wished me to say to them, but I have not always been able to say it. I think you should be a preacher'.[30]

Commenting on the incident over fifty years later, Howard recalled: 'Now at the time this made no appeal whatever to me; though I have since learned that perhaps Dr Parker was right, though if that were so, the kind of preaching for which I was to become fitted required long years of preparation quite other than that taught at Theological Colleges.'[31]

Parker's interest in phrenology is not attested in any of the biographies. As a science for determining human behaviour, it had fallen out of favour in Britain in the 1850s, but it was experiencing something of a revival in the 1860s and 1870s, as a result of the influence of the lecture tours of the American phrenologist Lorenzo Fowler.[32] Parker's suggestion may also have been influenced by the fact that he was about to establish an institute of homiletics for the training of preachers, and was keen to recruit. It would be interesting to know if feeling the heads of potential students was a standard part of the application process, and if so, whether anyone regarded this as unusual.

Whatever the circumstances of his termination of employment, Howard remained intensely proud of the fact that he had been

---

[30] This version is from Howard's own biographical notes, preserved at HALS DE/Ho/F17/10/2. It was an anecdote that Howard frequently repeated, including when talking to Osborn about his formative influences, and when he was interviewed for *The Spectator* on 5 June 1926: 'Mr Howard remembers an occasion when the preacher's fingers roved over the hills and dales of his head'. This expression is also found in a document Howard wrote about his lifetime achievements in 1926, preserved at HALS DE/Ho/F18.

[31] HALS DE/Ho/F18.

[32] Fowler founded his Phrenological Institute in Ludgate Circus in 1862, so it is quite possible that Parker had encountered him in the City. W.T. Stead published an account of a phrenological reading he had had at the Institute at the hands of Fowler's daughter in the 1880s. W.T. Stead, *The Review of Reviews* vol IV, November 1891, p. 600. https://attackingthedevil.co.uk/reviews/phrenology.php Available on the W.T. Stead Resource Site https://www.attackingthedevil.co.uk/ accessed 15 April 2022.

secretary to Dr Parker, who became one of the most famous preachers in late nineteenth-century Britain. Howard's first biographer, Dugald MacFadyen, claimed that he could quote long passages from Parker's sermons from memory.[33] As Parker was the earliest documented religious influence on Howard, it is worth exploring him and his Congregational context a little further. Parker's published sermons from his first year at the Poultry, some of which were transcribed by Howard, provide a valuable insight into his strand of mid-Victorian Congregationalism, as it wrestled with the implications of the various developments in science and theology which had emerged in the previous years. When he addressed his audience of male City workers, Parker's sermons were practical, and full of homely good advice and wisdom: 'Selfishness makes the world a very little place . . . love is the only ink that does not fade . . .'[34] He was always keen to emphasize the merits of hard work, sometimes in a manner which sounded at odds with the traditional emphasis on faith above works in Protestant theology: 'Make your desk an altar; turn your business into a means of grace; let your counting house be a sanctuary; and then heaven will be but the natural climax of your Christian progress.'[35] Parker presented himself as a staunch defender of orthodoxy:

> I am more and more assured that, as individual Christians, and as churches of Jesus Christ, *we need to be very clear in our doctrinal foundations* (italics in the original). Do let us get a distinct idea of the principal points in the Christian faith. Beginning with the doctrine of sin, let us strive after God's view of it.[36]

Taking a position on the status of the Bible and biblical criticism was a burning issue within the Congregational ministry, and Parker rarely missed an opportunity to demonstrate his contempt for the scholars, mocking them in a withering first person plural: 'We do our best by carnal criticism to cool the glow of many a text; we say that it cannot

[33] HALS DE/X1053/S8/14. MacFadyen, himself a Congregational minister, thought that 'it is probable that he owed the unconventional emancipated side of his thinking to the first teacher in the affairs of life that he took seriously'.

[34] Parker, *City Temple*, p. 313.

[35] Parker, *City Temple* p. 24.

[36] Parker, *City Temple* p. 24.

mean all that it appears to mean, and count ourselves very skilful if we can bring some transcendent passage within the range of common feeling and apprehension.'[37]

The Congregationalists had been the first of the orthodox Protestant denominations to feel the effects of historical-critical approaches to the Bible. In the mid-1850s, there had been a notorious case involving Samuel Davidson, a leading biblical scholar, who had been forced to resign from his post as professor at the Lancashire Independent College, on account of his promotion of German critical scholarship and his doubts about the plenary inspiration of scripture. The Davidson case had had a polarizing effect, with ministers becoming either sympathetic or, like Parker, hostile to his position. It also raised the whole question of the desirability of a college-educated learned ministry.[38] But the direction of travel was with the theological liberals. When Henry Allon was elected chairman of the Congregational Union in 1864, he used his inaugural address to attack the doctrine of the verbal inspiration of the Bible. Two years later, Allon became editor of the *British Quarterly*, with the result that this Congregational journal began to adopt a much more positive tone towards biblical criticism. Allon's concern, now becoming increasingly widely shared by other Congregational ministers and educated laity, was that attempting to hold on to the old doctrines in the face of the new knowledge would lead to widespread revolt.[39]

Parker's position seemed to acknowledge that scripture was not necessarily as straightforward as had once been believed, but also suggested that prodding it with linguistic tools was too risky. Far better to overcome such temptations, and live by faith: 'We may not be the greatest in critical exposition, we know little or nothing of the syntax of the New Testament; we may be condemned by grammarians and linguists, yet may we be able, by the power of the Holy Ghost, so to live as to throw an explaining lustre upon hidden passages and difficult

---

[37] Parker, *City Temple* p. 19.

[38] Dale A. Johnson, *The Changing Shape of English Nonconformity 1825–1925* (Oxford, 1999) p. 67.

[39] Michael R. Watts, *The Dissenters Volume III: The Crisis and Conscience of Nonconformity* (Oxford, 2015) p. 30.

expressions.'[40] The venom that he directed at ministers with academic pretentions reveals a loathing that was clearly deep seated. In a chapter on 'Unsuccessful Men' in a book of advice he wrote for young preachers, he had this to say:

> Another class of unsuccessful men may be ironically described as *hyper-super-intellectualists*, something, in spite of the ugly word, very aerial and sublime. These magnificent and unapproachable royalties, throned among the stars, and clothed with clouds of many colours, expend their lives in one desperate determination to say something that is not in the New Testament. The moment they are about to put one word of gospel into their sermons, they recoil from the vulgarity as from a temptation to be profane. As a consequence they excel in *not* preaching the gospel.[41]

He proceeded for the next few pages to excoriate ministers who took an interest in the ideas of the French positivist philosopher August Comte, declaring that their ministries were always doomed to failure.[42] As late as 1893, Parker was still urging the retention of the Bible 'exactly as my mother gave it'.[43]

Questions about the authority and status of the Bible were just one area in which nineteenth-century Christians found themselves having to take up new positions as new questions arose. An increasingly literate population and the explosion of popular literary reviews meant that ideas about human evolution, the possibility or impossibility of miracles, providentialism, the uniqueness of Christianity, and the claims of other religions, as well as questions about divine justice, theodicy, and the ethics of eternal punishment were all in wide circulation.[44] The religiously minded were no longer simply drawing

[40] Parker, *City Temple* p. 21.

[41] Joseph Parker, *Ad Clerum: Advices to a Young Preacher* (London, 1873) pp. 216–17.

[42] Many of the leading Nonconformist thinkers of this period were taking a critical interest in Comte. See David M. Thompson, 'The Emergence of the Nonconformist Social Gospel in England' in Keith Robbins (ed.), *Protestant Evangelicalism: Britain, Ireland, Germany and America, c.1750–c.1950 Studies in Church History Subsidia 7* (Oxford, 1990) pp. 270–3.

[43] Parker, *None Like It* cited in Watts, *Dissenters* p. 33.

[44] James C. Livingston, *Religious Thought in the Victorian Age: Challenges and Reconceptions* (New York and London, 2006) pp. 1–6.

their ideas from what they heard in the pulpit. Quite where Ebenezer Howard placed himself in relation to these debates is difficult to gauge. Probably he was beginning to find Parker's version of the faith too constricting – perhaps this was the 'intolerance' that he felt was a factor in the termination of his employment at the Poultry Chapel. Intriguingly, though, he provides a comment on Parker's preaching, which seems at odds with what we know from the printed sources:

> On one occasion Dr Parker preached a sermon on 'The Fall of Man'. He expressed the view, quite clearly, that in his opinion what is recorded in the Book of Genesis should be regarded as allegory not as history. He also very delicately suggested that the Fall had some subtle connection with the misuse of the creative faculties of man, and woman. The deacons did not at all like that sermon and although I well remember that he told me that he thought it was the best sermon he had ever preached, it was never published as his other sermons were.[45]

Did Joseph Parker present himself in print as more conservative than he actually was in order to make himself acceptable to his deacons? Perhaps he had received a warning shot from them, at the beginning of his London ministry, which had convinced him that there were boundaries that should not be crossed. Howard's reminiscence about Parker continues with an account of a clairvoyant he met in Letchworth around 1907. She was a regular worshipper at the City Temple, and claimed that she frequently saw Dr Parker, who had died in 1902, standing beside the current minister R.J. Campbell, and thereby signalling approval of Campbell's extremely liberal preaching. This episode well illustrates one of the themes in this book – the syncretic relationship between Protestant orthodoxy and the spirit world in the late nineteenth and early twentieth centuries.

Having left Parker's employment, Howard spent a couple of years working as a shorthand clerk with Pawle, Lovesey, and Fearon, a firm of solicitors in the Strand. In 1871, he was living at 18 London Wall, with his parents, elder sister Elizabeth, younger sister Tamar, and younger brothers Thomas and Henry, together with a general servant, and a female bakery assistant. The Howard children were aged

---

[45] HALS DE/Ho/F17/10/5.

between twelve and twenty-three. As the eldest boy, and with six years of employment as a City clerk behind him, Ben was presumably feeling that it was time to stretch his wings. Although he had recovered well from a serious illness, which had necessitated convalescence in Felixstowe, and rum and milk for breakfast,[46] the pollution levels in London were clearly having an ill effect, and his lungs were giving him trouble. The doctor suggested that a healthier environment would be desirable.

The American adventurer

The American Midwest was selected as the healthier environment. Howard grew to love America and visited periodically until 1925. American modes of thought, most particularly those of the American Transcendentalists, had a profound effect upon him. The adoption of the terminology of 'First Garden City' to denote Letchworth, 'Second Garden City' to denote Welwyn, and the habit of identifying streets by numbers clearly derives from American influences. Arbor Day, the annual festival of tree planting which he introduced to Letchworth, was something which he must have first encountered in America, for it was introduced in Nebraska in 1872, at the time that he was there. He also found the comparative lack of hierarchy – very different from the pecking order in a London office – very appealing. It was in America that he began to read seriously, and develop intellectually, and to observe in detail the design of other towns and cities.

Howard embarked on his adventure with his friend John Harrison, who was a draper's assistant, and Harrison's friend, John Jordan, a photographer's assistant. The Howard and Harrison families were closely connected, making the young men obvious travelling companions. The Harrisons lived at 9 Aldersgate Street, and it was here that Howard first encountered automatic writing. Ebenezer Harrison, a grocer, was one of the deacons at the Poultry Chapel. John Harrison's eldest brother Frederick married Howard's eldest sister Elizabeth; they were the first couple to marry in the new City Temple in January 1875, with the ceremony performed by Joseph Parker. Howard,

[46] HALS DE/Ho/F17/6/4.

however, was still in the United States, and missed witnessing this formal union of the two families.

The outward crossing by steam ship took eighteen days, due to an engine failure, but as a sea voyage was seen as part of the lung cure, Howard regarded it positively.[47] Arriving in late 1871, the three young Londoners seemed extremely ill prepared for survival in the wild west, with little planned beyond delivering a letter of introduction to a minister in Des Moines, Iowa, whom they would consult on what to do next. The minister suggested that they should join a small party of Irish Canadians, who were on their way to Nebraska. The party was, appropriately enough, bound for the newly established Howard County, which had only been formed in that year. It was an extremely bold enterprise for the three young Londoners. They were drawn to Nebraska by the provisions of the Homestead Act of 1862, which permitted settlers to claim 160 acres of free land in the east of the State. Nebraska also benefitted from good weather and prime agricultural land, perfect for cattle grazing. At an early stage, the little party founded a church, the Ebenezer Church – presumably so named in an allusion to stones being raised up,[48] and not in honour of the group's shorthand writer. Indeed, Howard claimed that his companions named their new congregation without being aware that he was called Ebenezer.[49] Unsurprisingly in view of his recent experience in the employment of Joseph Parker, he was called upon to be a regular preacher at Ebenezer Church, Howard County, although what he told the congregation is sadly unrecorded.

Howard and his two friends claimed their 160-acre homestead, and set about planting potatoes, maize, melons, and cucumbers. The three novice farmers lived together in a one-room cabin. Subsistence farming in this undeveloped land must have come as a considerable shock to all of them; if they had been hoping for a life far removed from the conventions and etiquette of the offices and shops of Victorian

[47] HALS DE/FJO/I35 Text of lecture delivered in WGC entitled 'Memories of Sir Ebenezer Howard'; by Mrs Edith Berry, December 1949.

[48] I Samuel 7:12. A church of this name still exists in a remote agricultural part of Howard County.

[49] He seems to have been known as Ben Howard for most of his youth. See also HALS DE/Ho/F18.

London, they would certainly have found it. It must have challenged any romantic 'back-to-the-land' notions that they had entertained, but Howard supplies relatively few reflections on his homesteading experience. His months of unsuccessfully tending his large plot – all the crops failed except the cucumbers – gave him the opportunity to think about questions of land holding, quite possibly sowing the seed for his later condemnation of the 'unearned increment' – wealth derived from nothing beyond the ownership of land and property. Furthermore, Nebraska provided him with first-hand experience of a radical land-transfer scheme, and one which was very much at odds with the quasi-sacred approach to landownership which pertained in Britain.

In the short term, simple survival was a challenge. Howard was five feet five inches tall, and while in Nebraska weighed little more than eight stone, suggesting that the physical exertion caused him to burn more calories than he consumed, rather than build muscle. The hard labour caused him to develop an abscess on his hand which needed to be treated by a surgeon, but the nearest one was fifteen miles away. The urgency of the situation was such that he rode an unsaddled horse through roadless terrain, something which he had never done before. On the way back, light-headed from the pain of the treatment and from 'restorative' whiskey, but now with a saddle, he fell off while galloping, but was so light, he sustained no injury.[50] The farming experiment was clearly failing, and by the autumn of 1872, he decided to give up his life as a homesteader, rather than risk a winter on the farm. Howard was clearly not ready to return to London, but he needed to find employment that matched his skills. He made the six-hundred-mile trip to Chicago, in order to find work as a shorthand writer.

Chicago in 1872 was rapidly rebuilding after a major fire which had destroyed about one third of the city in the October of the previous year. Tracts of the centre of the city presented what was virtually a blank canvas, and the new Chicago was quickly emerging, with a priority on tree planting and better-designed buildings, in keeping with its status as America's second city.[51] Chicago was also

[50] HALS DE/Ho/F17/10/8.

[51] Bessie Louise Pierce, *A History of Chicago: The Rise of the Modern City 1871–1893* (Chicago, 1957) pp. 3–19.

experiencing rapid population growth, with a large number of Irish and German immigrants. Howard secured employment with Ely and Burnham, a leading firm of Chicago stenographers. Ely had been secretary to General Ulysses S. Grant, (eighteenth President of the United States, 1869–77) and Sherburne Wesley Burnham was a highly distinguished astronomer, as well as a stenographer. They needed someone to cover proceedings in the law circuit at Waupaca, Wisconsin, and sent Howard there on a trial basis. He found the speed of the proceedings formidable, but adjusted to it, and within a short time, was earning the same wages as the other men.[52]

Back in Chicago, the office of Ely and Burnham was a stimulating environment, and Howard made friends with his new colleagues, and in particular with Alonzo Griffen, a Quaker who encouraged him to read seriously. Howard later commented that Griffen:

> Helped me greatly in the direction of perfect freedom of thought: and associated with this, a very deep sense of responsibility, and a clear perception that all values, to be rightly estimated, must be assessed mainly by their influence on the spiritual elements in our nature. Thus only can material conditions be widely and permanently improved. We became, as our friends remarked, like brothers.[53]

It was at this point that Howard's intellectual foundations became more firmly established. His thinking became shaped – and would remain shaped – by a mixture of influences. Particularly important were the American Transcendentalists, Ralph Waldo Emerson, Nathaniel Hawthorne, James Russell Lowell, and Walt Whitman. Howard seemed particularly drawn to Emerson, who combined the legacy of Puritanism with Romanticism, mysticism, and a certain practical devotion to the American way of life. He also read W.H. Draper's *Intellectual History of Europe* and Darwin's *Descent of Man*, together with various other scientific works. Like many of his generation, he struggled to make sense of the implications of scientific discovery for traditional religious belief. Significant cracks were now appearing in the faith in which he had been nurtured. He found that once he had become proficient with taking shorthand in the law

[52] HALS DE/Ho/F17/11/2–5.
[53] HALS DE/Ho/F18.

courts, his hand could do the work, leaving his mind completely free: a 'complete rest' for the brain, as he described it.[54] If he had found his work more taxing, perhaps he would not have been able to engage in such a systematic process of self-education as he began in Chicago.

Chicago in the 1870s was certainly a place of vibrant religious growth, as new churches sprang up to replace those lost in the fire, and to meet the needs of the expanding and diverse population. All the main Protestant denominations were represented, with tensions very evident between the supporters of the 'old time religion' and those expounding a liberalism that rejected the 'dead dogmas' of substitutionary atonement and eternal damnation in favour of evolutionary theory and biblical criticism.[55] Sometimes secessions resulted, as when the prominent Presbyterian minister David Swing, described as the 'Emerson of our American pulpit', was accused of heresy, was acquitted, but nevertheless established his own non-denominational congregation in 1875.[56] Although there were Congregational churches in Chicago, and Swing himself eventually became Congregationalist, the denomination had struggled to break out from its New England roots, and in Chicago was a pale and insignificant shade in a brightly coloured ecclesial tapestry. In the State of Illinois, only three per cent of the population were Congregational in 1890.[57] Chicago offered possibilities for spiritual exploration very different from what Howard had experienced at the Poultry Chapel or within London Nonconformity. Free thought societies of various types flourished in the city – in which members read and discussed the writings of Voltaire, Thomas Paine, Darwin, and Huxley – as well as those of the Chicago agnostic, Robert Ingersoll. It seemed as if Howard, in common with all the other freethinkers in the city, were working through a single booklist. Howard attended the Society of the Golden Fleece, which also seemed to function as an introductions agency for those in search of friends of the opposite sex. Every week the male

[54] HALS DE/FJO/I35 text of lecture delivered in WGC entitled 'Memories of Sir Ebenezer Howard'; by Mrs Edith Berry, December 1949.

[55] Pierce, *Chicago*, pp. 423–32.

[56] Pierce, *Chicago*, pp. 429–32.

[57] Edwin Scott Gaustad and Philip L. Barlow, *New Historical Atlas of Religion in America* (Oxford, 2001) pp. 90–3, 377.

members of the Society were sent a letter, naming a female member that they should escort to that week's meeting.[58] Howard became romantically involved with a Miss Kelhuiston, and perhaps he met her in this way.[59]

The young Englishman did, however, persist with Sunday worship and found a Congregational church to attend. Indeed, when his employer requested him to work on a Sunday, he refused.[60] In a much later biographical note to himself, he jotted down an event of 1873: 'Robert Laird Collyer, famous preacher in Chicago'.[61] Collyer was a former Methodist, originally from Yorkshire, who had been in America since 1850, and was a leading Unitarian preacher in Chicago at the time that Howard was there. He founded the city's second Unitarian church, known as Unity Church, which became one of the strongest Unitarian churches in the American West, with Collyer himself famed as a pulpit orator; a Unitarian equivalent to Joseph Parker. Howard presumably attended and was influenced by his sermons. Howard's strong belief in unity as a religious principle, which he expounded quite frequently in Letchworth, may perhaps have been awakened by Collyer.[62] Frederic Osborn commented on this as a particular feature of Howard's thought: 'He had a peculiar desire for *Unity* – based on a faith in the single control of the universe

[58] Robert Beevers, *The Garden City Utopia: A Critical Biography of Ebenezer Howard* (Houndsmill, 1988) p. 6. Beevers describes the 'Society of the Golden Fleece' as a church, but this seems unlikely, in view of the status of the golden fleece in Greek mythology, where it symbolizes kingship and authority. There are no golden fleeces in Christian theology, and the only fleece which makes a significant appearance in the Bible, the one which Gideon uses to test God (Judges 6:36–40) is not recorded of having been unusual in colour. It is, however, quite possible that Chicago's Society of the Golden Fleece adopted some of the characteristics of a church, with weekly Sunday services, and prayer before social and cultural events.

[59] HALS DE/Ho/F33/6/6 preserves a programme for an evening of music and amateur dramatics held by the Golden Fleece on 28 December 1874, and the event did indeed open with prayer.

[60] Osborn, 'Howard' p. 226.

[61] HALS DE/Ho/F17/6/4.

[62] For example, HALS DE/Ho/F3/14 Mss of a lecture on religious themes given to The Adult School, in The County Lower School, Letchworth, 25 September 1910.

(God) – and for universal Harmony, in which love would end all
conflict and transform individuals into a perfect community.'[63]

Howard experienced another new and very significant spiritual
influence in Chicago, which would intensify after his return to London. This was Spiritualism, which he first encountered at a meeting
conducted by Cora Richmond (who was also known as Cora Scott,
Cora Hatch, Cora Daniels, and Cora Tappan – she was married four
times). Howard and Griffen were sent to the meeting by the *Chicago
Times*, who had asked for a verbatim report of her address, and they
were much impressed by what they saw and heard.[64] Her method was
to speak on any subject that the audience voted for; Howard was
particularly thrilled on a subsequent Sunday, when the topic that he
had suggested was chosen by the majority vote, and he recorded that
she spoke eloquently for forty-five minutes on it immediately afterwards.[65] His topic was 'the woman of the future', which hinted at his
developing feminist sympathies. Wilbur Storey, the owner of the *Chicago
Times*, was one of the city's most prominent converts to Spiritualism, but
generally the American movement was less well received than in
Britain, even among those of advanced theological views. Books with
titles such as William A. Hammond's *Spiritualism and Allied Causes of
Nervous Derangement* indicated at least some of the prevailing attitudes.[66]
In this respect, American Spiritualism differed from its English version,
which meshed more easily with mainstream Christianity. Howard was
captivated by the beautiful and eloquent Cora Richmond and joined a
study group that met at her home. One of the texts that they studied
was Tom Paine's *Age of Reason*, and this, coupled with the teaching that
under the guidance of friendly spirits, the religious errors of the past
could be abandoned, and the true paths made known, was enough to
convert him as a Spiritualist freethinker.[67] He always remained a man

[63] HALS DE/FJO/I1/2. Notes made for a lecture to Welwyn Garden City
Literary Society, 3 November 1963.

[64] HALS DE/FJO/I35. Text of lecture delivered in WGC entitled 'Memories
of Sir Ebenezer Howard'; by Mrs Edith Berry, December 1949; HALS DE/Ho/
F18. Later correspondence suggests that Griffen also became a Spiritualist.

[65] HALS DE/Ho/F18.

[66] Pierce, *Chicago* pp. 436–7.

[67] Stanley Buder, *Visionaries and Planners: The Garden City Movement and the Modern
Community* (New York and Oxford, 1990) p. 10.

of faith, but he appears never to have returned to the Protestant orthodoxy in which his father had raised him.

Howard read widely, and there were other texts which made a particularly profound impression upon him, and to which he frequently returned. Towards the end of his time in Chicago, he read *Hygeia: A City of Health*, a pamphlet based on a lecture delivered by the distinguished medic and public health advocate Benjamin Richardson FRS.[68] The purpose of Hygeia, Richardson's imagined city, was to reduce the annual mortality rate to the lowest possible figure. He described in detail how houses should be built, and the way in which the hospital should be constructed and administered. He did not neglect other facilities which would improve public health, with guidance provided for the proper regulation of laundries, sewage, abattoirs, and cemeteries. The pamphlet made a deep impression on the twenty-six-year-old Howard, and elements of life in Hygeia, for example public and private gardens, and the factories located on the edge of the town, became embedded into his mind, and were worked into the book he would write in the 1890s, *To-morrow: A Peaceful Path to Real Reform*.

Richardson was a distinguished scientist at the top of his profession – too distinguished to be written off as a crank – and Howard saw that he not only dared to dream of his ideal city, but he also provided a carefully reasoned printed account of how it might be made into a reality. Hygeia was to be built from scratch; it did not involve making adjustments to existing buildings. Richardson's housing stock was envisaged as spacious, thoughtfully planned, and above all clean. A large army of public health officials would enforce compliance, and teetotalism was mandatory – Richardson had himself recently given up drink. The cultural life of Hygeia was only vaguely sketched, but it seemed to revolve around sports facilities, and artistic and educational activities. Richardson believed that the outcome of Hygeia would be a 'city of health' where disease was reduced to an unavoidable minimum of cancers, lung conditions, and inherited maladies, coupled with the occasional, but swiftly contained, outbreak

[68] Benjamin Ward Richardson, *Hygeia: A City of Health* (London, 1876). See also Patrick Wallis, 'Sir Benjamin Ward Richardson 1828–1896' *Oxford Dictionary of National Biography* (Oxford, 2008).

of scarlet fever or whooping cough. He predicted that in the first generation, the mortality rate would drop to an astonishingly low eight per thousand, and in subsequent generations drop lower still. Only a medical man could have credibly promoted much of Richardson's scheme, but perhaps Ebenezer Howard glimpsed in the section on the planning of the city a project that he could take forward, and was inspired by Richardson's firmly forward-looking vision, and unshakeable belief that once shared with 'the masses', his ideas would spread, like light between torches.

Shortly after he finished reading *Hygeia*, Ebenezer Howard decided to return to London. He was twenty-six. He had had adventures in rural America and gained first-hand experience as a 'back-to-the-land' homesteader. He had lived among the sophistication and religious pluralism of Chicago, and witnessed a city being rebuilt from the ground up, and been charmed by the egalitarianism of America, so different from the intricate interplay of class and status that existed in England. He had encountered American Congregationalism, the Society of the Golden Fleece, Unitarianism, and Spiritualism, and had quite possibly tasted other denominations as well. His intellectual horizons had been expanded through his varied and systematic reading, and through theological discussion with friends, and particularly with Alonzo Griffen, with whom he would remain in intermittent contact for the rest of his life.[69] He had gained in confidence and was now established as an experienced shorthand writer, who would be able to command good rates of pay, and interesting employment, in London. His health had improved, and he had practical experience of the link between improved health and a cleaner environment. He would always acknowledge that his years in Chicago had changed him profoundly, and that he had learned far more than he would ever have done if he had stayed in London. But it was time to go home and settle down.

---

[69] The two men renewed their correspondence shortly after the publication of *To-morrow* in 1898. They met for the last time in Detroit, in 1925. HALS DE/Ho/F25/27 and HALS DE/Ho/F18.

2
Laying the Foundations 1876–1889

Early married life

Ebenezer Howard arrived back in London in 1876, and the following year began work at W.B. Gurney & Co, a firm managed by Baptists, who were the official shorthand writers to the Houses of Parliament.[1] He was proud of the fact that he was the first 'Pitmanite' shorthand writer to be employed by them. The position permitted him to observe the workings of the political establishment at first hand, and to learn more about the policies and public face of government. On several occasions he broke through the barriers of class and convention which normally separated the clerks and minor functionaries at the Palace of Westminster from the men of power and influence. He discussed his Garden City ideas with the celebrated economist Professor Alfred Marshall, and with the prominent trade unionist and dockers' leader Tom Mann, when they were sitting on the Royal Commission on Labour, from 1891 to 1894. Marshall and Mann, whose social origins were fairly similar to Howard's, were evidently perfectly happy to chat with the stenographer, during breaks in the extremely lengthy proceedings. Howard's gradually expanding social circle illustrates the ways in which late nineteenth-century London was still a relatively small world, where interconnecting networks could be fairly quickly established among like-minded people.[2]

---

[1] Gurneys were the official shorthand writers to Parliament from the 1770s, until the post of Official Shorthand Writer was abolished in 2010. Clyde Binfield, 'Garden City Religion: The Free Churches of Letchworth and Welwyn' *The Chapels Society Journal* 2016, 2 p. 65 makes the Baptist connection.

[2] This is also noticeable in the interconnecting networks created by theologians and artists in London at this time. See Frances Knight, *Victorian Christianity at the Fin de Siècle: The Culture of English Religion in a Decadent Age* (London: IB Tauris, 2015) pp. 27–9.

Ebenezer Howard: Inventor of the Garden City. Frances Knight, Oxford University Press.
© Frances Knight 2023. DOI: 10.1093/oso/9780198790815.003.0003

Howard did not find it easy to settle into the status of an employee. He was impulsive and creative, and wanted to be free to pursue projects outside the rigidity of the workplace. After just two years, he left Gurneys and set up his own business, forming a partnership with William Treadwell, who was a more experienced stenographer. He put £250 into the business, which was almost certainly supplied by his parents. Treadwell was older and did not find Howard an easy business partner. The relationship broke down in 1884, after Howard had taken a prolonged leave of absence in New York, although for legal and practical reasons, the partnership limped on for a further four years. In 1888, Howard set himself up as a freelance stenographer, sometimes working for Gurneys, and from 1889, for the London County Council.[3] Because he never made any money from his Garden City idea, he was only able to retire completely from shorthand writing in his mid-seventies.

In other respects, his life was developing more pleasantly. His younger brother Thomas married Clara Bills, who was the daughter of Thomas Bills, the owner of the Newdigate Arms, a posting inn in Nuneaton, and a gentleman of considerable means. Clara's sister Elizabeth Ann (Lizzie) was a bridesmaid, and it was apparently love at first sight when she met her new brother-in-law Ben. Lizzie and Ben soon became engaged and were married on 30 August 1879 at St Saviour's Church Lambeth, with a honeymoon at the Hotel du Prince Albert in Paris. The wedding venue suggests that Lizzie may have been an Anglican, and that Ben was still feeling somewhat detached from Congregationalism; he clearly did not wish to pursue the option of being married by Dr Parker at the City Temple. Howard's mother was an Anglican, and his parents had been married in the Church of England, so he was falling in with family tradition. The honeymoon destination suggests that the young couple wanted to make a fashionable, romantic, and cultured start to married life.

The patient, intelligent, and practical Lizzie was to be the great love of Ebenezer Howard's life; her early death was to be the greatest tragedy that he ever faced. Some of the letters from the early years of

[3] Robert Beevers, *The Garden City Utopia: A Critical Biography of Ebenezer Howard* (Houndsmill, 1988) pp. 11–12; Stanley Buder, *Visionaries and Planners: The Garden City Movement and the Modern Community* (New York and Oxford, 1990) pp. 27, 29, 37.

their relationship were excerpted and typed by Frederic Osborn in 1967; unfortunately, the originals appear not to have survived. They convey a vivid sense of Lizzie: energetic, evangelical, and initially appalled by the religious views of the man who was about to become her husband, and yet also convinced that he could be 'reformed' and persuaded to adopt religious views in line with her own. She discovered that not only did Ben appear doubtful about the divinity of Christ, but also about the veracity of the Bible. She tackled these issues in a letter of February 1879:

Can I feel peace dear when I know that you are rejecting Christ and in rejecting him you deny God Himself, for Christ was God made manifest in the flesh. Your soul revolts from the suggestion of rejecting God, as a terrible calamity against your soul, but dear it is true. He that despiseth Him that sent me. I and my Father are One . . .

I come now to your letter of the 14th [presumably a St Valentine's day letter] . . . I feel almost too crushed in spirit to write at all. I have asked myself again and again have I dreamed this and then the full horror of the bitter truth swarms over my soul, and I feel utterly appalled. Is it possible dear, oh I must have misunderstood you, that you would have me take the Bible and say it is a lie. I pray God that my tongue may be paralysed ere I thus deny the truth that my life may now be quenched if it were possible that I should ever by word or deed come to believe or act as though the Bible were other than the Word of God. It is the Word of God let men deny it as they may.[4]

This letter seems to have prompted a forthright response from Howard, leading her to reply rather combatively: 'Think before you speak, and exercise more of the charity you have so enjoined upon me to display. Surely dear for once you lost sight of Him whose life was love. And as he forgives, so do I, and will try to efface from my memory all that I am sure you could not mean.'[5]

Lizzie tried a slightly more conciliatory tone in the following month, alluding to her own conversion, and emphasizing that because he had been brought up in a Christian household, his reconversion was entirely possible:

[4] HALS DE/FJO/I3 13 February 1879.
[5] HALS DE/FJO/I3 13 February 1879.

You ask me to convince you that by embracing Christianity you would become a better man. That you would is as certain as that I became a better woman. Oh if you had known me a few years ago you would have a strong proof of the power of Christianity; a more thoughtless, disobedient and self-willed girl than I was could not be. If you think there is any great or small change in my character or disposition to this, you know to what it is due. 'I am what I am by the grace of God'. Don't imagine that I see in you nothing but error. Your disposition and moral character is not that which needs converting. Why? Because in youth you implanted in your nature the love of <u>true religion</u>, the perfection you arrived at was Christ and that love has never been wholly eradicated and so the fruits of righteousness still grow though the soil is not as congenial as it once was. No Ben your <u>heart</u> is right but your head is <u>wrong</u>. I ask you to put the question to yourself honestly. Is there anything which ennobles and lifts up human nature more, or so much as Christianity, what else has the power to <u>utterly</u> change the lives of men and women as this does. I could if I had time, enumerate <u>dozens</u> of cases that have come under my immediate notice when the father once a <u>drunkard</u> and degraded almost to the level of a beast has been reclaimed, by what, Christianity.[6]

The correspondence provides an insight into the spirited attempts of an evangelical woman to influence the religious outlook of her fiancé. She was, no doubt, fearful that she was about to become 'unequally yoked' to a free-thinking rationalist[7] and nervous about leaving her friends and family in Warwickshire, for an unknown life in London with an impecunious stenographer. At the time of their courtship, Lizzie was living in Coventry. In some of her letters she seemed to be trying to put him off from visiting, asking that he postpone because she was busy with the dressmaker, or with friends. In early June, she wrote that she was feeling 'wretchedly dull and depressed', the first intimation in her letters of the depression that she would suffer later. She cast doubt on the public nature of their engagement: 'You are quite wrong in your supposition that our engagement is widely known . . . <u>Very few know</u>. Ben, dear, you must not make up your mind to be

[6] HALS DE/FJO/I3 11 March 1879.

[7] II Cor 6:14: 'Be ye not unequally yoked together with unbelievers: for what fellowship hath righteousness with unrighteousness? And what communion hath light with darkness?'

married yet . . . I have told you it is improbable that I could be ready by the end of September.'[8] But somehow, Lizzie was able to be ready, and in late August the bride and groom walked up the aisle at St Saviour's, Lambeth. It was a rather grand setting: a large and fine medieval church with box pews and a triple decker pulpit, which had escaped Victorian restoration. Later it was restored, and designated as Southwark Cathedral. 'It somewhat resembles Salisbury cathedral', wrote Edward Walford, in the year before the Howards married there.[9]

They settled at 4 Ildersly Grove in Dulwich, in a spacious bay-fronted semi-detached house with a garden, which would then have still been fairly new. Howard spent the whole of that November working in Dublin, and this separation necessitated the resumption of correspondence. Lizzie's tone was markedly different, her letters full of love and longing. As a wife, she may have felt that her moment of maximum influence had passed, and that her earlier tone of pietistic reproach was no longer appropriate. It may also be that, influenced by her husband's strong personality and ideas, she was already beginning on a path of significant transition in her own spiritual life. Ben's letters reveal his careful observations of a culture that was new to him. He found the Irish to be 'exceedingly kind and good natured' but he was homesick, and regretted that he had accepted the contract in Dublin, as he missed his wife:

> Dear girl I do long to have you in my arms again and tell you how I love you . . . I shall not easily be moved to leave my darling again, I can tell you . . . I do not quite like my work. To be in the pay of a Conservative Government seems to destroy my enthusiasm, but I so wanted to get our little debts cleaned off, that I accepted the offer without perhaps sufficient thought. Next time, dearie, before I leave like this I will consult your wishes more.[10]

The reference to debts, and to acting without giving sufficient thought to Lizzie's wishes, was to be a sadly repeated theme in the Howards'

[8] HALS DE/FJO/I3 9 June 1879.
[9] Edward Walford, *Old and New London: Volume 6* (London: Cassell, Petter & Galpin, 1878) pp. 16–29.
[10] HALS DE/FJO/I3 2 and 22 November 1879.

marriage, and fairly frequently he left her to cope alone for extended periods.

Howard was shocked by the poverty he saw in Ireland. He was clearly already concerned with artisan housing, about existing forms of land ownership, and the need to improve the urban environment. He fantasized about Lizzie and himself becoming model landowners with an Irish estate:

> The country though is the poorest and most wretched I ever saw, and I fear we English in our overhand manner have contributed in no small degree to this – though the comparative poverty of the soil and the want of minerals is the chief cause. The cottages of the country are most wretched – I quite wish I could be a land owner and for once without a tinge of selfishness. I did think that with your help we might make ours the most comfortable estate, so far as the poor tenants would be concerned, in Ireland . . . [11]

Visiting Phoenix Park, he was most impressed by the way in which nature was being brought into the centre of the city:

> A very pretty natural park – only a small part of it has been laid out . . . the air was delightfully fresh . . . do you know the gardeners have just laid out a lot of pansies in bloom. Could this be done in England do you suppose, dear. If so why need our gardens be so bare in winter. I never I think saw such magnificent holly covered with splendid red berries as I saw here . . . [12]

In addition to exploring Dublin's parks, the religiously curious Howard also took the opportunity to experience Dublin's religion. Although he could easily have attended a Nonconformist service, or one in the recently disestablished Church of Ireland,[13] he chose instead to visit a Catholic church, and reported the fact to Lizzie: 'Last Sunday morning I attended a service at a Catholic Church. The preacher was an earnest fiery and I believe thoroughly sincere man, and his sermon was quite practical.'[14] Although Howard viewed

---

[11] HALS DE/FJO/I3 22 November 1879.

[12] HALS DE/FJO/I3 30 November 1879.

[13] John Crawford, *The Church of Ireland in Victorian Dublin* (Four Courts Press: Dublin, 2005).

[14] HALS DE/FJO/I3 25 November 1879.

church attendance very much through the Nonconformist lens of judging the sermon, he did not appear to hold the anti-Catholic prejudices that were common among English Protestants at this period. His experience in Chicago seems to have given him an openness to religious expression in many varied forms that he would retain throughout his life.

During the 1880s, Lizzie was preoccupied with infants, financial pressures, and her husband's unpredictability. Kathleen was born in 1881, Edith (or Editha) in 1882, Arthur Cecil (known as Cecil) in 1883, and Doris Margorie (Margery) in 1890. There was another daughter, Muriel, who died in infancy in 1886, and was buried at the South Metropolitan Cemetery.[15] Lizzie managed the household with the help of one live-in servant, and it was a strain. Howard's failed partnership with Treadwell, and the move to freelance status meant that finances were unpredictable. His mind was preoccupied with designing a typewriter modification which would permit variable spacing – the specific problem was making the carriage move slightly more when the slightly longer letters 'w' and 'm' were struck, so as to avoid a cramped appearance in the text.[16] Having found a solution, his plan was to patent the idea and sell it to Remington, the major manufacturer of typewriters. From the 1880s until the final years of his life, Howard spent hours in the workshop at his various homes, fiddling with typewriters and stenography machines, as he attempted to produce improved technology for recording words and speech. As Osborn always insisted, Howard was first and foremost an inventor.[17] He became famous for inventing the Garden City, but he would have dearly loved to have also become famous for making the technological breakthroughs which would have rendered manual shorthand obsolete and produced typescript of print quality. The quest obsessed him for the best part of five decades. There were numerous frustrations and setbacks, and he invested large amounts of money which would have been better spent in other ways. But he never lost the sense that

[15] HALS DE/Ho/F25/39 Muriel Howard.

[16] HALS DE/FJO/I34 Notes from A.C. Howard, n.d.

[17] 'Howard – let me emphasise this – was not a political theorist, not a dreamer, but an inventor.' F.J. Osborn, Preface, in Ebenezer Howard, *Garden Cities of To-morrow* (1946 edition) p. 21.

he was on the verge of solving the complex technical problems associated with the early writing machines.

In 1884, Howard spent three months in New York trying to sell his solution to the variable spacing problem to Remington, who had launched their typewriter onto the market ten years previously. Early typewriters were extremely primitive and bulky (the first ones only typed in capitals) so there was plenty of scope for technically minded and entrepreneurial individuals to suggest improvements which, if adopted, might revolutionize typing and make their fortune. Howard's device connected the uppercase key lever with a spring, so as to give extra movement to the capital letters.[18] Armed with his 'improved machine', Howard sailed out on the SS Wyoming in August, sharing a cabin with a Jesuit bound for New Mexico whom he described as 'pleasant and lively' and an Irishman from Belfast, who was also good company. He reported to Lizzie that there were many Mormons on board, and that they were a 'queer lot' and that the other American passengers were 'ashamed of them'.

The high hopes that the Howards had had for the 'machine' at the beginning of the trip gradually evaporated. By late September, it was clear that negotiations over the typewriter were making little progress, and Howard was running out of money. Lizzie, at home in London with three children under four, was anxious and frustrated: why had he not borrowed money in London, instead of attempting it in New York? Not for the first time, he had to be bailed out at the eleventh hour by his father. But despite these tensions, her letter of 21 September was warm and loving, full of the positivity for which she would become known:

> If you are unfortunate you will not let the pecuniary loss trouble you in the least on my account, for believe me darling I care not so that I have you home once again well and happy. We should soon pull round and another year or two's squeeze would not be very much, so that we are all well and at home together so don't worry darling. God bless you my precious husband, your wifie loves you more than she can tell . . . Good night dearest, your babies send you lots of love and want you home badly but not half as badly as I do . . .[19]

---

[18] HALS DE/FJO/I3/2 notes supplied by Mrs Berry, relating to 1884.

[19] HALS DE/FJO/I3 21 September 1884.

Howard continued in New York, making further modifications to the typewriter, and discussing the terms for a sale of the patent. Mr Densmore, who was commercializing the typewriter on behalf of Remington, offered him the enormous sum of $7,500, but for some reason Howard refused. Lizzie was by now becoming severely stressed, and her mood had darkened. Her 'poor old nerves are nearly all used up. The anxiety and suspense one has to endure for inventions certainly ought to be taken into account, and the price fixed accordingly . . . Very disappointed you did not take Mr Densmore's offer, which to me seemed a good one, for now you will have a lot more worry and bother with the thing.'[20] Howard was on the voyage home as she wrote this letter, and she told him that she desperately hoped that he had agreed terms for the typewriter before leaving New York. She reported that she had bought a 'pretty coat' for one of the children 'and a few other pretty things, but I can assure you dear I bought sparingly for I felt in my bones that the machine was not sold and all the cash would be wanted for other purposes'.[21] Lizzie's premonition was correct. By the following year, Ebenezer Howard was looking for somewhere cheaper to rent, and as the family grew, money became ever tighter. A second trip to New York in 1886, three months after the death of baby Muriel, put further strain on the marriage and the finances, and again failed to sell the typewriter patent. The tone of Lizzie's letters indicate that she had become seriously depressed, and her physical health was probably also deteriorating. 'I tell you candidly that in all my life I have never spent such a time of wretchedness and had I been able to realise all I should never have consented to your going away just now. Well all I can say is come back <u>as soon as</u> you can for I can't hold out much longer without you . . .'[22] Howard hinted that he might like to move to America permanently. Lizzie replied that she did not care 'two straws' where they lived, as long as they were not apart. After seven years of marriage, Howard was not providing his family with the security expected of a Victorian husband, and his wife was on the edge of a full-scale mental breakdown.

[20] HALS DE/FJO/I3 31 October 1884.
[21] HALS DE/FJO/I3 31 October 1884.
[22] HALS DE/FJO/I3 27 June 1886.

Spiritualism

Amid these practical and emotional trials, the Howards had found a new form of support and inspiration: they both became deeply involved with Spiritualism. Once a poorly understood phenomenon that was believed to be on the eccentric fringes of late-Victorian culture, Spiritualism is now recognized as having been woven into the belief systems of people of all classes and backgrounds. Indeed, it has been suggested that it is now considered 'central to what many people think it meant to *be* a Victorian',[23] and if that judgement is perhaps a little too sweeping, much recent scholarship has focussed on the realization that an active interest in Spiritualism was compatible with both mainstream Christianity[24] and with science.[25] The interest shown by scientists in Spiritualism and by Spiritualists in science has provided a challenge to the older theory that Spiritualism was mainly a reaction to a perceived crisis of faith, in which people turned to it in a desperate attempt to prove the doctrine of the immortality of the soul. Although there were certainly plenty of Christians who found it straightforward to hitch their faith to the Spiritualists' wagon, there were also plenty of scientists who considered the investigation of psychic phenomena as potentially the key to unlocking various unexplained aspects of the physical world. Such scientists proceeded by means of empirical observation, rather than falling back on a rationalist faith which believed that psychic phenomena must necessarily be

[23] Jennifer Tucker, 'Foreword' in Tatiana Kontou and Sarah Willburn, *The Ashgate Research Companion to Nineteenth-century Spiritualism and the Occult* (London and New York) 2012 p. xiv.

[24] See especially Georgina Byrne, *Modern Spiritualism and the Church of England, 1850–1939* (Woodbridge, 2010) and Michael R. Watts, *The Dissenters Volume III: The Crisis and Conscience of Nonconformity* (Oxford, 2015) pp. 36–41. Watts highlights well the range of attitudes which Nonconformists had towards Spiritualism, from enthusiasm to disdain.

[25] Christine Ferguson, 'Recent Scholarship on Spiritualism and Science' in Kontou and Wilburn, *Ashgate Research Companion* 19–24. See also Richard Noakes, 'Spiritualism, Science and the Supernatural in mid-Victorian Britain' in Nicola Bown, Carolyn Burdett, and Pamela Thurschwell, (eds.) *The Victorian Supernatural* (Cambridge, 2004) pp. 23–43.

fraudulent. In Peter Lamont's words, these scientists were not suffering from a 'crisis of faith', but a 'crisis of evidence'.[26]

As noted in the previous chapter, Howard had first encountered Spiritualism through the influence of Cora Richmond in Chicago.[27] Born in 1840 in New York State, she had been brought up partly in socialist intentional communities[28] at Hopedale, Massachusetts, and Waterloo, Wisconsin, where as a teenager she began to manifest an ability to speak on any topic given her by an audience.[29] The unlikelihood that a young girl would be able to speak with the fluency and clarity that she displayed gave her a sense of authenticity and authority which lasted throughout her life.[30] She was said to have given three thousand different lectures in the course of fifteen years, channelling communications from, among others, Thomas Paine, Thomas Jefferson, and William Ellery Channing, as well as reciting spontaneously produced poetry.[31] Before the spirit-channelled 'discourse', she would begin with an 'invocation', in the form of a prayer and thanksgiving in the Christian style. She was a firm believer in the synthesis of science,

[26] Peter Lamont, 'Spiritualism and the Mid-Victorian Crisis of Evidence' *Historical Journal* 47, 4 (December 2004) pp. 897–920. For the alternative view that Spiritualism was a response to a crisis of faith, see Janet Oppenheim, *The Other World: Spiritualism and Psychical Research in England 1850–1914* (Cambridge, 1985).

[27] She is always called Cora Richmond, her final surname, in the Howard archive, but is usually referred to as Cora Tappan by contemporaries and scholars. Of the previous scholars who have worked on Howard, only Buder does justice to the influence of Cora Richmond. See Stanley Buder, *Visionaries and Planners: The Garden City Movement and the Modern Community* (New York and Oxford, 1990) pp. 8–13.

[28] An 'intentional community' is a residential community of like-minded people who gather together to live co-operatively, in accordance with a shared vision.

[29] The idea was that the spirits who had tutored the poorly educated Cora were ready to help her: 'A circle of spirits . . . were ready always and in attendance to give response; and whenever the subject was in the particular department that they knew, the one who gave the lecture would be the one who had the most knowledge on that special subject.' Cora Tappan, *Discourses through the Mediumship of Mrs Cora L.V. Tappan – The New Science, Spiritual Ethics* (London, 1875) p. xvi.

[30] Alex Owen, *The Darkened Room: Women, Power and Spiritualism in Late Victorian London* (Chicago, 1989) pp. 210–12.

[31] Erika White Dyson, '"Gentleman Mountebanks" and Spiritualists: Legal, Stage and Media Contest between Magicians and Spirit Mediums in the United States and England' in Kontou and Wilburn, *Ashgate Research Companion* p. 249.

Spiritualism, and religion, and the content of her discourses, and the style of delivery, were inspirational and positive. For a nineteenth-century audience her stage presence was arresting: a young female speaker with golden curls confidently addressing huge gatherings and speaking on all manner of subjects. At the time that Howard first encountered her, she was the pastor of the Spiritualist church in Chicago, and had recently returned from a two-year stay in Britain, which had resulted in the publication of *Discourses through the Mediumship of Mrs Cora L.V. Tappan – The New Science, Spiritual Ethics* (London, 1875), a seven-hundred-page account of the 'orations' that she had delivered. The 'new science' in the title was what she termed 'super-science [which] seems to have laws antagonistic to mundane laws' and which emphasized the limitations of existing scientific knowledge, with much yet waiting to be discovered.[32] C.M. Davies, the pioneer sociologist of religion, devoted a chapter to Cora Tappan (as she then was) on the basis of what he had witnessed at one of her meetings at Cleveland Hall in London. He was struck by her appearance 'dressed neatly in black, with a profusion of golden hair' and her eloquence, reproducing her 'inspirational address' in full, which was loosely based on I Corinthians 15.[33] Frank Podmore, writing in 1902, also praised her intelligence and eloquence, but was more critical of the content of her trance utterances. He considered that they were frequently verbose and littered with duplications and redundant phrases. He concluded that the spirits poured forth from her, but they did so monotonously, and without recourse to irony, humour, or any of the literary artifices adopted by ordinary speakers. 'The style is clear, as jelly is clear; it is the protoplasm of human speech, and it is flavoured throughout with mild, cosmic emotions.'[34] For Howard, however, she was captivating, and the embodiment of spirit-inspired wisdom and cosmic optimism.

Returning to London from Chicago, Howard found the environment very congenial for developing his interest in Spiritualism further.

[32] Tappan, *Discourses* p. 6.

[33] C.M. Davies, *Heterodox London: or Phases of Free Thought in the Metropolis* Vol 2 (London, 1874) pp. 42–85.

[34] Frank Podmore, *Modern Spiritualism: A History and a Criticism* (London, 1902) Volume 2 pp. 134–9.

It seemed as if everyone was interested in it. Indeed, a writer in the *The Times* admitted bafflement that 'in a generation which boasts of itself to be one of exact science and plain matter-of-fact belief the "epidemic" of spiritualism had gained an estimated twenty million adherents'.[35] Howard had absorbed Cora Richmond's theory that the supernatural phenomena associated with Spiritualism were on the cusp of being explained by science, and that once they were, this would open up striking new insights into the workings of the world, and the brain. Science was progressing rapidly, with new discoveries in astronomy, biology, chemistry, geology, medicine, physiology, physics, and zoology, and so the belief that there was still much to be explained was both rational and widely shared. Having been convinced by witnessing Cora Richmond's trance speaking, and meeting with her at her home in Chicago, Howard's interest in Spiritualism seems to have been largely focussed on the intellectual engagement with Spiritualist ideas, considered in the context of the scientific publications of men like the physicist John Tyndall.[36] Although it may be assumed that he attended séances, at this point they seem not to have been the aspect of Spiritualism that particularly attracted him.

After his return from Dublin in 1879, he joined the Zetetical Society, also known as the Holborn Literary and Debating Society. The Zetetical Society had been founded in the previous year, as a junior version of the more prestigious Dialectical Society, and although it brandished its progressive credentials by being open to both sexes, it 'consisted largely of young men who wanted intellectual exercise'.[37] No topic, theological or otherwise, was seen as off limits, as long as it was discussed with 'decorum'. The Society nurtured several early Fabians, including George Bernard Shaw and Sidney Webb, whom Howard rapidly befriended. Both were still very young, and

---

[35] 'Spiritualism and Science' *The Times*, 26 December 1872, p. 5. Cited in Richard Noakes, 'The Sciences of Spiritualism in Victorian Britain: Possibilities and Problems' in Kontou and Wilburn, *Ashgate Research Companion* p. 25.

[36] Howard seems to have been particularly influenced by Tyndall's *Light* (1873) and *Fragments of Science for Unscientific People* (1871) both of which were based on lectures that he had given and were intended for the general public.

[37] Norman and Jeanne MacKenzie, *The First Fabians* (London, 1977) p. 35.

neither was yet known to the public.[38] Indeed, Shaw was only twenty-three, newly in London and struggling to make a living; perhaps he regarded the older and more travelled Howard as sophisticated and emulated him by learning shorthand.[39] Webb was even younger, at just twenty-one. He had recently joined the Inland Revenue and was engaging in a rigorous process of self-education. The Zetetical Society advertised that their speaker on 14 February 1880, would be 'Mr Ben Howard' on the topic of 'Spiritualism'. The lecture was apparently well received and led to vigorous debate, and an invitation to speak again on the same topic. This was undoubtedly an important moment for Howard, and one that he looked back on with pride. It signalled his public reception by members of London's young radical intelligentsia, and it showed that he could hold his own in front of a lively and discerning audience. The long hours taking down in shorthand the debates in the House of Commons had evidently taught him the art of public speaking. The printed version, which appeared in the Spiritualist magazine *Medium and Daybreak*, ran to nine thousand words. It was a carefully argued text, underpinned by multiple references to the scientific theories of the day.[40]

The second lecture, delivered in late May, was more revealing. It began with scientific and philosophically precise definitions of the terms that he was using and addressed the objections that had been made during the debate on his first lecture. It then proceeded in the manner of a discourse on physics and chemistry. Howard's argument was that the existence of luminiferous ether was central to the workings of the universe. 'The luminiferous ether can exist in what is

[38] Beevers, *Garden City Utopia* p. 14.

[39] Shaw only became well known from the mid-1880s. There were similarities between his early life and that of Howard, and he too began tedious employment as an office clerk at the age of fifteen. After his arrival in London from Dublin in 1876, he saw the debating societies where political, social, and religious issues were discussed as the best, cheapest, and most stimulating means to make friends, develop his speaking skills, and discuss his reading. He taught himself Pitman shorthand in 1882. See Stanley Weintraub, 'George Bernard Shaw, 1856–1950' *Oxford Dictionary of National Biography* (Oxford, 2004).

[40] Ebenezer Howard, 'Spiritualism: A Paper Presented to the Holborn Literary and Debating Society, Feb 14, 1880' *Medium and Daybreak*, XI (April 16, 1880) pp. 241–5.

technically known as a vacuum; it can pass freely through glass; itself invisible; it makes visible; and by its motion the stream of all life, whether animal or vegetable, is kept flowing on continuously. It is, as it were, a great Weaver, and all the chemical substances are its materials.'[41] Belief in luminiferous (light-bearing) ether was still an accepted scientific theory in 1880. It remained so until 1887, when it began to be seen as increasingly less plausible. Until then, it was hypothesized that the Earth moved through a medium of ether, to carry light, and that this explained the way in which wave-based light could be propagated through empty space. As a means of providing a natural explanation for supernatural phenomena, Spiritualists frequently asserted the existence of a very powerful invisible force. It might be suggested that this was ether, electricity, magnetic fluid (favoured by the mesmerists), or odyle (a universal emanation posited by a German industrial chemist, Karl von Reichenbach).[42]

Howard was simply developing this line of thought, favouring luminiferous ether as a plausible explanation for the seemingly unexplained. He made frequent references to the works of the distinguished physicist Tyndall, who believed in the existence of luminiferous ether, but was a noted critic of Spiritualism, as well as to Dalton and Huxley.[43] Howard also turned his attention to one of the classic dilemmas of the human condition – that a person feels themselves to be more than a collection of molecules. He considered the possibility of non-materialist explanations in relation to the human body, asking, 'Is the thinking substance of man the matter of the brain, or is it some other substance which can exist and act independently of the brain altogether? Is the brain the Ego, or is it an instrument of the Ego? The former is the materialistic hypothesis, the latter the spiritualistic.'[44] He drew back from stating that it was the ether that was 'the thinking substance of man' but he did hint at it as a possibility. The lecture concluded with a sermonic peroration: he was willing to be written off as a 'mad enthusiast' but he urged 'that out of those phenomena of Spiritualism which many men of science scorn to

[41] HALS DE/Ho/F3/43 Mss paper on Spiritualism, 27 May 1880.
[42] Noakes, 'Sciences of Spiritualism' 37.
[43] Noakes, 'Sciences of Spiritualism' 42–4.
[44] HALS DE/Ho/F3/43 Paper on Spiritualism, 27 May 1880.

investigate will come lines of communication with unseen intelligences; and that the day will dawn, yea, even now has dawned, when men will learn to think of those who have departed from us through the portals of Death, no longer as dead, but as living in a new and perhaps more exalted plane of existence'.[45]

Howard had argued himself into the conclusion that science would show that death had been overcome, and Spiritualism had provided the means for making this realization. He felt exulted. The revelation was enough to take him back to Christianity.[46] Writing years later, he stated: 'I well remember that the following Sunday the very souls of the flowers, and the birds – all Nature seemed to have become nearer, more familiar, more real, more as it were a part of my environment and inner being and I felt that I had learned something of the secret of life.'[47] In 1910, he wrote that having broken away entirely from orthodox faith, the experience of delivering the lecture had brought him back to the realization of the supreme value of Christ's teaching.[48] A month before his death, he dictated notes to his son on how he wanted this incident handled by his biographer:

Look for Reports of Lecture given by me in 1879 [actually 1880] before the Holborn Lit & Debating Society. I want it brought out in my life that my absolute belief in a future life was one of those influences which made me dare to do anything for the cause I had at heart. I think you will find in addition to the printed report of my first lecture, the mss of a second lecture on a similar subject which I gave to the same Society. I sent a copy of my article to Sir Oliver Lodge [the distinguished physicist and Spiritualist] who made this remark in a letter which is somewhere about that though my views about light as expressed then, in 1879, [1880] were very far from being the views which are now held,

---

[45] HALS DE/Ho/F3/43 Mss paper on Spiritualism, 27 May 1880.

[46] Tim Larsen has identified other examples of freethinkers who followed Howard's pattern, finding their way back to Christianity through the Spiritualist route. Timothy Larsen, *Crisis of Doubt: Honest Faith in Nineteenth-Century England* (Oxford, 2006).

[47] HALS DE/Ho/F10/6/6. Notes for a lecture or speech concerning the Garden City movement, *c.*1910.

[48] HALS DE/Ho/F28/9 Spiritual Influences and Social Progress published in *Light* as two articles on 23 and 30 April 1910.

yet at the same time they showed an astonishing realization of some of the essential truths with regard to light.[49]

By the early 1880s, it appeared that Ben had reached an accommodation with Lizzie on matters of religion. He was happy to declare himself to be Christian, and to resume his association with Congregationalism. They were both happy to declare themselves as Spiritualists, and Lizzie was fully converted to it after meeting Cora Richmond in the summer of 1880.[50] Howard noted that when Richmond and her husband visited London 'my wife and I became very intimate with Mr and Mrs Richmond, attending a good many of her lectures, and on one or two occasions she visited us at home'.[51] Ebenezer Howard's nascent feminism, expressed in his positive attitudes concerning the equality and capabilities of women, may also have been influenced by what he had witnessed in Cora Richmond. Howard's two eldest daughters, Kathleen and Edith, interviewed many years later by Frederic Osborn, both attested to her influence on their father.[52] Edith remarked that once in a trance, she had told him that 'you are going to give of your engineering inventions . . . I see you surrounded by circles.'[53] Edith remarked that this was probably the reason that he had based his Garden City plan on circles. Osborn professed scepticism at this idea, but given the seriousness with which Howard took everything that Cora Richmond said, it does not seem beyond the bounds of possibility.

The turn to the social gospel and the housing and land questions

Howard's adoption of a spirituality that mixed elements of Spiritualism with elements of Congregational Christianity energized him to dream dreams and see visions. In the 1880s and into the 1890s, he

[49] HALS DE/Ho/F27/3 biographical notes dictated to A.C. Howard by Sir Ebenezer Howard in the presence of Lady Howard on Wednesday 11 April 1928.

[50] Buder, *Visionaries and Planners,* 11.

[51] HALS DE/Ho/F17/13/2.

[52] HALS DE/FJO/I35. The interview with Kathleen (Rawlinson) took place on 3 February 1968.

[53] HALS DE/FJO/I35 Notes of talk with Mrs Berry in WGC, 4 March 1944.

explored the foundations that would underpin *To-morrow*, and contemplated the practical steps that would be needed to create the
Garden Cities. The influences on him were very varied. They
included joining a church (Rectory Road in Stoke Newington)
where preaching the social gospel that was becoming a feature of
some sections of English Christianity was a central concern. Equally
important was his discovery of ideas about landownership which
sprang from older traditions of radical dissent, the widespread propagation of new economic theories, the ripples of socialism that were
washing over London, and utopian science fiction, which was also
concerned with perfected societies. Howard pondered what each of
these might contribute in his search to formulate a remedy for the
deteriorating urban conditions that he witnessed around him. As he
began to think about the alternatives, he developed an increasing
sense that he was the bearer of a special message for the world.

In 1883, Andrew Mearns and W.C. Preston anonymously pub-
lished *The Bitter Cry of Outcast London: An Inquiry into the Condition of the
Abject Poor*, a penny pamphlet on behalf of the Congregational
Union.[54] It was given large amounts of publicity by W.T. Stead, the
editor of the *Pall Mall Gazette*, who was a Congregationalist with a
powerful sense of religious and social mission which he activated
through crusading journalism.[55] Stead and *The Bitter Cry* authors
demanded to know why Christians were concentrating on building
new churches, when slum conditions, in which it would be impossible
to live a Christian life, were in their midst? They also demanded
action from the local authorities. This signalled the recognition of an
important theological shift: 'sin' was increasingly now seen as woven
into the fabric of unjust structures, not merely the result of the fallen
condition of humanity, who had turned away in disobedience
from God.[56] Mearns and Preston used evidence supplied by agents
of the London City Mission, and were unsparing in describing the

[54] Andrew Mearns is usually cited as the sole author. Mearns, *The Bitter Cry of
Outcast London*, ed. Anthony S. Wohl, (Leicester, 1970).

[55] Stewart J. Brown, *W.T. Stead: Nonconformist and Newspaper Prophet* (Oxford,
2019) pp. 49–52.

[56] There were, however, some Nonconformists who were unhappy with this
shift. See Watts, *Dissenters Volume III* pp. 291–2.

conditions that were being uncovered. There was enormous over-crowding, with families living in single rooms in dilapidated houses that had been subdivided in order to cram in the maximum number of tenants, which in turn could result in alcoholism, prostitution, abuse, and incest. The absence of sanitation led to illness and premature death. The authors coined the phrase 'the submerged tenth' to describe the ten per cent of the population who lived in these abject conditions.

Everyone read *The Bitter Cry* – from Queen Victoria to the Howards, and both Ben and Lizzie made regular references to the 'submerged tenth' when they spoke about social conditions in London: the reference clearly remained readily understood by audiences for some decades. The ability of Mearns and Preston to combine conciseness with carefully observed detail made their report compelling reading, and it had considerable impact in mobilizing what was becoming known as the social gospel. This idea influenced both Nonconformists and Anglicans, and was conceptualized by broadening both the concept of the state, and its legitimate sphere of activities, and the Christian doctrine of redemption, so that redemption was seen, at least by more advanced theologians, increasingly in societal, rather than in narrowly individualist terms.[57] The Congregational theologians R.W. Dale, J.B. Paton, and A.M. Fairbairn were at the forefront of promoting the social gospel in Nonconformist circles. Dale declared that it was the duty of the Christian citizen 'not to forsake municipal and political life because it is corrupt, but to carry into municipal and political activity the law and spirit of Christ'.[58] There were also various Anglican initiatives inspired by similar sentiments, including the university settlement movement, pioneered initially by Samuel and Henrietta Barnett.

---

[57] For a helpful analysis of the origin and meaning of the term, its relationship with the 'Nonconformist Conscience' and the specific contribution of Nonconformist thinkers, see David M. Thompson, 'The Emergence of the Nonconformist Social Gospel in England' in Keith Robbins (ed.), *Protestant Evangelicalism: Britain, Ireland, Germany and America*, c.*1750*–c.*1950 Studies in Church History Subsidia 7* (Blackwell, Oxford, 1990) pp. 255–80.

[58] R.W. Dale, *The Laws of Christ for Common Life* (London, 1884) pp. 187–8. Cited in Thompson, 'Emergence of the Nonconformist Social Gospel' p. 277.

One of the more immediate responses to *The Bitter Cry* was a two-day conference on the condition of the poor organized by the main Nonconformist denominations in April 1884, at which the Methodist leader Hugh Price Hughes urged the adoption of Christian Socialism, a term that at this date was often used as a synonym for the social gospel. In the midst of the general condemnation of abject poverty, there was a particularly new focus on housing, and the moral problem of the housing crisis became a prominent issue at the Methodist Conference of 1885. The Royal Commission on the Housing of the Poor (1884–5), requested by Queen Victoria, and with a membership which included the Prince of Wales and Cardinal Manning, was both a direct consequence of the publicity surrounding *The Bitter Cry* and a sign that the state was indeed beginning to think about the need to enlarge its sphere of moral responsibility. *The Bitter Cry* remains very frequently cited as the landmark event in the public discussion of poverty and its consequences in the 1880s.[59]

Another major influence of this period was the economic theories of the American journalist Henry George. His most famous book, *Progress and Poverty*, was published in America in 1879, and sold millions of copies worldwide; it could be purchased in England for sixpence. Awareness of him in the British Isles increased when he visited England and Ireland four years later. He expounded his ideas in a lecture at the headquarters of the Congregational Union, on 5 September 1882, and was found to be a charismatic speaker. Howard found George's theory extremely compelling, and it rapidly took hold in radical circles. He argued that what was needed to remedy the growing gulf between the rich and the poor was a single land tax on landlords' rent, to reflect the fact that they grew wealthy simply by owning land – what he termed their 'unearned increment'. The tax

[59] See, for example, D.W. Bebbington, *The Nonconformist Conscience: Chapel and Politics 1870–1914* (London, 1982) pp. 42–3; Thompson, 'Emergence of the Nonconformist Social Gospel' pp. 257–8; Sally Ledger and Roger Luckhurst, (eds.) *The Fin de Siècle: A Reader in Cultural History c.1880–1900* (Oxford, 2000) pp. 26–32; Seth Koven, *Slumming: Sexual and Social Politics in Victorian London* (Princeton, 2004) pp. 27, 228; Tristram Hunt, *Building Jerusalem: The Rise and Fall of the Victorian City* (London, 2004) pp. 291–4; Watts, *Dissenters Volume III*, pp. 133–8, 290–1, 307–8; Knight, *Victorian Christianity* pp. 157–9.

raised should be shared among society in order to reduce poverty. George stated that wealth created from land speculation was immoral not merely because it created fortunes amassed from idleness, but also because it resulted in overcrowded cities – higher rents meant poorer housing compared with what could be rented elsewhere – and an underutilized, stagnating countryside. George was expressing the centuries-old radical view that land was part of man's common inheritance, like air and water, and should not be bought, sold, or speculated upon.[60] The idea of land being held in trust, and the rent and rates being paid by the people who occupied it being used first to pay off the costs of the purchase, and then to fund social projects for the benefit of the occupiers, was to become a central edifice of the Garden City idea.

Howard found an earlier iteration of a similar idea in the 'land plan' of the late eighteenth-century radical Thomas Spence. Spence, together with James Murray, a radical Presbyterian minister, had been enraged by a proposal to enclose common land in Newcastle, prompting Spence to argue that land was a common property, and that all had the right to sustain themselves and their families upon it as a 'natural right and privilege'. Parishioners should therefore appoint a day to take control of the land of their parish, and form themselves into 'corporations' to manage it. Land belonged in the hands of the citizens, not in the hands of landowners, or indeed of central government authorities. His plan was that the land, and any other natural resources such as rivers or mines, would be rented out to the highest bidders who would work them efficiently. The rent they paid would be used to finance public amenities for the benefit of all, and to provide an income, to be divided equally among all citizens each quarter- day. In this way, poverty would be eliminated. Although Spence intended to deprive the rich of their land, he did not envisage stripping them of their other forms of wealth, and he envisaged that workers would be self-employed, or part of co-operative ventures. Spence first delivered these views in a lecture to the Newcastle Philosophical Society, where they were not well received, leading to a sequence of events which

[60] For the influence of Henry George upon Howard, see Beevers, *Garden City Utopia* pp. 17–18; Buder, *Visionaries and Planners* pp. 14–25.

resulted in Spence's ostracism in Newcastle, and removal to London, where he became a radical pamphleteer.[61] Some of his other publications imagined utopian island communities, 'Crusonia' and 'Spensonia', where people lived harmoniously on shared land. Spence's pamphlet *The Real Rights of Man*, based on his Newcastle lecture, was reprinted by H.M. Hyndman, the founder of the Social Democratic Federation, in 1882, together with his own notes and commentary, under the title *The Nationalisation of the Land in 1775 and 1882* and it was this that Howard read.[62] Spence's overriding focus on land, and the use of land rents, together with his gentle acceptance of individual wealth and freedom fed directly into Howard's thinking. The question unanswered by Spence was precisely how the parishioners should gain control of the land in their parish, and what should be done in the face of landowner resistance. Jean-Yves Tizot has suggested that although Ebenezer Howard appeared enthusiastic about Spence's plan in *Tomorrow*, in fact he edited Spence's text to remove the most radical elements, thus sanitizing it so that it would not frighten the capitalists who he hoped would support his scheme.[63]

Howard found yet further confirmation of the view that land should not be privately owned in the first, and little-known book of the philosopher Herbert Spencer, *Social Statics*, published in 1850, and encountered by Howard during his time in Chicago. Spencer stated the argument with an elegance that was lacking in Spence:

> Equity, therefore, does not permit property in land. For if *one* portion of the earth's surface may justly become the possession of an individual, and may be held by him for his sole use and benefit, as a thing to which he has an exclusive right, then *other* portions of the earth's surface may be so held; and eventually the whole of the earth's surface may be so held; and our planet may thus lapse altogether into private hands . . . Supposing the entire habitable globe to be so enclosed, it follows that if the landowners have a valid right to its surface, all who are not

[61] For an account of Spence, together with his collected political works, see H.T. Dickinson, *The Political Works of Thomas Spence* (Newcastle, 1982).

[62] Beevers, *Garden City Utopia* p. 21.

[63] Jean-Yves Tizot, 'Radical Legacy or Intellectual Indelicacy? Ebenezer Howard's use of "the most admirable project of Thomas Spence" in the Garden City Concept' MIRANDA 13, 2016 https://doi.org/10.4000/miranda.9173

landowners, have no right to its surface. Hence, such can exist on the earth by sufferance only.[64]

Ebenezer Howard found Spencer's logic intoxicating, and it provided him with the philosophical foundation that he needed for arguing for common land ownership.

Edward Bellamy's utopian science fiction took Howard in a very different direction from the English Dissenters. He was lent a copy of *Looking Backward 2000–1887*, shortly after it came out in America in early 1888, and was instantly captivated, reading it overnight in one sitting. 'I was transported by the wonderful power of the writer into a new society, which, having solved for itself the industrial elements of the social problem, had its face turned towards the problems of the higher life, which will become yet more real and urgent when we have solved such problems as those of unemployment, of insufficient housing and the care of the nation's children.'[65] As he walked through the crowded narrow streets of London the following morning, Howard had an epiphany: 'There came to me an overpowering sense of the quite temporary nature of nearly all I saw, and of its entire unsuitability for the working life of the new order – the order of justice, unity, and friendliness . . . the writer had permanently convinced me that our present industrial order stands absolutely condemned and is tottering to its fall, and that a new and brighter, because a juster, order must ere long take its place.'[66] He felt compelled to ensure the dissemination of Bellamy's work in Britain, and called on William Reeves, the radical publisher, urging him to issue an edition for the British market. Reeves was sceptical but agreed to arrange publication when Howard offered to take the first hundred copies of the print run and compile an index. According to Robert Beevers, Reeves made a small fortune from the publication, but Howard was not even paid for the index.[67]

[64] Herbert Spencer, *Social Statics: Or, the Conditions Essential to Human Happiness Specified, and the First of Them Developed* (London, 1851) pp. 114–15.

[65] HALS DE/Ho/F28/9 Spiritual Influences and Social Progress published in *Light* as two articles on 23 and 30 April 1910.

[66] HALS DE/Ho/F28/9 Spiritual Influences and Social Progress published in *Light* as two articles on 23 and 30 April 1910.

[67] Beevers, *Garden City Utopia* 28.

What was it about *Looking Backward* that so enchanted Howard? It was a detailed description of life in Boston in the year 2000, in a world where equality, the sharing of resources, and kindness had broken out, and where servility and selfishness were seen as outmoded and discredited concepts from the past.[68] The virtues of brotherhood and working for the common good were practised by citizens living in light and spacious houses equipped with technological gadgetry: sermons were delivered to the whole population down the telephone. The people gathered together in elegant public dining rooms to eat communally prepared dinners and enjoy a range of recreational activities. There were, however, elements of authoritarian control in Bellamy's vision, for example an 'international committee' who intervened to decide on trade rules between nations, and when he re-read the book for a second time, Howard found these elements, and the fact that society was organized as a big business corporation, abhorrent. Certainly, Bellamy's Bostonians seemed rather fixated on the familiar capitalist pursuits of visiting shopping malls and acquiring possessions. The central conceit in *Looking Backward* is of a Bostonian who falls into a deep sleep in 1887, and wakes up in the year 2000. This device permits the bemused time traveller to make constant comparisons between the Boston of the late nineteenth century, and the city that it has become, and he is aided by his well-educated host, who provides him with numerous explanations and comparisons between his own time, and the present. In the final chapter, the time traveller finds himself back in 1880s Boston, and is filled with precisely the kind of revulsion that Howard evidently also experienced as he walked around London having read the book.[69]

Howard's deep interest in descriptions of alternative communities where land is managed equitably – Thomas More's *Utopia* and its many later parallels: Hygeia, Crusonia, Spensonia, a Boston of the

[68] For a recent scholarly edition, see Edward Bellamy, *Looking Backwards 2000–1887* edited with an introduction and notes by Matthew Beaumont (Oxford, 2007).

[69] Nathaniel Robert Walker, *Victorian Visions of Suburban Utopia: Abandoning Babylon* (Oxford, 2020) p. 2 suggests that Howard 'began his engagement with settlement reform, not as a professional architect or planner, but rather as the reader of utopian science fiction' (i.e. Bellamy).

future – is evident. With the obvious exception of More, it is significant that most of these authors – Spence, Spencer, George, and Bellamy – were rooted in the Dissenting tradition of which Howard himself was part. Although he associated with Fabian friends, and others on the left who would create the Labour Party, it is striking that he did not become a Fabian, and never mentioned Marx as having been an influence. Howard's proposal for land management never included state ownership, and although he believed in equality and disliked hierarchy, he did not propose a radical overhaul of the existing class structure.

The Howards were, in the 1880s, experiencing their own middle-class version of the London housing crisis. As already noted, the house in Dulwich was proving too expensive, and Ben was looking for something cheaper, reporting back on his fruitless search to Lizzie. He had looked at some properties in Clapham and concluded that although they were 'nice inside' with fitted bathrooms and electric bells but 'instead of gardens, [they had] little strips not as big as the kitchen'. The rents were between £38 and £50 a year. He suggested a different plan, a cooperative housing solution in which the Howards, at this date a family of five, would share a large house with his parents, his brother Harry, and his sister Annie. He tried to persuade his wife of the merits of this proposal:

> Suppose we took a house at a rent of £80 or £90 a year our expenses would be less than they are now. We could have a really nice garden for the children to play in, with perhaps a lawn tennis ground. There would be a saving in many ways. One kitchen fire would serve for both families. A joint of meat would not have to stay about for days but we might have far more variety of food . . . If I did not come home in the evening you would not be nervous. We should of course have our own private sitting room, so that we could have all the privacy we have now, and even more for little Nem [their children] could sometimes adjourn to Father's sitting room and we could spoon together . . . I am sure as I can be of an untried thing that it would possess great advantages . . . You think it over and let me know. Don't allow your mind to be too strongly prejudiced in favour of separate houses, but try to picture the advantages as well as the undoubted small disadvantages.[70]

This plan for cooperative housekeeping for the extended Howard family did not materialize, although it did resurface in the Homesgarth and Meadow Way Green cooperative living schemes in Letchworth some decades later.

The Howards spent the remainder of their years in London renting smaller homes in Stoke Newington, North London, fairly close to Howard's parents, who resided in a large house in Evering Road with eight other members of their extended family.[71] Although the streets in which they lived, Norcott Road and Durley Road, were both marked as red, signifying 'well to do' in Charles Booth's tinted map, the social investigator described the area as having 'no symmetry or convenience or natural order of any kind . . . All seems haphazard'[72] – something which Howard would have found troubling. According to Booth, Congregationalism was the 'most typical religious organisation' in this part of London, and also the most 'complete and successful'. He provided a detailed description of the thriving North London Congregational churches, with their packed Sunday services, ambitious programmes of weekday activities, their middle-class membership, and well-paid ministers.[73] The Howards joined Rectory Road Congregational Church, where his parents were also members, on 31 October 1889. They almost certainly spent some earlier period as attenders, before taking on the formal commitment of membership.

The minister, C. Fleming Williams was like Howard a protégé of Joseph Parker, and active in London's radical circles. He was highly regarded by his large and well-heeled congregation, who were presumably sympathetic to his progressive views.[74] The church was

[71] Information from the 1891 Census. In addition to Ann and Ebenezer senior, other family members were their daughter Elizabeth, her husband Frederick Harrison, an artist, and their two children; their youngest daughter Tamar, a thirty-five-year-old 'typewriter operator'; a niece, Millicent Tow, who was also a 'typewriter operator and stenographer', and another niece and nephew from the Tow family. These family members had evidently embraced the cooperative living arrangement that Ben had contemplated some years earlier.

[72] Charles Booth, *The Life and Labour of the People in London: Third Series: Religious Influences Vol 1 London North of the Thames: The Outer Ring* (London, 1902) p. 115. The date of his enquiry into the area was 1897–8.

[73] Booth, *Life and Labour* pp. 119–24.

[74] For Fleming 'Flaming' Williams, see Binfield, 'Garden City Religion' p. 65 and *Congregational Year Book*, 1938 p. 674.

visited by one of Booth's researchers in the late 1890s, who noted that
the Sunday evening service attendance was between eleven and twelve
hundred, and that there were many young men dressed in frock coats
and carrying top hats, and the women were dressed equally smartly.
Fleming Williams on that occasion preached on a popular and
recently published novel, Hall Caine's *Christian,* contrasting its message with that of the New Testament. On other Sundays, he held
question-and-answer sessions, where members of the congregation
raised issues that were bothering them, including: how should a
young man act whose parents disapproved of his views on religion?
What should a girl teach her Sunday school about heaven and hell?
The researcher concluded that 'on all these questions the replies given
were very thoughtful; those of a true leader of his people. One could
not but recognize how great a position such a man holds.'[75] This was
the religious world into which the Howards had been settled for the
previous decade, and where Lizzie began her own public speaking
career by reading papers on Tennyson. Unsurprisingly, the couple
became firm friends with Fleming Williams, who was known as
'Flaming Williams' because of his periodic outbursts against the
exploitation of working people. He was elected an alderman on the
London County Council, and in cooperation with fellow Congregationalist John Williams Benn, James Branch, and other Progressives,
campaigned against slum housing. Indeed, Williams served on the
Public Health and Housing Committee from 1890 to 1906, and was
its chairman from 1893 to 1895.[76] Clyde Binfield commented that the
Rectory Road church 'resembled the LCC at prayer'.[77] This social
gospel and slum clearance activist was the ideal minister, from the
perspective of Ebenezer Howard, and it was among these North
London Congregationalists that he found the support he needed to
launch his Garden City ideas upon the world.

[75] Booth, *Life and Labour* pp. 224–6.
[76] Bebbington, *Nonconformist Conscience* pp. 43–4; Buder, *Visionaries and Planners*
pp. 36–7.
[77] Binfield, 'Garden City Religion' p. 65.

3

The Days before *To-morrow* 1890–1898

Early drafts and speeches

In October 1890, when General William Booth of the Salvation Army published his famous book, *In Darkest England and the Way Out*, Ebenezer Howard immediately sent him two papers that he had read at Rectory Road Congregational Church.[1] The three-hundred-page text of *In Darkest England* was divided into two parts: the first described the terrible conditions endured by the urban poor, and the second outlined the Salvation Army's schemes for their 'deliverance'. A multitude of social projects were designed to rehabilitate the destitute so that they might move through a sequence of 'colonies': from city to farm, and then to colonies that would be established in the British Empire overseas. The book had been ghost-written by the journalist W.T. Stead, who ensured that it was launched with maximum publicity.[2] Events included 'a great gathering' at London's Exeter Hall, at which Booth made a typically combative speech, promoting his schemes as the panacea for saving those lost in soul and body, and defending his work from its numerous critics. He brushed aside criticisms that he was unwilling to cooperate with others, or to allow his fundraising to be subject to the scrutiny of trustees. In outlining his scheme, he repeated the idea of souls

[1] HALS DE/Ho/F27/26. The papers were returned to Howard on 11 November 1890, with a note informing him that 'General Booth . . . has perused them with interest, and thanks you for them'. It is not clear which papers these were, but presumably early drafts of his plans for building new communities.

[2] Stewart J. Brown, *W.T. Stead: Nonconformist and Newspaper Prophet* (Oxford, 2019) pp. 109–13.

Ebenezer Howard: Inventor of the Garden City. Frances Knight, Oxford University Press.
© Frances Knight 2023. DOI: 10.1093/oso/9780198790815.003.0004

drowning in a sea of misery, an image which figured prominently in the text and in the litho print 'Work for All' which was the frontispiece to the volume. The meeting was well attended, and the report in *The Times* noted the presence on the platform of a number of notable Nonconformist leaders, including the Baptist John Clifford.[3]

It is likely that also present was the Congregational minister of Rectory Road, Stoke Newington and London County Council alderman, C. Fleming Williams. As a prominent London-based exponent of the social gospel, Williams was rapidly formulating his own response to Booth's well-publicized plans. Two days after Booth had spoken at Exeter Hall, Williams convened his own meeting to discuss Booth's project. Ebenezer Howard was on hand to transcribe the proceedings, and he noted that it was a 'a large gathering and it was expected that some definite proposal would be made.'[4] The 'definite proposal' was for the setting up of a district social reform league, comprising the churches of North East London. But the greatest significance of this event was probably its effect on Howard himself. He marked in his longhand text the places where Williams emphasized the importance of stemming the flow of country people to the city: 'this invasion of country people first of all increases the real mass of pauperism . . . it also displaces the weakest and least potent of those already engaged in work in the city and binds them in the same position of helplessness and almost hopelessness.'[5] The trend was for employers to lay off ageing warehousemen and clerks in order to employ fitter, stronger, and younger men who had arrived from the country.

Williams's criticism of Booth was muted, but evident. Booth and his followers 'have unfurled the banner of faith and said that they will deal with the social problem' but it was no longer enough for one denomination to imagine that it could do this. Times were changing, and society had grown more complex and interdependent. He agreed with Booth on the need to set up labour bureaux, provide better homes, help the 'most hopeless cases', and ban drinking and gambling at his

---

[3] *The Times*, 'In Darkest England' 18 November 1890 p. 7.

[4] HALS DE/Ho/F10/15 Speech of Mr Williams (Fleming Williams) at a Special Meeting called just after the publication of *In Darkest England*.

[5] HALS DE/Ho/F10/15.

Salvation Army projects. But he went much further than Booth in believing that the slums of London needed to be demolished and rebuilt. This required having the powers to tackle slum landlords, which in turn required close cooperation between Christian social activists and secular bodies such as Parliament and the London County Council. Simply focussing on plucking lost souls from a churning sea of sin without this more substantial action was, he implied, fruitless: 'With the support of the philanthropy of England and his co-workers, [Booth] could empty the sea of misery if he could deal with whatever it is that drives people from the country to the town, and then drives them to drink. But with the forces that disallow the rebuilding of London in a wholesome way still in place, those forces would simply reproduce the old crop and that sea would be full again tomorrow with a more despairing crowd of sinking wretches.'[6] Williams' speech must have reinforced for Howard two ideas that he would always emphasise. First, that there had to be a curb on the constant drift of population from country to city, and secondly, that for desirable changes in planning and building to be achieved, co-operation had to be secured among a broad spectrum of interested parties.

In 1890 Ebenezer Howard, now forty years old, wrote what is the earliest surviving version of his vision for a new society. It survives on thirty-one flimsy pages and is now very faded. It stops rather suddenly, suggesting either that the remainder is lost, or that he lost confidence in his writing, and realized that it had become wordy, and overladen with detail.[7] The style is indeed wooden and passive, and quite different from the compelling rhetorical style that he developed a few years later. He entitled his paper 'City of Health and How to Build it', which was a homage to Benjamin Richardson's *Hygeia: A City of Health* which he had read fourteen years earlier in Chicago. He began by providing a resumé of *Hygeia*, describing Richardson as the 'poet of hygiene'. After this he provided a description of a community to which he gave the American-sounding name Unionville, which was

---

[6] HALS DE/Ho/F10/15.

[7] HALS DE/Ho/F1/5 'City of Health and How to Build it' n.d. (1890–1). Another early paper which survives from around 1894 is 'The Revenues of Unionville and How it is Obtained' (HALS DE/Ho/F3/32).

in many respects identical to the Garden City that he would describe in *To-morrow*. Unionville is a complete circle, one thousand acres in size and with a population of thirty thousand. It is enclosed by a belt of nine thousand acres of agricultural land, making fresh agricultural produce cheap and easily available. The city is divided by three main boulevards into six equal wards. In the centre are the public buildings – trade hall, concert hall, lecture halls, library, museum, picture gallery, and theatre. There is an inner ring, with alms houses, orphanages, and sports fields. There is a free circular electric tramway running around the town, close to a circular glass corridor which functions as a covered market and shopping arcade. There is a winter garden, where flowers bloom all year (reminiscent of the winter pansies he had seen in Dublin's Phoenix Park). There is an outer ring, with circular railway line and factories, warehouses, dairies, markets, and technical schools. Housing is arranged in a series of belts, and freedom is permitted in styles of architecture, as long as plans are approved by a building committee. Tenants living in accommodation blocks have the option of eating in a communal dining hall, while others may choose to do their own cooking. All of these ideas survived into later iterations of the Garden City plan. Only a few did not, including a proposal for circular glass local stores dotted around the boulevards, and a plan for children's playgrounds with attached work rooms for mothers equipped with sewing and knitting machines. Howard explained that he hoped this would allow mothers to 'enjoy the society and help and advice of each other, and divide the labour of looking after the little ones for whom suitable toys and games are amply provided' but perhaps this plan for garment manufacture with communal child minding seemed too reminiscent of a sweat shop to survive into later versions. Howard imagined this community being funded from money raised by mortgage debentures. Several classic Ebenezer Howard tropes are found in this early description of an imagined city of health. The city is an 'invention' and the key to its creation is 'simple'. Both town and country are within walking distance. Freedom of thought and individual liberty are continuously stressed, although they are exercised within the framework of an overarching and detailed plan.

Howard showed this document to someone, for there are pencil annotations in another hand, questioning some of Howard's assumptions and figures. 'Cities grow', said the annotator, 'they are not made to order, and this would cost too much'. The annotating hand also questioned some dimensions and acreages, pointing out that the circular glass shopping arcade would be two miles and three hundred and twenty yards in circumference. But Howard was undeterred. There was much in Unionville which became First Garden City, and the circular glass shopping arcade survived into later versions. This idea seems particularly fanciful, but Beevers points out that Howard's first marital home had been within sight of the glass towers of Sydenham Hill, where Joseph Paxton's glass exhibition halls from the 1851 Great Exhibition had been re-erected. Howard acknowledged the inspiration he had received from Paxton.[8]

Howard is said to have had a beautiful speaking voice, and he was probably aware that he was better as a public speaker than as a writer. By 1892 he had prepared a lecture entitled 'Common Sense Socialism' which he toured round various audiences and congregations in London. It was illustrated with lantern slides which permitted the new city he described to be appreciated in visual terms, and gave the audience something to imagine, while he rattled through the figures on acreages, costs, and percentages. These slides are the first version of the circular diagrams which appear as the plates in *To-morrow*. As noted in the previous chapter, Howard did not acknowledge Marx as an influence, and he began his lecture with his own definition of 'Socialism':

> Socialism is a state or condition of life in which every endeavour is made by Society and by the individuals who compose Society to satisfy from the bountiful reservoirs of Nature the needs of Society as a whole and the needs of individuals who compose Society. Such a state of Society in which human need is made the touchstone of individual and collective action is undoubtedly an ideal state and represents a condition which to many seems unattainable. But it is essential to have an ideal as showing us the direction in which we should move.[9]

[8] Robert Beevers, *The Garden City Utopia: A Critical Biography of Ebenezer Howard* (Houndsmill, 1988) p. 53.

[9] HALS DE/Ho/F10/8/1 'Common Sense Socialism, 1892'.

He concluded the lecture by stressing that his form of socialism involved no physical force or restriction but depended entirely upon the power of intellectual and moral persuasion, and common sense. His first draft was somewhat more political before editing: a reference to mine owners was crossed out and changed to those 'who live in idleness out of the energy, and the skill and the labor (sic) of others'. Landlords, however, were explicitly condemned, and would not exist in the 'new city.'

> God gave the land for the use of man, and He never intended that there should be any intermediary between Himself and the recipient who, as such intermediary, should take for himself a special share of the gift. The landlord is in every-day-life what the priest is in religion. He says in effect 'If you want to go to God's earth you must go through me'.[10]

This anti-landlordism was drawing directly on Spence and Spencer, and the analogy with the priesthood was intended to resonate with his Protestant audiences. Likewise, 'common sense' and 'socialism' (variously understood) were concepts to appeal to his Christian socialist, social gospel-influenced Nonconformist constituency. This was a sounder strategy than advertising a lecture on building 'new cities', which could have appeared simply irrelevant and utopian. Howard became skilled at taking an audience with him in incremental stages: he began by setting out the familiar problem, the iniquities of urban overcrowding and deserted rural areas, and only after these had been detailed and described did he begin to make proposals for what at this date he was calling the 'new city'. The community envisaged was almost identical to that described in the 'City of Health', although here he makes it explicit that the 'new city' will attract people of all types, who have taken responsibility for improving their situation through collective action:

> Men, women, children, architects, engineers, bricklayers, builders, carpenters, tradespeople, teachers, doctors, artists, etc. – having become so profoundly convinced that the congested life of our great cities is bad for their health, moral, intellectual and physical, and being bad for their health must therefore tend to lessen their productive powers. Having

[10] HALS DE/Ho/F10/8/9.

become profoundly dissatisfied, these people 'have banded themselves in a great migratory effort' having seen that this is much better than each person attempting it on his own, they have realised that they need to arrange to purchase out of their collective resources, and by an appeal to the interested public sufficient money to purchase or to secure the option of purchase of a large estate, and they have now built themselves a city in the form I now place before you...[11]

Howard suggested that £300,000 was needed to fund the city, but that this was 'paltry' and would be easily obtained if enough publicity was given to the project. He assumed that the money could be borrowed at an interest rate of four per cent per annum, and that the freehold of the estate would be vested in trustees on behalf of the residents. He reminded his audience of Isaiah's promises concerning the restoration of Israel: 'wherefore will ye spend money for that which is not bread? And your labour for that which satisfieth not?'[12] In reality, of course, £300,000 was an enormous sum in the 1890s, and many must have come out of his meetings with a sense of the impossibility of what was being proposed. But there were others who were captivated by his message, and he began to gather a band of supporters.

In the years between 1891 and 1894, Howard was employed intermittently as a court reporter for the Royal Commission on Labour, which meant that his professional and personal preoccupations coincided. He noted in a memoir prepared in 1926 that he had deliberately given up more lucrative work, in order to make himself available for the Labour Commission.[13] The Commission was enquiring into the relations between employers and employed, the conditions of labour and recent trade union disputes. It heard evidence from William Booth, amongst others, and it was here that Howard got to know the economist Professor Alfred Marshall and trades union leader Tom Mann. As his reputation on London's progressive and Nonconformist lecture circuits began to grow, he became drawn into the arguments of some of the other individuals and groups who were interested in promoting colonies and new forms of communal living.

[11] HALS DE/Ho/F10/8/7.
[12] HALS DE/Ho/F10/8/13, citing Isaiah 55:2.
[13] HALS DE/Ho/F18.

There was the Nationalization of Labour Society, who promoted the ideas of Edward Bellamy, and the Land Nationalization Society, who believed, as Howard did, that a colony should at the outset own its own land. Howard was by this time disillusioned with Bellamy's vision for a centrally managed community, in which members had to relinquish significant personal freedom. Howard's friend, J. Bruce Wallace, a Congregational minister who founded his own Christian socialist Brotherhood Church in Southgate, and who moved with him to Letchworth, was a prime mover in the campaign to establish an English colony. Discussions in the autumn of 1892 centred on fleshing out some of the plans, and concluded that it should be built within a thirty- or forty-mile radius of London, and close to a railway line. It was envisaged as laid out in the pattern of a spider's web, with the public buildings in the centre. These ideas may well have originated with Howard, and they are certainly ones of which he would have approved.[14]

It was decided to hold a public meeting to promote these ideas at the Congregational Union's Farringdon Memorial Hall on 11 February 1893. The press was invited, and the event was reported in the more Liberal London newspapers.[15] The meeting was chaired by James Branch, a radical Liberal member of the London County Council and Congregational deacon at Rectory Road, who would also become one of the Letchworth pioneers. In the audience were Bruce Wallace, Fleming Williams, and presumably other progressive London Congregationalists. Howard spoke for an hour, outlining his ideas for a community of thirty thousand people on nine thousand acres of land, created by common landownership. A member of the Nationalization of Labour Society then expressed the more extreme, Bellamyite position, suggesting that their colony would be established once the one proposed by Howard had been set up, and within its borders. Howard's vision was presented as simply a first step. The discussion which followed was generally critical of Howard for not being socialist enough. Nevertheless, Branch's presumably skilful

[14] Stanley Buder, *Visionaries and Planners: The Garden City Movement and the Modern Community* (New York and Oxford, 1990) pp. 54–61.

[15] Beevers, *Garden City Utopia*, summarizes a report from the *Morning Leader* but the event went unreported in *The Times*, *Telegraph*, and *Sunday Times*.

chairing ensured that a resolution was passed, establishing a committee who were charged with raising £20,000 and finding a site.
Although a nine-hundred-acre site near Hockley in Essex was located,
the money was never forthcoming, and the scheme was abandoned.
Bruce Wallace, and the minister of the other Brotherhood Church, in
Croydon, J.C. Kenworthy, continued with their experiments in
setting up small and often short-lived communities and colonies,
based on the Christian socialist ideas of the Russian novelist Leo
Tolstoy. Kenworthy's short-lived intentional communities were in
Croydon (1894) and Purleigh (1896). The best-known and most successful Tolstoyan community was at Whiteway, in the Gloucestershire
Cotswolds, which was founded by a Quaker, Samuel Veale Bracher, on
a forty-one-acre plot in 1898.[16] Meanwhile, Ebenezer Howard spent
his spare moments over the next few years working on the text of
To-morrow and with his ruler, compass, and water colour paints carefully
preparing the seven illustrations that would enliven the text.[17]

The Howard family in the 1890s

Many years later, Howard's daughter Editha recalled that her father
had worked on the book on the dining table in the family's home,
which was by this time in Kyverdale Road in Stamford Hill, with the
family all around, doing various jobs. 'When our dear old maid Mary
came in and said "clear", we just had to clear.'[18] She marvelled at her
father's ability to write in this hugger-mugger fashion, without any
form of privacy. Howard certainly had excellent powers of concen-
tration, and as he noted in relation to his work as a shorthand writer,
was able to focus on one task, while thinking about something entirely
different.

He had to cope with several painful family circumstances during the
decade that he was writing the book. From the late 1880s, his wife
Lizzie's health was in a steady decline. She had a goitre in the throat,
which made speaking difficult, and possibly other undiagnosed

[16] Nellie Shaw, *Whiteway: A Colony in the Cotswolds* (London, 1935); Joy Thacker,
Whiteway Colony: The Social History of a Tolstoyan Community (London, 1993).

[17] Buder, *Visionaries and Planners* 62.

[18] HALS DE/FJO/I3/2 Mrs Berry's collection of press cuttings.

conditions. In the language of the day, she suffered with her nerves. Trips to south coast seaside resorts saw her becoming interested in special cures, and later on, seeking out Spiritualist doctors. In 1887, she reported to Ben that she had met 'an energetic lady of 72 who is a total abstainer from alcohol, milk, meat and vegetables and lives almost entirely on bread and butter. A religious fanatic but very nice . . . very fond of Dr Parker, now that he was sound on the atonement.'[19] The following year, when she was away and unwell again, Ben instructed her to 'keep your faith bright and your health will no doubt improve', adding rather mysteriously, 'you will though I hope continue the use of the means which God has appointed'.[20]

Late in 1893, they had to deal with the death by suicide of Ebenezer Howard's younger brother Harry after he jumped from a railway bridge in Sheffield. Resident in that city, Harry was a travelling salesman for Remington typewriters, and had long struggled with acute depression. In the mid-1880s, correspondence between Ben and Lizzie shows the couple holding out hopes that Harry's new-found enthusiasm for Spiritualism would result in a 'marvellous change in him . . . because hitherto he has seemed almost hopefully certain that there was no hereafter'.[21] In June of the year in which he died, Harry wrote to his elder brother Ben to congratulate him as 'an exceptionally happy husband and father', a letter which perhaps hints at the unmarried Harry's own feelings of loss and absence.[22] As he travelled around Britain, Harry was deeply affected by the poverty and suffering which he witnessed, and apparently gave away all of his money and spare clothing to striking miners, before jumping from the bridge. It was appalling news for the Howard family, and Howard was called upon to identify the body. In Sheffield to attend his brother's inquest, he wrote to Lizzie: 'I feel convinced the affair was a pure accident – of course that would not have occurred but for his mental

[19] HALS DE/FJO/I3 28 August 1887.

[20] HALS DE/FJO/I3 25 August 1888.

[21] HALS DE/FJO/I3 4 March 1885. Harry consulted Cora Richmond, and received a communication from her spirit guide Ouina, on 13 July 1885. HALS/DE/Ho/F25/38.

[22] HALS DE/FJO/I3 30 June 1893.

condition.'[23] The verdict at the inquest was suicide during temporary insanity, and Harry Howard's distress at the coal strike, together with the consumption of large quantities of potassium bromide which he had taken to remedy insomnia, were presented as the aggravating factors.[24]

During the 1890s Howard's four children were entering their teenage years, and his parents were reaching what was for the period advanced old age. Family letters tell of concerns over the health of his mother, and also 'that even at this late period of their lives Father and Mother may become united in their religious experience'.[25] Ann Howard seems to have abandoned her earlier attachment to the Church of England, and Howard records his pleasure at taking his mother to the services at Rectory Road Congregational Church. A birthday letter survives from Ebenezer senior to Ebenezer junior, when he turned forty-eight. It is the only time that we hear from the octogenarian baker, as he summoned up his literary powers to write to his son:

My dear Ben

This comes with the old and good wishes for many happy returns of your natal day. This far your frail bark has been brought safely over lifes rugid way Hither to the Lord hath helped you and I do hope that at least you may reach the heavenly rest. Surely there is no need to be in any doubt of this.

'I am the way the truth and the life'

[23] HALS DE/FJO/I3 24 November 1893. The evidence is that Harry died in Sheffield, not Newcastle as Beevers suggests. Beevers, *Garden City Utopia* 43–4. The confusion with Newcastle comes from a reminiscence supplied to Osborn in 1928 from Howard's niece Ethel Cole. But the references in the correspondence of 1893 indicate clearly that the death happened in Sheffield, and this is given further weight by the fact that the miners' strike of 1893, which was suppressed particularly brutally and seems to have triggered the suicide, was centred on the Featherstone pit near Wakefield in Yorkshire. Howard's daughter Editha (Mrs Berry) also recalled that Harry 'worked in the slums of Sheffield'. HALS DE/FJO/I35 Notes of talk with Mrs Berry in WGC, 4 March 1944. The fact that Harry gave away his money and possessions shortly before his death is an indication that he planned to end his life, and that it was not accidental or spontaneous.

[24] *Sheffield Evening Telegraph* 25 November 1893.

[25] HALS DE/FJO/I3 4 March 1885.

'Him that cometh unto me I will in no wise cast out'.

I am thankful to have my hand as steady as it is after having done ten hours of pretty tough work.

I sometimes think I am a miracle when I think of what I have been brought through none but the allmighty will ever know.[26]

Ben was never able to convince his parents about his plans for the Garden City, although they were both in the audience at Rectory Road when *To-morrow* was launched there. The couple, who had both been born in 1817, died on the same night, on 24 November 1900.[27]

To-morrow: A Peaceful Path to Real Reform

To-morrow: A Peaceful Path to Real Reform was published in 1898. The path to its publication was not a smooth one. Publishers did not consider it likely to be a commercially viable proposition, and none was prepared to take it on without a subvention. In the end, it was the Spiritualist network which rescued the project. Through their mutual connection with Cora Richmond, the Howards had become friends with Josephine and George Dickman, wealthy Americans who lived in Hampstead. George Dickman was the managing director of the British arm of the Kodak Company. On one occasion when Lizzie was taking tea with them, Dickman asked about progress on the book, and Lizzie explained that no publisher was prepared to take the risk. 'Thereupon, George Dickman said, "Go tell Ben that if £50 is any use, he can have it as a loan which he need never return, and perhaps this will enable him to get the book printed and published." '[28] Swann and Sonnenschein were willing to take the book on this basis, with Howard supplying printed sheets, which they bound and distributed, charging him for the service. There were of course no royalty payments and neither author nor publisher sought copyright. But the first edition received generally positive reviews and sold surprisingly

---

[26] HALS DE/FJO/I3 29 January 1898. The original spelling and punctuation have been retained.

[27] HALS DE/FJO/I3/2 Mrs Berry's Collection of Press Cuttings.

[28] HALS DE/Ho/F17/19 1897–8.

well – it was rapidly re-issued in paperback and had sold three thousand copies by the turn of the century.[29]

The text was just over 150 pages, divided into fourteen chapters. Howard assembled his material extremely skilfully, anticipating and answering all the questions and objections that were likely to be raised. The tone was upbeat, but also realistic about the potential difficulties, and in particular the challenge of raising the huge sum that would be needed to bring the ideas described in the book to fruition. In the introduction he advanced his central premise, that the constant stream of people flooding into overcrowded cities from depleted country districts was universally deplored. Indeed, he suggested that in a society often divided into hostile camps by religious and political questions, this was the *only* issue on which all could agree. The authorities he cited in support of this included politicians (the Liberal Lord Rosebery and the Conservative Sir John Gorst), clergy (Dean Farrar), and trades unionists (Ben Tillet and Tom Mann).[30] Howard's skilful ability to build consensus by drawing on a wide range of sources, and holding together opinions that were usually seen as in opposition is apparent throughout the book. Whenever he asserted that in the Garden City there would be co-operation and community-funded social projects, he also quickly stated that there would be private enterprise and a high value on individual freedom and initiative. Although the town would be built to a plan, there would be freedom of choice in the style of individual buildings. There would be communal dining facilities, but houses would also be provided with proper kitchens, so that families could maintain privacy, and cook for themselves. It would be left to the residents to decide whether they wished to have licensed premises, and Howard showed no desire to enforce his own teetotal views.

Although he made it clear that there would be no private landlords because the people would be their own landlords, he toned down the anti-landlord rhetoric which had appeared in his 'Common Sense Socialism' lecture. He was fully aware that he needed to make his plan attractive to business interests and investors and devoted a chapter to

[29] Buder, *Visionaries and Planners* p. 62. Beevers, *Garden City Utopia*, pp. 57–8.

[30] Ebenezer Howard, *To-morrow: A Peaceful Path to Real Reform* (London, 1898) pp. 1–4.

outlining the limitations of socialism, making it abundantly clear that he was not envisaging a socialist colony. 'Most socialistic writers appear to me to exhibit too keen a desire to appropriate old forms of wealth, either by purchasing out or by taxing out the owners, and they seem to have little conception that the truer method is to create new forms and create them under juster conditions.'[31] If his project was to stand any chance, it was imperative that he persuade large numbers of people to invest in it. Aware that he needed to excite the interest of several very different audiences, he skilfully wove the visionary elements, in which he described plans for, and life in, the Garden City, with chapters which amounted to the working out of a detailed business case, bristling with figures, costs, acreages, revenues, and returns. For those who were interested in the intellectual origins of the plan, there were chapters in which he discussed the thinkers who had shaped his thinking. He acknowledged in particular the influence of Edward Gibbon Wakefield and Alfred Marshall (for the proposal for an orderly migratory movement of people of different backgrounds and skills), of Thomas Spence and Herbert Spencer (for stressing the importance of common land tenure), and James Silk Buckingham (for a model city). He argued that his plan was stronger and more viable because it combined the best of their ideas and dropped the weaker, and particularly the more autocratic, elements. He proudly stated that he had created from these sources 'A Unique Combination of Proposals.'[32]

Overall, the book focussed on the delivery of practical outcomes. The point of creating the Garden City was to create higher wages for the working classes, by ensuring that they could live in the country without having to work in agriculture. It was to show how the population could be 'demagnetized' so that it would not, like iron filings, be irresistibly drawn to the city. The famous 'Three Magnets' diagram was the first of seven which appeared in the text, and it provided a clear visual representation of the advantages and disadvantages of the town and the country, and an indication of how the best of both worlds could be had in the 'town-country'. Perhaps Howard had

---

[31] Howard, *To-morrow* pp. 119–20.
[32] Howard, *To-morrow* pp. 102–15.

noted the way in which a picture diagram illustrating the ideas in the text had been used as the frontispiece to *In Darkest England* and had decided to copy the idea, for the benefit of less literate readers. The diagrams, based on some of the lantern slides that he used to illustrate his lectures, certainly made his ideas easy to grasp.

The antithesis of the Garden City was London, a looming sooty presence throughout the text. It was perhaps inevitable that Howard would focus on London, rather than presenting his readers with a generalized depiction of the problems of the late Victorian city. It was the city that he and his 1890s audiences knew best, and the plan was to set up the Garden City not too far from the capital, so that Londoners, and London business owners, would be prepared to make a mass migration. Howard was careful to stress that one experimental Garden City should be built first, and that if it succeeded, then a cluster of interconnected 'Social Cities', with a total area of sixty-six thousand acres and a total population of two hundred and fifty thousand should be constructed. He provided an outline for this in diagram number seven, which he headed 'Group of Slumless Smokeless Cities'.[33] For those who remained in London after the Garden Cities had sprung up, he predicted a rapid improvement in the quality of life. As population decreased and businesses moved out, house prices and rents would fall dramatically, meaning that the poor would be able to afford to move to the more spacious and sanitary housing that had been previously occupied by the middle classes. In this scenario, slums would become worthless, and eventually, London would be reconstructed.[34] Howard had very limited interest in the historic significance of cities. They had 'done their work' and were 'entirely unadapted for a society in which the social side of our nature is demanding a larger share of recognition'. Desiring to live in the same place as one's ancestors he saw as akin to cherishing 'the old superstitions which a wider faith and a more enlarged understanding have outgrown'.[35] He considered that little in the built environment was worth preserving if it was more than sixty years old, although he

[33] Howard, *To-morrow* pp. 130–3.
[34] Howard, *To-morrow* pp. 142–52.
[35] Howard, *To-morrow* p. 135.

was willing to make an exception in the case of universities, schools, churches, and cathedrals.[36]

As was obvious from the title, the whole thrust of *To-morrow* was towards the future. Howard expected that religious and cultural activities would transfer easily and naturally from city to Garden City, and that people would become more social, more creative, and less hidebound by distinctions of class and gender. He envisaged religion being organized along the voluntarist principles typical of his Congregationalist faith: 'sites are reserved for churches of any denominations which the religious feelings of the people may select, and which they are prepared out of their own funds to erect and maintain'.[37] Schools should be built first, and could serve in the early years as places of worship, as well as for meetings and concerts, until more suitable public buildings were constructed.[38] If it occurred to Howard that wherever he built his Garden City, it would fall somewhere within the parochial boundaries and diocesan structures of both the Church of England and the Roman Catholic Church, he did not think to mention it. In his imagination, the site was a blank canvas of agricultural land, free from any pre-existing religious claims.

A plethora of references in the text to newspaper items which he had spotted in the early 1890s indicates that Howard wrote *To-morrow* over a period at least six years, and it is clear from 'City of Health' and 'Common Sense Socialism' that his vision for the Garden City was almost fully developed by the beginning of the 1890s. He found writing the book difficult, and emotionally taxing. In a lecture to the London Spiritualist Alliance in 1910, Howard described in detail the struggles that he had had with it. Although he acknowledged the many sources which had fed into it, he saw the whole as coming to him as a supernatural vision, and himself as a messenger, struggling with personal unworthiness:

> So, as I have said, the Garden City idea came to me as the result of very careful study and of much thought, and a good deal of earnest patient effort: and yet when the idea did come to me, I could not, for a single

[36] Howard, *To-morrow* p. 123.
[37] Howard, *To-morrow* p. 16.
[38] Howard, *To-morrow* p. 38.

moment, think of it as my own idea, as something I had created. I knew then, and I know with still greater certainty now, that the idea exists in the spiritual atmosphere which envelopes and pervades the lives of us all, in far greater clearness, brightness and beauty than I have ever yet realised it. (Applause). There was you see a conscious effort on my part, and there was also a clear sense of the revelation coming into my mind from some mysterious source . . . But what happened when I had received this revelation? Did I, when this message came to me – knowing with certainty that I had discovered a path which, wisely followed, would lead this and other nations to a splendid goal – at once go out into the world, and seek to get it realised – giving up all, as did the disciples, to follow the truth that would lead me forth? No I did not. I was timid and anxious and self-conscious, rather than conscious only of my message. But that was not all: my timidity, anxiety and self-consciousness would have been easily overcome if this had been all that was keeping me back. What was keeping me back? I will tell you. I will not go into details – that is quite unnecessary – but I was not leading a true life – I was even guilty of doing a real injustice to a dear friend – and while this state of things lasted it was as though I could not press forward – my message would not out; for I was an unworthy messenger. And then what happened? I confessed freely and fully to my friend all that I had said and done, and was freely, oh, so freely and fully forgiven! Never shall I forget the peace that then came into my heart – peace that not only filled my soul, but filled my body too; for a physical glow, as from a new and entirely fresh and delightful source of energy, streamed into my physical body.[39]

This account has something of the tone of a classic evangelical conversion narrative, although instead of repenting from sin and seeking forgiveness from God through Christ, Howard relies upon the forgiveness of his friend as the means of his spiritual liberation. The episode had great psychological resonance for him, and it fits with a pattern that can be observed elsewhere, in which Howard describes himself as suddenly liberated from a difficulty or a doubt, and as the bearer of a message to humanity from a higher power.

His account of the book launch, held at Rectory Road Church on 3 December 1898, is similarly revealing, with a detailed description of

[39] HALS DE/Ho/F28/9 Spiritual Influences and Social Progress. Delivered as a lecture on 14 April 1910, and published as two articles in *Light* on 23 and 30 April 1910.

how he was struck dumb, and then suddenly had his powers of speech restored:

> Soon after the publication of my book 'To-morrow' I arranged with my friend, the Rev Fleming Williams, Alderman of the L.C.C., that I should have the use of his church for a lecture on the Garden City Movement. I had lectured previously, but this was the first time I was to do so after the publication of my book. I arranged with Mr Young, Past President of the Society of Actuaries, a very able speaker and, naturally, a master of facts and figures to take the chair. I had a number of lantern slides prepared, and engaged a lanternist, and I had large posters printed, and small hand-bills. I then allowed myself three days in which to prepare the lecture . . .

> To my astonishment, when I awakened on the first morning I found I had no voice except a whisper voice, though there was no soreness in my throat. However, I, for some unaccountable reason was not at all upset, and went on with the preparation of my paper as if nothing had happened. The next morning, and the next – which was the day on which I was to speak – I experienced the same difficulty but still proceeded as though nothing were wrong. I had my lecture written a short time before I was due at the church. I had written it on small slips of paper so that at a glance I could turn over each slip and read it. I then went into the church – some little time before the time for starting – and told Mr Fitzhenry, a Deacon, in a whisper voice that I had not been able to speak, except in a whisper, for three days, and asked if he would be kind enough to read my lecture for me. Not unnaturally, he refused. I really cannot understand my mental condition, but this did not disconcert me in the least. I went on the platform, took a verbatim note of the Chairman's opening speech, and then began to give my lecture with a short preface as to my experiences of the last three days. It is no exaggeration to say that I could then have spoken to three or four thousand people without any difficulty.[40]

This account is slightly reminiscent of the story of Zachariah in Luke's Gospel, who was temporarily struck dumb after expressing scepticism that his ageing wife would have a son, who turned out to be John the Baptist.[41]

---

[40] HALS DE/Ho/F17/16/1–2 1898.
[41] Luke 1:5–64.

To-morrow: A Peaceful Path to Real Reform attracted considerable attention. A second edition of the book was produced under a revised title, *Garden Cities of To-morrow* in 1902. The new title sounded rather more domesticated and less revolutionary than the original one, and although it was clearer, Howard was irritated by it, disliking the loss of the words '*Real Reform*'. The second edition contained a signed photograph of Howard as the frontispiece, an indication of his transition from relative obscurity to minor celebrity in the space of three years: his hairline was receding, but the walrus moustache was still brown. There were fewer illustrations than in the original version. The Three Magnets diagram survives, as does the 'Garden City' diagram, which depicts the settlement in the midst of its agricultural land, and 'Ward and Centre', which provides a close-up of one segment of the Garden City. But by 1902 a very large note had been appended to both of these illustrations, indicating that they were 'Diagram only' and that plans could not be drawn until a site had been selected. Howard had clearly suffered from literal interpretations of the diagrams in the first edition, and in particular the criticism that he was obsessed with circles. The other illustrations had been removed, and the highly stylized diagram depicting the seven cities that would exist in harmony and interconnection as new Garden Cities sprang up was replaced with a sketch map of Adelaide in Australia, and a diagram showing a detail of how cities might develop at a distance from one another, without encroaching on the surrounding countryside. Adelaide was chosen as an example of a city that was developing without compromising surrounding parkland.[42]

The cover, designed by the celebrated Arts and Crafts artist Walter Crane, was spectacularly inappropriate: it showed a medieval princess, flanked by potted olive trees and holding a miniature Gothic city in the palm of one hand and a lily stem in the other. The marketing of *Garden Cities of To-morrow* had become softer, feminized, and unthreatening. But the changes were more to the presentation of the text, than the text itself. With the exception of new material about Adelaide in the chapter 'Social Cities', changes in the text were relatively minimal. They amounted to the replacement of one quotation from John

---

[42]   Ebenezer Howard, *Garden Cities of To-morrow* (London, 1902) p. 129.

Ruskin with another, at the head of the first chapter, the disappearance of the original Chapter Nine, which was a short and rather inconsequential summary of the previous three chapters, and the removal of many of the quotations with which Howard had started his chapters in the original version. By 1902, it was presumably considered a distraction to interrupt Howard's flow with masthead quotations ranging from Charles Dickens to Victor Hugo.[43]

Reflecting on the book several years later, Howard told his audience at the London Spiritualist Alliance that he had realized that people of all classes were not yet ready to embrace a social order that would embody the essential teachings of Christ, and so 'I endeavoured to devise an experiment which would appeal to the idealist – to the man who loves justice and order, and wishes to see the reign of justice and order established – and also to the so-called practical man, who must be convinced that the so called departure is on sound lines; that it does not interfere with bread and butter politics, but will rather make the production of wealth forms more easy.'[44] The combination of proposals in *To-morrow* was uniquely his own, but he made it clear that he saw himself as simply the latest in a line who had endorsed the same idea, from the Garden of Eden to the experimental communities of his own day. The names in the line are revealing: Moses, Plato, Christ, St Paul, Thomas More, William Morris, Ruskin, Professor Marshall, Tolstoy, and Peter Kropotkin. Howard would always credit supernatural assistance for the fact that he had got his proposals into print and into wide public discussion. This being the case, translating the vision from the page to a four thousand-acre site in Hertfordshire seemed to him entirely possible, if the divine blessing held out.

---

[43] Beevers suggests that Howard may have removed the quotations and reduced the number of diagrams as a result of critical comments in a review by Edward Pease, secretary of the Fabian Society. Pease was particularly scathing about Howard's 'pretty plans designed with ruler and compass' and his use of quotations, which were 'like plums in the unpalatable dough of his utopian scheming'. Beevers, *Garden City Utopia* p. 71, citing *Fabian News* December 1898.

[44] HALS DE/Ho/F28/9 Spiritual Influences and Social Progress.

4

The Path to the First Garden City 1899–1904

The Garden City Association

On 21 June 1899, just six months after the publication of *To-morrow*, the Garden City Association, which had become a legal entity eleven days earlier, was launched in the familiar venue of the Congregational Hall in Farringdon Street. In the chair was Sir John Leng, a nonconformist newspaper man who was also the Liberal Member of Parliament for Dundee. Leng was on the radical wing of the party, and an advocate of devolution and the taxation of land values. Howard had presumably encountered him in Westminster and knew that he would be sympathetic to the cause. Once more, James Branch was on hand to propose a motion, which was seconded by Mrs Annie Grant (wife of the lawyer Corrie Grant, who would be elected Liberal MP for Rugby in the following year). That she was the seconder hints at the significant role which women would play in the early plans for the Garden Cities. The motion was that 'many of the evils arising from life in crowded cities might be largely, if not entirely, removed by the construction of Garden Cities, and by arrangements being made for securing to the communities to be gathered in such cities the full advantage of the increased value accruing to the land from their own exertions'.[1] Beyond a brief account in *The Morning Post* the launch generated little interest in the press, and it was reported subsequently that the GCA had begun with just thirteen members, and with capital

---

[1] *Morning Post* 1 July 1899.

Ebenezer Howard: Inventor of the Garden City. Frances Knight, Oxford University Press.
© Frances Knight 2023. DOI: 10.1093/oso/9780198790815.003.0005

of only thirty shillings.[2] Of those who can be identified as present at the launch event, almost all were Congregational in denominational allegiance, or associated with Bruce Wallace's Brotherhood church. Several were associated with the London County Council.

How did the Garden City Association develop so rapidly from this tiny band of like-minded friends and co-religionists to a nationally significant organization that was able to begin to put its ideas into practice in Letchworth after only four years? This chapter addresses this question, and it is clear that several factors proved immensely beneficial. First, the GCA received frequent and largely positive coverage in the national and regional press. Secondly, certain individuals worked tirelessly to make Howard's vision palatable to those who might have been suspicious of it. With the appointment of Ralph Neville as chairman and Thomas Adams as secretary came a strong focus on the business sense and practicality of the Garden City scheme. They began to distance the project from a narrow identification with the ideas set out in *To-morrow* and took steps to ensure that the scheme would not be perceived as naively utopian. Neville and Adams were skilful in capitalizing on the support of the leading industrialists who had already built model villages for their workers, and particularly George Cadbury at Bournville and William Hesketh Lever at Port Sunlight. Meanwhile, the preponderance of Congregational ministers associated with the project helped to make it more acceptable to the 'Dissenting lay grandees' and businessmen whose names soon appeared on the supporters lists, such as John Leng, Lever, Albert Spicer the paper merchant, J.H. Whitley the Halifax

---

[2] *Morning Post*, 31 October 1899. The names of the thirteen original members present when the GCA came into legal existence on 10 June, who included the ministers W. Charter Piggot, Bruce Wallace, and of course Howard himself, are listed in Dugald MacFadyen, *Sir Ebenezer Howard and the Town Planning Movement* (Manchester, 1933) pp. 25–6. Many of these men had connections with Rectory Road Congregational Church. We may assume that they were all present at the public launch eleven days later, together with James Branch, the Revd Thomas Child, Annie Grant, Henry Holiday, Lizzie Howard, the Revd Fleming Williams, and others unidentified. The reference to thirty shillings comes from an article Howard wrote for the *Daily Mail*, 25 July 1905.

cotton spinner, and the Cadburys.[3] Thirdly, but more intangibly, it was evident that the Garden City idea had been born at an opportune historical moment; it originated during a time of hopes and fears brought about at the *fin de siècle*, and it came to fruition just at the point when the Liberal party was reviving its fortunes. It coincided with the peaceful interval between the Boer War and the Great War, and it benefitted from the active participation of women, which was seen as not only desirable, but expected. But its particular timing also meant that certain ideas that were quite alien to Howard – for example Garden Cities as a means of regaining English racial superiority – became hitched to the concept. Some of these factors will now be considered in more detail.

The importance of the press at the *fin de siècle* is well attested[4] and it proved very useful for publicizing Garden City ideas. Cecil Harmsworth, younger brother of the newspaper magnates Lords Northcliffe and Rothermere, served as chair of the GCA from 1911 to 1919, and became a close friend of Howard. The *Daily Mail*, which they had founded in 1896, gave many years of enthusiastic support. Other newspapers which they owned or founded, including the *Daily Mirror*, *The Times*, and a large number of regional titles, could all be relied upon to provide full accounts of GCA meetings, and usually positive editorial interventions, as could the *Daily Telegraph*, which remained independent of the Harmsworth empire. Stories that had appeared in the nationals were often recycled the following day in the regional newspapers, and some regional titles regularly featured a 'London column' from a correspondent, who might on occasion report a recent conversation that they had had with Ebenezer Howard, or the speeches at the latest GCA meeting.[5]

---

[3] Clyde Binfield, 'Garden City Religion: The Free Churches of Letchworth and Welwyn' *The Chapels Society Journal* 2016, 2 p. 66.

[4] Margaret D. Stetz, 'Publishing industries and practices' in Gail Marshall (ed.), *The Cambridge Companion to the Fin de Siècle* (Cambridge, 2007) pp. 113–30; Laurel Brake, *Print in Transition 1850–1910: Studies in Media and Book History* (Houndmills, 2001); Andrew King and John Plunkett (eds.), *Victorian Print Media: A Reader* (Oxford, 2005); Stewart J. Brown, *W.T. Stead: Nonconformist and Newspaper Prophet* (Oxford, 2019).

[5] The *Derby Daily Telegraph* was an example of this type of supportive regional coverage.

This positive press coverage was already in evidence by the time of the GCA's first annual meeting, in September 1899. Subheading the article 'How to Plant Perfect Towns in England', *The Mail*'s reporter noted that the meeting contained a group of reformers 'from all classes and parties', and he was enthusiastic about what he heard from Howard, 'visions of the ideal city, ample and beautiful' but also a plan that was carefully thought out in all its aspects. At the meeting Howard argued that if individual wealthy industrialists like George Pullman, Andrew Carnegie, Sir Titus Salt, and the Lever brothers could create well-planned towns of their own, then how much more could be achieved by groups of firms, inspired by high social principles?[6] This strategy presented his idea as simply the next stage in an evolutionary process that had been initiated by great men – the next phase would allow smaller-scale entrepreneurs to achieve something significant by working together. When the newspapers editorialized, they generally sought to reassure readers: the *Sunday Times* declared that the project might have a Utopian air about it, 'but wilder Utopias have been tried experimentally, and there is no reason why a practical trial should not be given of the "the garden city" ... there is ample room for this among the numerous social experiments of which the times are prolific, and few of which have so great a practical value'.[7] After a few years, and once it could be assumed that readers would be familiar with the basic principles behind the Garden City idea, a newspaper might hint at a potential weakness, such as its possible unattractiveness for urban factory workers: the *Manchester Courier* suggested that no working man who had to be at work by six o'clock would want to leave 'his dwelling under the bell of the factory or workshop, and go and live in a model cottage four miles away' although it conceded that young married couples might find the idea appealing.[8] Generally, however, the press could be relied on to follow the developments that led to the creation of the first Garden City carefully, and to report them fully. By 1900, there was little

---

[6] *Daily Mail*, 27 October 1899. See also *The Times, Gloucester Citizen*, and *Morning Chronicle*, all of the same date.

[7] *Sunday Times*, 24 June 1900.

[8] *Manchester Courier*, 26 April 1902.

excuse for any regular newspaper reader to be unaware of the plans to develop Garden Cities.

At its inauguration, the Garden City Association was closely associated with the Land Nationalization Society, with F.W. Steere as the honorary secretary of both organizations, and a corner of the LNS office designated as the headquarters of the GCA. The LNS had been founded in 1881 under the presidency of Alfred Russel Wallace (a Spiritualist as well as a distinguished scientist) with the objective of promoting state ownership of land. The idea was that landowners would be bought out, great estates broken up, and the land then turned into parcels of low-rental small holdings, which would be let to a class of 'independent yeoman' who would live healthily by working the land, within a system in which capitalism could still flourish.[9] Howard was immensely attracted to this vision, and knew that wrapping the idea in the Garden City packaging would make it more palatable for middle-class supporters who were still wedded to the sanctity of private property. The GCA was also in its early days closely associated with the London County Council. Its first chairman was Thomas Howell Williams Idris, chemist and soft drinks manufacturer, LCC member and Welsh nationalist, and as we have seen, the Congregational Garden City promoters Fleming Williams and James Branch were also LCC members. The GCA's first appeal for funds, launched early in 1900, shows that the Council were thinking like somewhat jaded London County Councillors, suggesting that the Garden City could be built for a sum 'considerably less' than that being spent by the LCC on clearing slums from the Strand. The GCA promised 'real homes' in place of a 'huge sky-scraping city-barrack'[10] that was being built on Aldwych and Kingsway.

The tone changed in early 1901, when Ralph Neville joined the Council, apparently at Howard's invitation, and shortly after was elected as chairman. Neville, a public school and Cambridge educated lawyer was cut from a different cloth to most of the rest of the board. His influence was decisive until 1906, when his appointment as

[9] C.B. Purdom, *The Letchworth Achievement* (London, 1963) p. 3; Robert Fishman, *Urban Utopias of the Twentieth Century: Ebenezer Howard, Frank Lloyd Wright and Le Corbusier* (New York, 1977) pp. 55–6.

[10] *Daily News* 1 March 1900.

a high court judge necessitated his resignation. His political experience had been shaped by eight years as a Liberal MP for a Liverpool constituency, and his professional experience had been gained in the Court of Chancery. Given his background, he was unusual in arguing that property in land was a concept unknown in common law, and should instead be viewed as a form of tenure held under the crown.[11] Although, as we shall see, Neville and Howard were to lock horns on a number of issues, their shared position on the critical issue of land tenure in the Garden City provided enough common ground for an initially positive working relationship.

Neville's arrival at the GCA marked a new emphasis on the 'practical' and 'business-like'. In April 1901 he was joined by Thomas Adams as secretary and the first paid official. Adams was a youthful Scot with a flair for administration (something Howard lacked) and public relations. The newspapers were quick to pick up on the change of tone, and were uniformly positive about the efforts of Neville and Adams, who began to get as much, if not more, coverage than Howard himself. In an editorial that August, the *Sunday Times* devoted significant space to promoting the Association's proposals as the only sensible remedy for the urban housing crisis. Utopianism was not even mentioned, and nor was Howard. Instead, the emphasis was on the roll call of 'many practical men' who had recently become vice presidents, and 'the eminently practical lawyer' Ralph Neville, who had become chairman.[12] The list of vice presidents was certainly impressive. By the following year there were 110 of them, with the added glamour of Daisy Warwick (Frances, Countess of Warwick) the socialite and socialist, at the head of the list. The Countess of Warwick had announced her support for the Garden City movement in 1900, when she attended a flower show in East London 'organised by children, for plants grown on slum window-sills'. The *Daily Telegraph* reported that 'her ladyship gave an instructive and entertaining address to the large company present, and advocated the "Garden City Association"'.[13] The vice presidents' list for 1902 showed the breadth of support that

[11] Robert Beevers, *The Garden City Utopia: A Critical Biography of Ebenezer Howard* (Houndsmill, 1988) p. 73.
[12] *Sunday Times* 11 August 1901.
[13] *Daily Telegraph* 14 July 1900.

the GCA had gained within just a couple of years. A wide spectrum was represented from the veteran freethinker George Jacob Holyoake, to the industrialists William Hesketh Lever, George Cadbury, T.H.W. Idris, and members of the Harmsworth family. There were thirty-one MPs and ten members of the LCC There were, unsurprisingly, prominent Nonconformists, including John Clifford, F.B. Meyer, J.B. Paton, Fleming Williams, Bruce Wallace, Percy Alden, J. Williams Benn, and Stopfold Brooke – but there were also prominent Anglicans, including the bishops Winnington-Ingram (London), E.S. Talbot (Rochester), and John Perceval (Hereford), and clergy, including Henry Scott Holland, Dean George Kitchin, and William Moore Ede. There were a smattering of artists and writers: Walter Crane, Marie Corelli, Sarah Grand, Henry Holiday, and H.G. Wells, and there were some academics and scientists, including Alfred Marshall, Alfred Russel Wallace, Sir John Gorst, and Tempest Anderson.[14]

Thomas Adams had organized the GCA's first two-day conference in collaboration with George Cadbury at Bournville in September 1901. It was attended by three hundred delegates, and a large press corps. Cadbury acted as host, showing off his industrial village, and attracting much favourable publicity thereby. Ralph Neville and Earl Grey chaired the proceedings, and papers were delivered by a number of prominent supporters who enthused about particular aspects of the proposed scheme. Ebenezer Howard was the sixth speaker and summarized his plan in the manner described in his book. *The Times* reported that his paper prompted a long discussion 'with several speakers pointing out the practical difficulties of the scheme, particularly in inducing manufacturers to transfer their works'.[15] Earl Grey, in concluding the proceedings, sounded decidedly lukewarm when he stated that 'he saw certain difficulties in the way of the adoption of Mr Howard's scheme; but if other manufacturers could only realise that it was good business for an employer of labour to plant his works in the fields outside the cities there would be a greater desire on their part to follow the noble and splendid example which Mr Cadbury had set'.[16]

[14] Garden City Collection (GCC) LBM3056.33.31 Garden City Association Fourth Annual Report, 1902.

[15] *The Times* 23 September 1901.

[16] *The Times* 23 September 1901.

This critical appraisal from such a prominent individual on such an occasion might reasonably have caused Howard some distress. But he swallowed his pride and declared himself delighted with the publicity that the Bournville conference had brought.

There was another prominent critic of Howard's financial model present at Bournville, although whether Howard knew of the extent of his criticism is less clear. George Bernard Shaw, who had known Howard since they were both young men learning debating skills at the Zetetical Society, had attended the Bournville conference, where he had 'raised a laugh' by asking what would happen if a gold mine was discovered in the Garden City? He received the sober answer that the increment would be used for starting other Garden Cities. Wrapped up in his humorous point was a significant and serious objection: those promoting the scheme must provide for the contingency that the original community might sell their interest and enrich themselves on the unearned increment.[17] Shaw was so exercised by the inadequacy of the response that immediately after the conference, he wrote a letter to Neville. In draft, and running to twenty pages of quarto in a tiny hand, it is preserved at the British Library. Shaw argued that the GCA, and Howard in particular, were deluded if they thought they could limit the freedom of capitalists by imposing upon them a trust deed, which was what was proposed. It was a very valid point. As a Fabian socialist himself, he pointed out that the average capitalist business entrepreneur would regard the plan as unadulterated socialism, and completely unpalatable. He reminded the GCA that since socialism was an alternative to private enterprise, private enterprise which aimed at socialism was simply aiming at suicide. For a similar reason, it could not be demanded as a condition of investment in the Garden City that business entrepreneurs be obliged to accept trades unionism, temperance, cooperation, or moral reform. 'The House of Commons and not the Board Room is the proper place for social legislation'.[18] Howard would probably have responded to this by on the one hand, assuring the businessmen of his belief in

[17] *Daily Telegraph* 23 September 1901; *The Times* 23 September 1901.

[18] BL Add Mss 50,513 ff.247–67. Beevers, who discovered the draft letter at the British Library, quotes from it extensively, and provides further context, in *Garden City Utopia* pp. 73–8.

private enterprise, and on the other, appealing to their altruism, while invoking the intangible concept of more morally elevated times coming.

Shaw was a complex critical friend of the Garden City. He seemed more aware of the pitfalls, and more willing to articulate them, than any of the GCA's other early supporters, and yet he remained extremely committed to the idea, investing sizable sums in both Letchworth, and two decades later, in Welwyn. In 1906, he selected the old rectory at Ayot St Lawrence, a hamlet near Welwyn, as his country home, and from there he was able to keep in close touch with the development of both communities, until his death in 1950. As we have seen, he remained sufficiently close to Howard to be considered as a potential biographer by some members of the Howard family. The complexities of building a Garden City were explored in his stage play of 1904, *John Brown's Other Island*, in which the lead characters, English and Anglo-Irish civil engineers Broadbent and Doyle, visit 'Rosscullen' in rural Ireland on behalf of 'Land Development Syndicate', apparently with the intention of creating a Garden City, like the one 'near Hitchin'. In the first act, Howard's book, and the circular maps, are produced as a stage prop, to underline the point. As the play unfolds, however, it emerges that the real intention of the duplicitous developers is to build a golfing hotel at Rosscullen, and the talk of a library, a non-denominational polytechnic, an art school, a gymnasium, and a cricket club, and the restoration of the round tower, were simply a front for a hard-headed business plan. Keegan, a somewhat mystical priest suspended for being 'cracked', emerges as the voice of conscience, pointing out in the final scene that the plan is simply the latest in which the English and the Anglo-Irish will extract money from Ireland, and that 'when the hotel becomes insolvent' the biggest losers will be the residents of Rosscullen.[19] The play is a dramatized version of Shaw's letter to Neville: the Garden City idea is immensely attractive, but the funding must come from capitalists, whose primary aim will be to make money. If they cannot make it pay, they will abandon it, with no thought to the consequences for the local community.

[19] George Bernard Shaw, *John Bull's Other Island* (First published 1904, Project Gutenberg Edition, 2009).

Neville must have been aware of the salience of Shaw's critique, and yet he also needed to build alliances with those with capital to invest. His personal wealth and social standing undoubtedly benefited the cause. Meetings at the Congregational Hall were dropped in favour of more glitzy venues, to which prominent members of London society were invited. GCA public meetings began to be publicized as occasions when ordinary folk could rub shoulders with celebrities: the 1902 gathering promised the presence of Earl Grey, William Hesketh Lever, several bishops and MPs, the Countess of Warwick, and the feminist novelist Sarah Grand. As the *Derby Daily Telegraph* accurately noted: 'The number of notables who will attend of all shades of opinion is remarkable.'[20] Other gatherings were by invitation only. In 1904, Neville hosted a fundraising reception for six hundred at the Royal Institute of Painters, Piccadilly, and offered to contribute £1000 himself, if the remainder of the £12,000 urgently needed was pledged in sums of £500.[21] This was in stark contrast with Howard's own fundraising efforts, which involved going around London's streets from door to door, trying to persuade householders to buy one pound or five pound shares in the Garden City Pioneer Company.[22] The social gulf between Howard and the other directors was very apparent. Howard always assumed that he would go to live in an ordinary house in the Garden City as soon as it was feasible to do so. He thought about the project in the second person plural, from the perspective of himself and other potential residents, as well as from that of employers and manufacturers. With the exception of the civil engineer Howard Pearsall, who also moved to Letchworth, for the other directors, taking up residence was never an issue. They saw Garden Cities as places for the lower orders to live in; their purpose was to deal with some of the problems of London and other cities, and

---

[20] *Derby Daily Telegraph* 30 May 1902.

[21] *The Times* 22 April 1904.

[22] HALS DE/FJO/13a. The maps that Howard used have been preserved. They are pages detached from *Philips' Handy-Volume Atlas of the County of London* (1902). Howard annotated them when calling on prospective subscribers. He wrote names and addresses on the backs of maps, in about their actual positions. The subscriptions came mainly from the middle-class and lower middle-class north London suburbs with which he was most familiar. The map of wealthy Kensington is conspicuously unannotated.

at the same time to create a sober and healthier workforce, who would improve British productivity.

This leads to the third suggested explanation for the rapid rise in support for the CGA; its coincidence with the particular climate of anxiety and opportunity brought about at the *fin de siècle*. This can be seen in various ways. Anxieties about the poor physical state of the British male, which were heightened by the Boer War, abounded, and are reflected in some of the speeches made at the Bournville confer- ence, and subsequently. Ralph Neville proclaimed at Bournville that improvements in housing and working conditions were measures essential to prevent national degeneration and the 'decadence of the race'. Britons were known to be less fit and healthy than the Germans and it was, he said, a question of 'national rivalry'.[23] Earl Grey lamented that the children of Londoners were 'narrow-chested gutter snipes, very different from the breed of Englishmen that had been the glory of this country'. Furthermore, workers who believed themselves to be cogs in a machine concluded that it was their duty to be shirkers.[24] The blunt language may have upset some members of the audience, who would have expressed their concerns about the children of London's poor and alienated workers in rather more charitable terms, but if this was the case, their irritations went unrecorded.

Clearly some of the movement's publicists gave the Garden City idea a much harder edge than Howard would have anticipated. This included some who dressed the message up in overtly religious terms. John McNeill, writing in the Belfast-based *Monthly Missionary Herald* linked a declining interest in religious matters with the degraded quality of home life, which he saw as fatally impaired in squalid city conditions. Evoking Ezekiel's vision of the valley of dry bones, he characterized the urban space as infested with a constantly replen- ishing community of 'thieves, harlots and evil-doers'. He proposed the creation of Garden Cities, with the accompanying restoration of home

---

[23] *The Times* 21 September 1901. At the GCA's annual meeting in December 1901, he repeated the idea that Garden Cities were needed so that industry could be undertaken under healthy conditions in order for the English race to maintain its position in the world. *The Times* 12 December 1901.

[24] *Daily Telegraph* 23 September 1901.

life, as the only way to restore the people's spiritual welfare and to combat 'corruption, blank atheism and unbridled license'.[25] Whether he envisaged these new communities as inhabited by the destitute 'submerged tenth' (which was not part of Howard's proposal) or by the contented worker, seeking to be closer to his work place (which very much was) was not entirely clear. His article reveals that a GCA fundraiser could seem astonishingly scathing about the people that he was seeking to help. Perhaps he was simply seeking to employ the kind of language that he thought would resonate with a conservative evangelical readership.[26]

There were, however, other strands of Christian opinion that were equally eager to promote the ideas of the GCA. The progressive Anglican Christian Social Union invited Ebenezer Howard, and other GCA lecturers, to speak at their branch meetings,[27] and there was significant religious representation at the Bournville conference. George J.H. Northcroft, who had been Wesleyan Methodist minister at Newlyn in Cornwall, was appointed organizing secretary of the GCA in 1903, and maintained good links with Methodism in the South West, once he joined the circuit of nationally deployed GCA speakers, which included Howard and Thomas Adams. Northcroft was fond of describing his Garden City collaborators as 'the apostles of decent environment'.[28]

Standish Meacham argued that the people founding the Garden City movement refashioned Howard's ideas for their own purposes, as they sought to recreate an imagined version of a rural English past. Those who were fearful of what the future seemed to hold, with anxieties about physical degeneration, class conflict and democracy, sought refuge in an idealized version of the Garden City that promised physical and mental health, and defused social tensions into class harmony. Worries about uncontrollable change and 'end-of-century

[25] John McNeill, 'Home! Sweet Home!' *Monthly Missionary Herald* 1 April 1900.

[26] McNeill also wrote for Henry Scott Holland's Christian socialist magazine, *The Commonwealth,* providing a review of Howard's book, and a very positive evaluation of the Garden City idea, in the November 1899 issue. *Commonwealth* 4,11 (1899) p. 344.

[27] *Bucks Herald* 22 March 1902 and *Western Times* 5 December 1904.

[28] *Western Times* 13 February 1905.

malaise' caused straight-laced capitalists 'to depart from the bondage of laissez-faire ideology and to welcome intervention, when not to do so appeared to threaten the interests of a citizenry vulnerable to social decay and disorder'.[29] This explanation sheds some light on the motivations of the wealthy industrialists amongst the GCA's early supporters, but as the vice presidents' list makes clear, support was drawn from many sections of society, and there were many agendas in play. Meacham's focus on the Arts and Crafts style architectural idiom of Barry Parker and Raymond Unwin, who designed many of the early properties in Letchworth, perhaps serves to overemphasize this sense of English village idealism, repackaged and domesticated for the early twentieth century. As for Howard himself, the cultural influences on him were almost as much American as English. He had spent five formative years living in the United States, and had been profoundly influenced by numerous Americans, including Walt Whitman and James Russell Lowell, Edward Bellamy, Henry George, Alonzo Griffen, and Cora Richmond.[30]

Another important characteristic of the early Garden City movement redolent of the *fin de siècle* was the prominent role of women. It is significant that, in a highly unusual reversal of the expected word order, Howard paid tribute to the 'Englishwomen and Englishmen [who] have for years been seeking a solution to the great housing problem'.[31] He may have been thinking of well-known housing reformers such as Octavia Hill, but frustratingly, apart from noting the contribution of his wife Lizzie, he says little about who the women directly involved with the Garden City movement were, or what they did. Some were aristocrats – we have already noted the support of the Countess of Warwick, and her daughter Marjorie, Viscountess Helmsley also supported the movement. A women's branch, which aimed to promote the work 'from the standpoint of wives and mothers' was established in 1903, and this was relaunched as the

[29] Standish Meacham, *Regaining Paradise: Englishness and the Early Garden City Movement* (New Haven and London, 1999) pp. 3–7.

[30] Meacham does in fact concede the importance of the American influences on Howard. *Regaining Paradise* p. 56.

[31] Ebenezer Howard, 'Life at Garden City by its Founder' *Daily Mail* 25 July 1905.

Women's League in the following year, with Lady Helmsley as secretary, in which capacity she also hosted drawing-room meetings in her home in Knightsbridge.[32] Other early supporters were more self-consciously political, with the Women's Liberal Federation backing the GCA as early as 1902, with a stirring speech from 'Miss Tillyard of Cambridge'.[33] When the location of the first Garden City became known, the close proximity of Letchworth to Cambridge, and the fact that Girton College had been originally founded in Hitchin, just four miles from Letchworth, naturally aroused further interest in Cambridge women. It was, however, Henrietta Barnett who was the best-known woman associated with the GCA, although her plans, for garden suburbs rather than cities, were deeply inimical to Howard. Barnett was a well-known Anglican social reformer, who with her husband Samuel, had been the founder of the Toynbee Hall Settlement in Whitechapel. She had lived in St Jude's parish in East London and been active in the world of religious philanthropy for several decades before she became interested in land use and planned communities. In 1903 she began a successful campaign to save eighty acres of Hampstead Heath from unsympathetic development. A result was Hampstead Garden Suburb, for which she was the driving force. She imported some of the elements of Howard's philosophy – a new community for people from different social groups, bound together by shared educational, religious, cultural, and social institutions – as well as the Letchworth architect Raymond Unwin. But the suburb was essentially a dormitory for London commuters, and encouraged the growth of an already overgrown city, and it was to this that Howard most strongly objected. Neville, no doubt for sound political reasons, was at pains to cultivate Henrietta Barnett, inviting her to address the GCA, and describing her scheme as 'of extreme importance'.[34] Howard was noticeably less enthusiastic.

The Garden City idea was, unsurprisingly, picked up and widely reported in the women's press. By the 1890s, there were many women journalists, and an increasing number of journals and columns within

[32] *Daily Mail* 25 July 1903 and 11 October 1904. *The Times* 5 December 1903.
[33] *Cambridge Independent Press*, 9 May 1902.
[34] *The Times* 6 March 1906.

newspapers aimed at a female readership.[35] The *Lady's Pictorial* ran an early article on Howard, casting him as a seer of the future, with plans to build 'ideal cities which shall make England altogether lovely'. The item was picked up by the 'Woman's World' column in the *Sheffield Evening Telegraph*, who applauded the principle but pondered how Howard would keep jerry builders at bay, and prevent his concentric communities widening into ugly suburbs. But, the writer concluded, in a manner which again hints at *fin de siècle* anxieties just below the surface, if the '"Garden City Association" can perform all its promises, then life will not be quite so terrible as we picture it in the coming by and by, when electric railways and flying machines and motors shall have made it possible for the townsfolk to push their residential way farther and farther into the now peaceful country'.[36]

The final years of Lizzie Howard

The woman who did most in the early years to promote Howard's version of the Garden City idea was Lizzie Howard. She was an active worker in the movement, and the only woman to sit on the nine-person council of the GCA. Had she lived longer, she might have achieved a reputation to equal that of Henrietta Barnett. It was well attested that she was 'a very good talker', and a frequent speaker at fund raising drawing room meetings hosted by wealthy women, such as Lady Marjorie Helmsley, Mrs Elizabeth Lever, and an unidentified 'lady millionaire' in Oldham. Given that she suffered with a goitre that made talking difficult, her success was particularly impressive; she wore cleverly designed dresses in order to conceal the lump on her neck.[37] She had learned the art of public speaking by giving talks to women's meetings at Rectory Road Church. The text of one such talk survives; it is about Enid, a character in Tennyson's poem *The Idylls of*

---

[35] In 1903 Alfred Harmsworth launched the *Daily Mirror* as a women's paper with an all-female staff. This revolutionary concept proved to be ahead of its time. The paper had to be re-launched in 1904, but the fact that it was possible at all indicates the large numbers of women involved in the newspaper industry by the turn of the century.

[36] *Sheffield Evening Telegraph* 6 November 1899.

[37] A photograph of Lizzie can be viewed at GCC LBM41.16.

the King. Enid is portrayed in the poem as completely obedient to her irrational and irascible husband Geraint, and she was, Lizzie Howard believed, an 'inestimable' role model for women. That she used a fairly recent literary work to make a theological point would have caused little surprise in the world of North London Congregationalism:

> We sit at her [Enid's] feet, like Mary at the feet of the Great Teacher, and learn of her that perfect womanhood consists in doing the small deeds nobly, in sweet home services, in the surrender of our wishes to the dictates of love, in the gentleness that compels all things, in the strength of purity which uplifts and ennobles man. Not by force of arms shall this world be won to Godliness and true living, but by the almighty force of love, and thus was Geraint redeemed by love.

It seems from this that Lizzie would probably not have identified herself with the first wave feminist movement that was challenging some of the traditional roles of women in the 1890s, but she had no difficulty at all in taking on a public role, semi-independently from her husband. Her interest in the Enid and Geraint story as a paradigm for married life suggests that she saw parallels between her patient self-sacrifice, and the rather stubborn and self-absorbed behaviour of her husband. Her fondness for Tennyson is attested by her daughter's recollection that she read his poems to the bug-infested women at the Hoxton mission, where she visited weekly in order to help them with their needlework. She had to give up volunteering at the Hoxton mission after catching the bugs herself, passing them on to her children, who then spread them around at their schools.[38]

Lizzie's experiences at the Hoxton mission meant that when she spoke of the horrors of London housing in the elegant drawing rooms of the wealthy, she was doing so on the basis of first-hand knowledge. Typescripts of some of her lectures survive, in a file annotated in Ebenezer Howard's hand as 'papers read by my darling'.[39] In one of these lectures, 'Garden Cities: a solution to the housing problem' she began by outlining the 'house famine' as an affliction in all large English towns, and most villages, deploying the 'bitter cry' imagery that was evidently still familiar to her audiences from Mearns'

[38] HALS DE/FJO/I35.
[39] HALS DE/Ho/F11/1.

publication of 1883. Building at scale was needed, and she proceeded to outline the advantages and disadvantages of the large schemes that would be necessary to address London's housing crisis. Building in London deprived Londoners of light, space, and air; building adjacent to London merely enlarged it, made it difficult for Londoners to get out to the country, and caused them to waste time commuting to work. The solution, therefore, was to move workers and their work right away from London, and build new cities, 'on a foundation of equity and justice'. She then outlined a plan for a circular city exactly as described in *To-morrow*, emphasizing, as Ebenezer Howard always did, that there would be a mixture of planning regulation and freedom for individuals to build and design. She also emphasized something that was being increasingly ignored by many of the wealthy supporters of the Garden City movement, that the new community would be for everyone, and not 'merely a manufacturing town, peopled by artisans.' She specifically mentioned ministers of religion, doctors, lawyers, artists, dentists, architects, engineers, teachers, shopkeepers, and people of leisure, taste, and independent means as the types that she wanted to see living in the Garden City. Women, she believed, had a particular responsibility in solving the housing problem, because a woman spent practically her whole life in her home. She ended by quoting Tennyson: 'The old order changeth giving place to the new' and declaring that 'on the eve of great social upheaval' it was 'high time the ethical teachings of Christ were put into practice'.[40] Much of Lizzie Howard's content was similar to that of her husband, but her emphasis on the 'bitter cry' of the slum dweller, and the need for justice for the labouring classes gave an edge of radicalism to her speeches which her husband's sometimes lacked.

A few surviving letters between the couple in these final years of their marriage reveal how enterprising she was. While being treated at the Matlock Hydro, she accepted an invitation to take part in a Women's Institute debate, and when convalescing in Hastings, she

---

[40] HALS DE/Ho/F11/2 'Garden Cities: a solution to the Housing Problem' n. d. Other versions of her lectures, some with her pencil annotations, and either undated or with dates ranging from 1900 to 1903, are located at HALS DE/Ho/F11/3; HALS DE/Ho/F10/14/15; HALS DE/Ho/F11/5 and HALS DE/Ho/F11/6.

met someone who knew a woman who wrote for *Field and Farm* and thought that this woman might be persuaded to review *To-morrow*. When the *Daily Mirror* was launched as a women's paper in October 1903, she wrote immediately to the editor with suggestions for stories, including that they should interview her about the Garden Cities.[41] By this time poor health was limiting the range of her public speaking activities, and she had to pull out of a prestigious engagement at the Mansion House, with Howard forced to deputize for his wife, 'a poor substitute' according to their daughter.[42] Lizzie Howard spent increasing amounts of time at the south coast, staying with Spiritualist friends and seeking advice from Spiritualist doctors. She provided a particularly full account of a consultation with Dr Stenton Hooker, in Hastings, who was medically qualified but anxious to try out a 'spirit diagnosis' because she was a fellow Spiritualist. The diagnosis included information about her son, 'a great joy to you' and her husband, 'he is *very* busy, he has great energy', as well as something about her medical problems. The doctor informed her that he was 'shown a cancer, and that was quickly wiped away'. He concluded that her throat was in a serious condition, but an operation was inadvisable, ascribing much of her trouble to her 'nerves'. Lizzie reported that she had attended the consultation 'thickly veiled' so that the doctor could not make any form of physical assessment. She was delighted with the 'wonderful accuracy' of his observations, and continued to put her faith in spiritual healing, although she was depressed by its lack of tangible results. She was surprised when another clairvoyant doctor failed to see that her sickness was caused by growths in her throat, suggesting instead a stomach problem.[43]

As she approached the final months of life, Lizzie Howard continued to blend strong Spiritualist beliefs with the evangelical Christianity that had first shaped her. She was under a great deal of emotional, financial and physical strain, and continued to refuse surgery, on the grounds that if the growths were removed, new ones would just grow back. Her husband was frequently away, giving lectures to promoting the Garden City Association, and once again,

[41] HALS DE/FJO/I3.

[42] HALS DE/FJO/I3/2.

[43] HALS DE/FJO/I3.

she was left to manage the household alone. Presumably aware that she had not much longer to try to influence his spiritual state, she did not hold back:

> I wonder why it is that just now when you most need to realise the Power of God you most realise the Power of mortal and evil.

> What can Pearsall[44] really do, he can make a silly suggestion, does that interfere with God's purpose and plan. If you could but give up this *fear* of self, and realise that *you are* the Son of God and that his wealth and his intelligence and Power were yours by right to draw upon then surely all these doubts and fears would be dispelled. If you are remembering past failures then you are doing wrong, for all these past errors are wiped out as a black cloud to be remembered against *you no more for ever* . . . Do dear get a penny edition of the Gospel of St John and read it all the way up from B'ham . . . It will I hope clear away the cobwebs that have gathered over your spiritual vision. May we not say with Whittier:

> > 'Yet in the maddening maze of things
> > And tossed by storm and flood
> > To one fixed stake my spirit clings
> > I *know* that God is good'[45]

Osborn noted that she elaborated further on this, but he did not include it in his transcription, and the original letter is now lost. Her emotions exploded in her final surviving letter, which was written a month before she died. Her daughter, Editha, believing that the many challenges that her mother had faced were unlikely to be fully appreciated by the public, wished that this letter be given due weight by biographers. The context for her letter was one received from Ben the day before, in which he told her that he planned to make up an annual salary of £500, comprising £150 from lecturing for the GCA, £100 from his director's fee and £250 from shorthand writing. She replied:

[44] Howard D. Pearsall was a civil engineer, director of the GCA, Fabian socialist and son of a Congregational minister.
[45] HALS DE/FJO/I3. The lines from Whittier come from his poem 'The Eternal Goodness' and are slightly misquoted. The third line should be 'To one fixed trust my spirit clings'.

My dear Boy,

I am glad you have a fair measure of success at your meetings and hope they will prove a stimulus.

Gurney Slater, as I think I told you, spoke to me about the conditions under which you lectured and I told him that you always returned your fee to the Association [the GCA]. Now as to your ideas re Asso. The Asso has in hand at the present time a few pounds only and its income is considerably less than it has been – under these circumstances I don't see how it is to pay you a sum of £150 to lecture, especially as there was quite a difference of opinion as to whether Mr N [George Northcroft] should receive £25 extra for the 30 lectures he has booked himself for. It was thought that a man of leisure should be sought who will lecture for us, or that he be offered £25 for the season. Now in face of all this I can hardly imagine they will jump at the £150.

Why is it necessary that our source of income should continually come up for discussion? First, that you should get your income as Director; then past income [for] shorthand for three months, then a switch back to shorthand with a fee from Directors and a little larger fee from the Asso. which, so far as I can see, has all its work cut out to pay its way now and badly needs more funds.

I could wish that the good Lord who made you a Social Reformer had also given you the wherewithal to reform on. The last few years of *knowing what to expect* has rather spoiled me for the *rough experience* of *old times* and I confess there is no charm for me in [the] sublime uncertainty of not knowing how and when my housekeeping funds will be available. I may be selfish in this matter, but if I am I fear there are lots of selfish people, for surely all men and women desire the peace which comes from a *settled* method of living.

Do make up your mind, if you can, *once* and *for all* how your income is to be made, and if you intend to act as Director let that be done with the devotion you used to give to the work when all you did cost us solid cash.[46] This continual change of policy is one of the most trying experiences for us both and I am quite sure your work will never be as effective as it might be until you have *method* in your work and in your pay. I think dear sometimes you are very like the child crying for the moon – you want to do the impossible. You want to be on the *free leg* as

---

[46] Presumably a reference to the money Howard spent working on typewriter modifications, and on trips to America.

far as finance goes, well if you were a *free man* like Bruce [Wallace] that would be all right and quite delightful, but you are not free, and cannot lightly play with responsibilities that are ours already. Of course, it would be delightful to work without fee or reward, *but*. Well you can imagine what the 'but' stands for.

All this about filthy lucre.

Now dear I must finish and do something towards supper.

With love from the chicks and your loving wife.[47]

Lizzie died just over a month later, on 11 November 1904, at the age of fifty-one. Although she had been unwell for years, her death seems to have been relatively sudden and unexpected. Friends from Rectory Road who had seen her the previous week had not anticipated it: although she was in pain, they thought she would improve with rest, as she had before.[48] The cause of death was given as congestion of the brain, presumably a stroke. Her daughter attributed it to her having used her brain too much during lecturing, because she had 'never used her brain before', a view which seems rather extraordinary to be holding as late as 1949, when Osborn interviewed her.[49] Thyroid or throat cancer, or complications resulting from the goitre, seem more likely as the underlying cause of her death.

Lizzie was buried in the churchyard of St Mary the Virgin, Letchworth, with an Anglican service conducted by an Anglo-Catholic, W.F. Cobb, the rector of St Ethelburga's Bishopsgate, who had been a personal friend. Condolences flowed in from industrialists, Spiritualists, church members and clergy. For Edward Cadbury, she showed 'unselfishness and devotion to the Garden City ideal';[50] for William Lever, she was 'a noble woman';[51] for Cobb, the rector of St Ethelburga's 'to know Mrs Howard was to receive inspiration'.[52] The Spiritualists unsurprisingly dwelt on Lizzie's new spiritual status, and continuing influence in the next life: Alice Callow, of the Higher

[47] HALS DE/FJO/I2/10/3a.
[48] HALS DE/Ho/F23/3/32.
[49] HALS DE/FJO/I35.
[50] HALS DE/Ho/F23/3/7.
[51] HALS DE/Ho/F23/3/26.
[52] HALS DE/Ho/F23/9. Cobb had been assistant secretary of the English Church Union from 1892–9, an Anglo-Catholic society.

Thought Centre, observed that she had been 'called to pass into another phase of the One Life.'[53] Ellen Malgarth commented that Lizzie would 'go on serving with fuller knowledge and wisdom than we can attain before "crossing the bar."'[54] The church secretary at Rectory Road also echoed the sentiment that Lizzie would continue to serve the cause, and assist Howard 'by the inspiration of her spirit. I sincerely trust that this comradeship may continue until the reunion on the higher plane'.[55] It sounds as if he too had strong Spiritualist leanings. A friend, Lily Rose, made a point that was unlikely to have been lost on other mourners: 'It is indeed strange that your wife should be the first to enter Garden City through the gate of Death'.[56]

Opening the Letchworth estate

After the launch of the GCA Howard began to travel frequently, taking the messages to audiences outside London for the first time. An early lecture was in Sheffield, particularly significant as the place where his brother Harry had lived and died. The audience, which included local clergy and politicians, were far from won over and 'agreed that important essentials had been overlooked in framing the scheme' and in particular that inducements would need to be given to manufacturers to relocate.[57] Howard remained the movement's best-known publicist, although, as we have seen, there were others who were also busy on the lecture circuit, including Lizzie Howard, Thomas Adams, George Northcroft, and Ralph Neville. A team of peripatetic lecturers were needed, not least to support the regional branches of the GCA that had been established in Manchester and Edinburgh.[58] As the 'founder' Howard developed a certain celebrity

---

[53] HALS DE/Ho/F23/3/24.
[54] HALS DE/Ho/F23/3/27.
[55] HALS DE/Ho/F23/3/33.
[56] HALS DE/Ho/F23/3/30.
[57] *Sheffield Independent* 16 October 1900.
[58] Both branches were in existence by 1904. The Scottish branch had offices in Edinburgh's Princes Street, and pursued its own campaigns, with plans for Garden Cities at Rosyth, on the Firth of Forth, and Foyers, in Inverness-shire. It appeared to operate largely independently of the London-based organization, although Thomas Adams, a native of Edinburgh, was a regular speaker.

status, although in some respects he was more like a partially self-supporting itinerant evangelist, working for a professionally organized mission society.

How else could he be deployed? It was not clear that his skills would transfer into executive leadership, but when the Garden City Pioneer Company was incorporated in 1902, he was given the title 'Managing Director' and a small salary, and tasked with promotional activities and searching for a suitable site for the first Garden City. One of his first duties in this new role was speaking at the GCA's second conference, at Port Sunlight, hosted by W.H. Lever. Lever used the event to promote his industrial village of Port Sunlight and his soap manufacturing operation, in the same way that Cadbury had at the Bournville conference in the previous year. After Lever had made a speech emphasizing that he was not a philanthropist, but simply interested in good business and profit sharing, Howard had to speak next, emphasizing that the Garden City ideas were 'not Utopian'.[59] Lever's involvement with the GCA was relatively short-lived, and he fell out with them in 1904, when the directors refused to back his demand that freehold sites in the first Garden City be sold to speculative builders. But while it lasted, Howard clearly enjoyed having one of the richest men in Britain among his circle of friends. The Howards stayed with the Levers on at least one occasion, and Howard proudly remembered travelling in Lever's coach to Rivington Pike, a beauty spot close to Lever's Rivington estate, near Bolton.[60] Lever was also a Congregationalist and built several Congregational churches, but whether the Levers and the Howards ever discussed religion is, sadly, not known.

Howard and Thomas Adams, who had moved from the GCA to be employed as secretary of the Pioneer Company, travelled about England prospecting for land. Before Howard Pearsall suggested the estate at Letchworth, they had visited possible sites in Warwickshire, Staffordshire, Essex, and Nottinghamshire, and were seriously interested in a site at Chartley Castle in Staffordshire. They lectured when visiting a town, but had to conceal their real purpose, for fear of landowners hearing about their interest, and raising prices; Howard's

[59] *Manchester Courier* 26 July 1902; *Gloucester Citizen* 28 July 1902.
[60] HALS DE/Ho/F17/6/1–4 and HALS DE/Ho/F25/45.

entire scheme was premised on land being purchased at agricultural values. This dissimulation did not come easily to Howard, who regarded candour as a virtue that should be displayed on all occasions. It was clear that the business interests on the board of the Pioneer Company (Edward Cadbury; Thomas Ritzema, business manager of the Cadbury-owned newspaper, the *Daily News;* Thomas Idris the soft drinks manufacturer; Aneurin Williams, an iron master and Franklin Thomasson, a cotton manufacturer) were determining the policy. In assessing plots, their first priority was its suitability for trade and manufacturing; transport, communications and access to labour supply were next on the list, and only then was the desirability of the site for residential purposes considered. There was division within the board about whether proximity to London was an absolute requirement; this was favoured by Idris, who wished to move his drinks factory from Camden, and he was eventually successful in persuading others.[61] The decision to select Letchworth was not therefore one in which Howard played a major part. He did, however, negotiate the purchase of the estate with a firm of Hitchin solicitors, one of whom remembered him as 'an insignificant little man, who, to a piercing eye, did not appear to be worth many shillings'.[62] Fifteen mainly agricultural properties were purchased from fifteen different owners in order to create a parcel of land slightly less than 4000 acres, which was smaller than Howard had proposed in *To-morrow*. When all the purchases were complete, Howard's estimate from nearly twenty years earlier was shown to have been remarkably accurate: the average cost per acre was almost exactly £40.[63]

Having purchased its land, on 1 September 1903 the Pioneer Company reconstituted itself as the First Garden City Ltd, with an authorized share capital of £300,000. W.H. Lever briefly joined the Board at this point, with the other directors remaining the same. A prospectus was issued, with an invitation to the public to subscribe to the first issue of £80,000 in £5 ordinary shares, with a dividend restricted to five percent per annum. The first £40,000 worth of

[61] Beevers, *Garden City Utopia* pp. 82–5.

[62] R.L. Hine, *Relics of an Uncommon Attorney* (London, 1951) p. 45.

[63] Beevers, *Garden City Utopia* p. 86; C.B. Purdom, *The Building of Satellite Towns* (London, 1949) p. 54.

shares were quickly snapped up by supporters of the GCA and those who had been members of the Pioneer Company. The dividend restriction, about which Howard had been explicit in speeches and publications throughout the 1890s, was central to his financial model, and it was not a disincentive for Garden City enthusiasts. For ordinary investors, however, it presented more of a problem. They wanted to invest in shares that would rise with the market, with no artificial limit on the dividend paid, and a guarantee of some annual return. In arguing for the five percent restriction, Howard was supporting a practice well established in late nineteenth-century finance, the principle of 'philanthropy at five percent', which had been adopted by the housing reformer Octavia Hill, and others.[64] But it was no longer seen as commercially viable in 1903. Neville became exasperated as Howard refused to concede: yes, he was correct to assume that Garden City investors would be people of goodwill, but no, he could not assume that they would be willing to invest if their dividends were restricted or deferred. Neville remarked that 'I think many people would subscribe £1,000 if they saw a reasonable chance of getting the return promised who would probably not give £100 if they found an indefinite future fixed for the payment of dividend'.[65] Howard was unpersuaded. Every city in the history of the world had been built on laissez-faire and speculation: he insisted that the Garden City should be built on altruism and cooperation.

Then word got back to the other directors that Howard had made a speech in Hitchin, just four miles from Letchworth, in which he had apparently declared that what was needed were investors who were prepared to take risks, philanthropists who would invest in the full knowledge that the whole project might fail. Neville, who had devoted the previous three years to persuading potential investors that the project was sound, was by now thoroughly exasperated by what he saw as an act of extreme foolishness:

> For months the Board have striven to put the investment on a business footing and have abandoned cherished projects on the very ground that from mere philanthropy without hope of return the money would not

---

[64] Fishman, *Urban Utopias* pp. 16, 46–7.

[65] HALS DE/Ho/F25/51 Neville to Howard 23 June 1903.

be forthcoming ... you must bear in mind that there is another side to the ethical question, and that is loyalty to the Board. I appreciate your reluctance to ask poor people to invest their savings but there is all the difference in the world between refraining from soliciting and depreciating investment. You cannot loyally do the latter ... I feel sure that you have not realised the inevitable effects of such remarks as these quoted. They can be made in one speech; they cannot be explained away in a hundred.[66]

Howard's unwavering views on philanthropic investment and speculation marked the end of his executive role with First Garden City Company. The day before Neville sent his letter, the board drew up a new job description for him. His new role involved working for the Company for nine months in the year, mainly as a publicist, giving lectures and writing to the press. He might show visitors around the estate, but he was not to interview manufacturers, unless specifically asked to do so by the board. Presumably aware that these were significant limitations to be placing upon the movement's founder, they agreed that he should be paid £350 'to give special attention to the work of first designing the Town' although as Parker and Unwin had just been selected as the architects, it was not clear what this meant. It was Parker and Unwin's plans for the arrangements of streets, and the design of houses, that would be put into practice at Letchworth. In this context, the £350 seems to have had the unmistakeable characteristics of a pay-off. Howard seems to have been aware of his own shortcomings as a managing director. Writing lengthy reports, which he enjoyed doing, was no substitute for dealing with the many issues that needed immediate attention and action. Other members of the board were no doubt aware that removing Howard from office would permit power to flow to Thomas Adams,

[66] HALS DE/Ho/F25/51 Neville to Howard 13 November 1903. The notes that Howard wrote in preparation for his speech in Hitchin are at HALS DE/Ho/F3/28. They indicate that he was planning to describe to the audience how the communities in Hitchin and Baldock would be affected by the development of nearby Letchworth. He made reference to Bournville and Port Sunlight, something of which other board members would have approved, and planned to show some slides of those places. His notes contain nothing about the risks of investment. Perhaps he departed from his script or was responding to a question.

who was bright, ambitious and highly efficient. Adams was duly promoted from the position of company secretary to manager of Letchworth Garden City, in 1904.[67]

The unsettlement created by Howard's falling out with the board provides the context for the letters Lizzie wrote him, which were quoted earlier. His confidence was badly bruised, and his future income looked precarious. His highly prized principle of democratic self-government for the residents of the Garden City, in which power gradually transferred from shareholders to residents, had been stamped upon. What the board had in mind was the creation of a town similar to Bournville and Port Sunlight, but with operations in the hands of several manufacturers, rather than one single owner-industrialist. This was, indeed, an idea that Howard had been partly responsible for promoting, as was seen in his speech to the GCA's first annual meeting, which was quoted at the beginning of this chapter. As Beevers points out, Howard's failure to tackle in his book the issue of how power would flow from the trustees to the community made him partly responsible for the muddle. It was inadequate to fall back upon vague declarations about 'an honest landlord, namely ourselves', and calls for a trust to be created to purchase the estate from the shareholders for the benefit of the inhabitants 'at a later date'.[68] Equally, the strategy pursued by Neville and Adams of repeatedly linking the Garden City with the communities already built at Bournville and Port Sunlight had successfully domesticated the Garden City concept in the public imagination, and had made it seem respectable and achievable.

The Letchworth estate was formally opened on 9 October 1903, amid mud and speeches. It was the climax of a week of rain-soaked activity, during which the GCA laid on special trains from King's Cross. The *Sheffield Daily Telegraph* reported that 'a little army of Pressmen' arrived two days before the opening but ventured no

---

[67] Adams went on to have a highly successful career as a pioneer of town planning in Britain, Canada and the United States. He published widely, and held visiting professorships at Harvard and Massachusetts Institute of Technology. See Michael Simpson, 'Thomas Adams, 1871–1940' *Oxford Dictionary of National Biography* (Oxford, 2004).

[68] Beevers, *Garden City Utopia* p. 90.

further than the lunch marquee outside the temporarily erected station, re-embarking without seeing the estate. On the day itself 'about a thousand people, mainly philanthropic old ladies and gentlemen, and Pressmen' arrived and struggled through the biting wind, the mud ruining their clothes; tall hats, frock coats and patent leathers proved unsuitable attire for the depths of the Hertfordshire countryside in a wet autumn. But once they had reached the site the situation improved:

> Conveyances were there ready to convey the people around the estate, about six square miles . . . the country seems very pleasant and pretty, and the company appear to have made a good speculation. The land is high, the soil good, and the climate all that could be desired. The estate is right in the heart of the country, and London, 28 miles away, is the nearest large place. If everything that is said about the city be true, the inhabitants should be happy people. They will have small rents, nice houses with gardens, and plenty of recreation grounds. It is also proposed to have no public houses unless the population desire them. In case they are desired, the profits will be devoted to counteracting influences.[69]

Earl Grey performed the opening ceremony, expressing the same tone of lukewarm endorsement that he had articulated at Bournville:

> The plan, he thought, was calculated to modify, not remove, those growing evils which they all so much deplored. It was admitted on all hands that the ill-regulated and anarchic growth of the large cities had become the very cancers of the body politic and were sapping the strength and poisoning the character of the nation. The poor people had nothing to relieve the squalor and depressing monotony of the slums except the public houses and music halls, and unless some effective steps were taken to counteract their influence on the character, temperament and physique of the people, they would not be able to retain their present leading position in the world. (Applause).[70]

Howard, who we may imagine shivering in the mud with the increasingly frail Lizzie at his side, might have reflected that these sentiments were not the ones that had inspired him to take up his pen at his dining

---

[69] *Sheffield Daily Telegraph* 10 October 1903.
[70] *Sheffield Daily Telegraph* 10 October 1903.

table, and express his ideas for *To-morrow*. Over the previous four years, the interventions of aristocrats, imperialists, industrialists, and politicians had recalibrated the message of the GCA from the one articulated at the launch at the Congregational Hall, where the emphasis had been placed on the agency of the garden citizens, who would take advantage of accruing land values for the benefit of their community, in a spirit of co-operation and self-determination. Howard had prepared a speech to make at the opening, but he was not called upon to deliver it, a fact that he attributed to the inclement weather.[71]

[71] The notes for the speech he had planned to make can be found at HALS DE/Ho/F3/25. He had wanted to talk about the role of journalists in spreading the Garden City gospel.

5

Howard in Letchworth 1905–1914

Moving to the Garden City

In April 1905 the opening of the railway station at Letchworth, and the introduction of a regular service to King's Cross,[1] made it practical for Howard and his children to move to the Garden City. They occupied an inner terrace at 2, Norton Way, which was one of the first homes to be built in Letchworth, designed by the estate architects Barry Parker and Raymond Unwin. It was typical of their Letchworth style: a cluster of three spacious cottages designed as a single building, with deeply pitched roofs and gabled windows.[2] The family at this point consisted of the youngest daughter, Margery, fifteen, and the adult children, Kathleen, twenty-four, Editha, twenty-three, and Cecil, twenty-two. Editha would later tell Frederic Osborn that her father had insisted on bringing a 'slum family', the Hughes, from London to live in the adjoining property, and that they were noisy and dirty, spoiling life for the Howards, and eventually had to be 'kicked out'.[3] Letchworth's early residents tended to be self-segregated into different districts divided by the familiar boundaries of wealth and occupation, so the arrival of a slum family in a Parker and Unwin Norton Way property does suggest direct intervention from Howard, and perhaps his desire to enact the transcendence of social divisions that he hoped to see. It seems likely that his elder daughters joined their father as regular Letchworth-to-London commuters for as long as they remained unmarried. The family connection with Remington, in Gracechurch Street, where Howard's sister Annie had been

---

[1] *The Times*, 17 April 1905.
[2] See photo at GCC LBM4067.21
[3] HALS DE/FJO/I35.

Ebenezer Howard: Inventor of the Garden City. Frances Knight, Oxford University Press.
© Frances Knight 2023. DOI: 10.1093/oso/9780198790815.003.0006

employed from 1886 as one of the firm's first female typists, was strengthened when Editha joined the firm in 1900. Annie remained in the company until 1917, retiring as head of the copying office when she was seventy. Kathleen and Cecil may also have found early employment as shorthand typists, as this had become established as the occupational norm for the whole family, with Cecil making his living as a shorthand writer at the time of his father's death. The house in Norton Way became emptier after Kathleen married in 1906 and became Mrs Rawlinson. The ceremony was conducted in the ancient parish church in Letchworth village, where her mother had been buried. Editha married in the following year and became Mrs Berry, choosing Letchworth's Free church hall for a service conducted by the family's old friend Bruce Wallace, the Congregational minister and founder of the Brotherhood church. Cecil also got married in 1907.

Howard himself re-married a few weeks after Editha's wedding, on 25 March 1907. He was ignoring the advice of his first wife Lizzie who had regularly told him that if she died, he should never marry again, because he 'was the sort of man who should not be married' on account of his lack of interest in a regular income.[4] In comparison with the considerable evidence that survives for Lizzie, relatively little can be reconstructed about Howard's second wife, Edith Annie Hayward. She was the daughter of a Lincolnshire farmer, and at the time of her marriage was forty-two, fifteen years younger than Howard. She had not previously been married and was living with her sister on a small private income in Norton, one of the villages which became part of the Letchworth estate. Most of what is known about her is filtered through the interviews which Howard's daughters gave to Osborn, and Osborn himself, who had been acquainted with her, and had formed a very negative opinion. These sources paint a picture of a 'most unfortunate marriage' and a 'disaster' which the family had strongly counselled against. But Howard, who became more stubborn as he grew older, would not listen, and 'nothing could alter him'.[5] It was not unusual for widowers to re-marry fairly swiftly, but there was

[4] HALS/DE/FJO/I35.
[5] HALS/DE/FJO/I35.

a degree of bafflement as to why Howard married a woman who appeared to be completely uninterested in both him, and his ideas. Perhaps it was simply that he believed he could not cope without a woman at home, and with the departure of the second of his adult daughters, he sought an urgent domestic replacement, without giving much attention to the particularities of his bride. The wedding was an Anglican ceremony, held in the tiny parish church in Temple Bruer, a hamlet thirteen miles south of Lincoln. Edith's father William Knight Hayward, who farmed locally, and was one of the witnesses. The absence of some or all of Howard's children provides evidence of the family's disapproval. A couple of scrappy letters from Edith Howard to her husband (signing herself as 'Nancy') survive from 1908. They seem hastily written in response to one from him in which he lamented that he had not 'received a letter [from her] for *such* a long time'.[6] A rare photograph of Howard and the second Mrs Howard is preserved in the Garden City Collection, showing them attired in historic fancy dress, at Letchworth's May Day celebrations in 1910. Edith, in a tightly laced faux regency style dress, squints unsmilingly at the camera from beneath a large lace trimmed bonnet, while Ebenezer peers out through his spectacles from under a tricorn hat. It seems that the photographer had captured a tense moment in the re-creation of Merrie England.[7] The 1911 Census records the couple living on their own in Wilbury Road, Letchworth, in a six roomed house; Edith's sister Kate lived nearby, with Charles Purdom and a suffragette, Jane Short, who operated under the alias of Rachel Peace, as her lodgers.[8] Howard was described, as he had been on his marriage certificate, as a 'shorthand writer'; the words 'Director of First Garden City' had been entered in his handwriting on the census return, but then struck out. The absence of even a single live-in servant, something which Howard had always managed at the time of earlier censuses, indicates that his finances had seen little

---

[6] HALS DE/Ho/F25/36.

[7] GCC LBM559. None of the other figures in the picture look particularly 'merrie', including a man dressed as a town crier, a man in Cambridge academic dress, and a tall woman with some children.

[8] A photo of the interior of their house in 1911 can be viewed at GCC 1961.46.138.

improvement. The couple separated later that year, although when confronted with the difficulties of advancing age and frailty, and probably also further financial pressures, they moved in together again in Welwyn in the 1920s. Notwithstanding the May Day photograph, it is noticeable from newspaper reports that Edith was never recorded accompanying her husband to events which other men's wives attended, and it was said that she played no part in the life of the town.

The contrast with the energetic and vivacious Lizzie, who, had she lived, would have naturally assumed the position of 'first lady of Letchworth' is striking. Lizzie's considerable reputation led to her being commemorated in the Garden City's first public building, the Mrs Howard Memorial Hall.[9] The laying of the foundation stone, in July 1905, and the opening of the Hall, in the following April, were events reported in the national and regional press, providing further evidence that Mrs Ebenezer Howard had been a well-known figure in her own right.[10] The Hall was built at a cost of £1,100, with the money raised by the 'women associated with the late Mrs Howard . . . the Hall designed in harmony with the old Gothic buildings of the district by Mr Raymond Unwin.'[11] The Hall was, and remains, a permanent memorial, but there were other ways in which Lizzie's influence continued to be felt. As an ardent Spiritualist, Howard clearly considered it normal to seek to maintain contact with his deceased wife. What the conventions and sensibilities were surrounding maintaining contact with one's first wife after having married another is a topic which might repay further investigation. Howard had relied on Lizzie's advice and support for the previous quarter-century, and evidently regarded contacting her as desirable, and probably necessary. Little is known about what such séances produced, although when the lighting was adequate, he preserved the messages received from the spirit world in shorthand.[12] After

[9]   See photos of the Mrs Howard Hall at GCC LBM4312.26, LBM4312.5 and LBM4312.27.1.

[10]   *The Daily Telegraph*, 12 April, 24 & 25 July 1905; *Manchester Courier*, 2 April 1906.

[11]   *The Times* 3 April 1906.

[12]   It seems likely that these messages were among the many papers destroyed by Edith Howard, after his death.

attending a Spiritualist meeting in Letchworth in 1926, Howard wrote sorrowfully to the organizer: 'I came to your gathering hoping very much for a message from my late wife, and went away really disappointed'. A message had been received, which was 'You have accomplished more than you know. Do not be impatient – go steadily on' but Howard felt insufficiently convinced that it had come from Lizzie, or that it was meant specifically for him. He asked the medium, Mr André, if he could not try again, to seek a further, more specific message from Lizzie. André tactfully declined, emphasizing that the members of his 'Developing Circle' were still working on developing their psychic powers, and could not get Howard what he wanted.[13] Even twenty years after her death, Howard remained deeply emotionally invested with Lizzie in the spirit world.

Building Letchworth

Early Letchworth is rightly celebrated as the substantial creation of the architectural duo Barry Parker and Raymond Unwin, who won the contract to design the estate layout, and were then retained as consulting architects, which meant that all building proposals submitted for the estate had to pass through their office. Howard's ideas had focussed on how the Garden City community should be created and how its members should relate to each other; he offered no thoughts on what its buildings should look like, beyond the obvious requirements that they should be spacious, healthy, and affordable. Parker and Unwin, who were brothers-in-law, as well as the closest of friends, were also early admirers of Howard. Looking back from the 1940s, Parker remembered 'how attracted to Howard I was and how completely sympathetic we were in our aims and views'.[14] Unwin had attended the Bournville Conference in 1901, and it seems likely that both men had read *To-morrow* at the time of its publication, and had recognized Howard as a kindred spirit. They keenly embraced the task of designing a town that bore a passable resemblance to Howard's

[13] HALS DE/Ho/F25/1.
[14] Parker interviewed in *Letchworth Citizen* 5 March 1943. Cited in Standish Meacham, *Regaining Paradise: Englishness and the Early Garden City Movement* (New Haven and London, 1999) p. 103.

diagrams. Their commitment to winning the contract was revealed in October 1903, when Unwin moved into lodgings in the hamlet of Letchworth, on the edge of the estate, so that he could repeatedly tramp the site as he worked on their entry for the competition. Their winning entry is recognisably derivative from the diagrams in *To-morrow*, showing a radial pattern of roads fanning out from the central point, with gardens and public buildings at the centre, and two inner ring roads providing linkage between the spokes. Howard's 'Grand Avenue' and north and south boulevards would become the Broadway, and the routes that would fan out from the hub, Gernon Road, Pixmore Way, South View, and West View were faithful to his design. As Howard had clearly stated, when a Garden City was built, the architects would need to adapt his plan to the terrain and the existing features. In Letchworth, the most significant of these was the railway line. Parker and Unwin took the decision to place the centre of the Garden City about a quarter of a mile from the railway, in the expectation, which was realized, that the station would be built in the spot where the railway ran closest to the centre. This made Letchworth convenient for commuters and for visitors, but as the railway snaked round to the north west side of the town, it effectively compressed the development on that side, meaning that the elegant symmetry in Parker and Unwin's design could never be fully realized. It also meant that steam trains puffed their way through the Garden City, something which Howard, who had imagined an electrically powered circular railway, had not intended. There were other natural features that were retained, the most important of which was the Icknield Way, the ancient highway stretching from Norfolk to Wiltshire which passed just north of the railway line, and was incorporated into the scheme as an east–west route through it. Norton Common was retained as an open space, and Pix brook became a defining boundary line between the central and outer developments. The centre of the Garden City was placed on the highest point, and north of the Baldock to Hitchin road, which meant that the centre of Letchworth would move north to the Garden City, and away from what would become known as 'old' Letchworth village, with its historic parish church.

Having won the contract as estate architects, Parker and Unwin moved their architectural practice from Buxton to Baldock, in order to give their undivided attention to the building of Letchworth. Unwin was forty-one, and Parker thirty-seven. They were a well-respected and experienced partnership, but still youthful and energetic, and strengthened by the bonds which enabled them to act as a single family unit.[15] Their manifesto had been set out in their influential publication of 1901, *The Art of Building a Home*.[16] Parker was the more visually gifted and artistic, and Unwin, who had trained in engineering, was the more politically and theologically engaged. A childhood spent in Oxford, where his father had enrolled as a mature student and then stayed on as a private tutor, had led to Unwin's early exposure to various forms of *fin de siècle* culture. While a pupil at Magdalen College School he had heard John Ruskin and William Morris lecture, and was influenced by Arnold Toynbee and Samuel Barnett. He consulted Barnett on whether, like his elder brother, he should become a clergyman, and Barnett advised him to consider whether he was more concerned about humanity's sinfulness, or its unhappiness.[17] It was a characteristically pragmatic response from the settlement movement's founding father.

Unwin made the interesting decision to take up an engineering apprenticeship in Chesterfield, rather than the scholarship at Magdalen College Oxford, which was also offered to him. It was in Chesterfield that he became acquainted with the Parker family, who were his cousins, and whose daughter Ethel he would marry. He also became friends with Edward Carpenter, the socialist and homosexual rights campaigner who had briefly been an Anglican clergyman.[18] Carpenter had purchased about seven acres of land at Millthorpe,

[15] Standish Meacham, *Regaining Paradise: Englishness and the Early Garden City Movement* (New Haven and London, 1999) pp. 79, 110. They designed a double house for their two families in Letchworth Lane.

[16] Barry Parker and Raymond Unwin, *The Art of Building a Home: A Collection of Lectures and Illustrations by Barry Parker and Raymond Unwin* (London, 1901).

[17] Andrew Saint, 'Sir Raymond Unwin 1863–1940' *Oxford Dictionary of National Biography* (Oxford, 2004). See also Meacham, *Regaining Paradise* p. 73.

[18] Carpenter was ordained in 1870 and served as curate to F.D. Maurice at St Edward's Cambridge, but took advantage of the Clerical Disabilities Act, 1870, to relinquish his orders in 1874. Thereafter he remained committed to spiritual exploration in various forms. See Chushichi Tsuzuki, 'Edward Carpenter, 1844–1929' *Oxford Dictionary of National Biography* (Oxford, 2004).

between Chesterfield and Sheffield, in order to develop a 'simple life' community, based on market gardening, sandal making, vegetarianism and teetotalism. Unwin lived at Millthorpe for some years in the 1880s, and then moved to Manchester, where he became branch secretary of William Morris's Socialist League. He met William Morris again, and also Ford Madox Brown, who was painting his frescoes in Manchester Town Hall. Returning to Chesterfield as chief draughtsman to the Staveley Coal and Iron Company, he engaged in his first formal collaboration with Barry Parker, designing St Andrew's church for the mining community of Barrow Hill. He also designed his first workers' cottages and threatened to resign if bathrooms were not included.

The Arts and Crafts style which would predominate in early Letchworth was an unsurprising choice for this period. It could seem somewhat at odds with Howard's relentlessly futuristic thinking, but its conscious use of space to promote both sociability and wellbeing chimed very much with Howard's ideas. As well as William Morris, Unwin was also influenced by the Viennese town planner Camillo Sitte, who advocated the human scale and 'organic' principles that he discerned in the seemingly haphazard construction of medieval towns, with their mixed roof lines, streets of irregular widths and building overhangs. He made a conscious attempt to recreate something of that atmosphere in Letchworth.[19] It was a visceral reaction against the miles of tiny-roomed monotonous terraces, run up by the speculative builders of the previous generation, which the Arts and Crafts architects considered too small and bleak for wholesome family life.

Individual styling and open plan living spaces predominated. Several other architects besides Parker and Unwin, including M.H. Baillie Scott, Courtenay M. Crickmer, Cecil Hignett, H. Clapham Lander, Thomas Geoffry Lucas, and the firm of Robert Bennett and Benjamin Bidwell, were also involved in designing the town's first homes.[20] They wanted to design cottages, including large

[19] Raymond Unwin, *Town Planning in Practice: An Introduction to the Art of Designing Cities and Suburbs* (Second edition, London, 1911). See especially pp. 309–10; 346–8.

[20] Josh Tidy and Aimee Flack, *Arts and Crafts in Letchworth* (Letchworth Garden City, 2017).

cottage-style middle class family homes, that looked anchored in the landscape, with cosy inglenook fireplaces for family and friends to gather.[21] They were building rural homes on generously sized plots in Hertfordshire, which was still an overwhelmingly rural county. But if the completed houses were vastly more 'garden' than 'city', the Arts and Crafts philosophy of the unity of form and function, simplicity of design and integrity in the use of materials and techniques of manufacture, fitted perfectly with the broader aims of the Letchworth project, as well as with the prevailing aesthetic of what constituted 'good taste' in progressive early twentieth-century circles. The Letchworth Arts and Crafts style evolved into one in which 'healthy living' was given centre stage. Sunshine, natural light and ventilation were very important, and some of the elite housing was designed with verandas or sleeping porches, to accommodate the Edwardian belief in the desirability of sleeping in the fresh air.[22] Gardens, and gardening, were of course mandatory for residents of all classes. The 'Letchworth look', with its sweeping red tiled roofs, and rough cast render to conceal the locally produced Arlesey white bricks, which were considered unacceptably pale, emerged as something visually different from the slate-and-brick of many early twentieth-century villa semis or small terraces.

The result was that some fabulous Arts and Crafts residences were built in Letchworth, and some good quality, though relatively expensive, artisan housing. In the absence of benevolent and wealthy industrialists such as Lever, the Cadburys or the Rowntrees, there was no one to underwrite the costs of working-class housing, as there was at Port Sunlight, Bournville and New Earswick. Workers' cottages had to try to pay their way by being built as cheaply as possible. Unwin, who loathed tiny rooms and had a particular horror of 'useless' front parlours (which working-class women generally wanted) advocated saving money by leaving walls unplastered; but the aesthetic attraction of an unplastered wall probably only appeals to someone who can afford to plaster it, should they wish to.

---

[21] Parker and Unwin, *Art of Building a Home*.

[22] See GCC LBM701.31 for a photo of Crabby Corner owned by Howard Pearsall, a Parker and Unwin house designed to facilitate sleeping in the fresh air.

In 1905 the Cheap Cottages Exhibition was organized in Letchworth by Thomas Adams, on the suggestion of John St Loe Strachey, the editor of the *Spectator*. The intention was to show a range of cottages, constructed in a variety of styles and materials, that could be built for £150, while simultaneously publicizing Letchworth. Over 125 cottages were built for the exhibition, and over 60,000 people visited Letchworth between July and September in order to view them, with cheap excursion trains laid on from Liverpool, Manchester, Newcastle, Bradford, Leeds, Edinburgh and Glasgow, as well as regular inclusive tickets from London and Birmingham.[23] Not all of the visitors were impressed with the unfinished state of the town, or the quality of the cottages, some of which were made from timber, or concrete, and seemed to be of flimsy or unfamiliar construction.[24] There was a significant cohort of middle-class Londoners in search of second homes, who had been encouraged by articles such as that in the *Daily Mail* which had promoted the exhibition under the headline 'Bolt-holes for weekends', and as the place to find 'a cheap, simple airy cottage, in close proximity to London'.[25] Controversy broke out about whether some of the cottages could in fact be built for £150. The figure appeared more accurately to reflect the cost of building materials only, and seemed not to include architects' fees, transporting materials to the site, builders' profit, fencing or indeed the bath; a bath was regarded as essential in new builds, if bathing was ever to become an established habit amongst the working classes. When all these costs were included, the cost of a cottage was more like £200.[26] The negative publicity about the true cost of workers' housing in Letchworth was unhelpful.

In October, shortly after the exhibition had closed, the London Housing Reform Union held a conference in Letchworth, to consider the lessons learned. Howard was reported as having said that it was 'necessary, if the best results were to be attained in garden cities, that landowners, builders and owners of buildings should loyally

---

[23] *Hull Daily Mail; Manchester Courier* 14 September 1905.

[24] For photos of the Cheap Cottages Exhibition, see GCC LBM4308.16 and LBM2492.

[25] *Daily Mail* 13 January 1905.

[26] *Daily Mail* 25 September 1905.

co-operate'[27] which sounded like code for 'be willing to forego profit'. Howard had devoted a chapter entitled 'Pro-municipal Work' in *To-morrow*, expounding the idea that once common ownership of land was achieved, 'pro-municipal agencies' meaning charities, religious societies, educational agencies, banks, building societies, trades unions and cooperative societies would be able to work together to form 'building societies' to build homes for the people. What was needed was the organization of this co-operative effort:

> If labour leaders spent half the energy in co-operative organisation that they now waste in co-operative disorganisation, the end of our present unjust system would be at hand. In Garden City, such leaders will have a fair field for the exercise of pro-municipal functions...and the formation of building societies of this type would be of the greatest possible utility.[28]

The dream of common landownership had evaporated well before 1905, leaving Howard with no alternative but to appeal for cooperation from property owners and business interests. Throughout the first decade of the twentieth century, the cooperative movement was asked to throw its weight behind the Garden City, but it declined to do so. It was undoubtedly powerful, with more than two million members organized into 1,600 local societies, which in 1903 sold £92 million of goods and distributed £10 million in profits. In the same year, cooperative societies had either built or advanced money for 37,000 houses, and the movement's factories were producing more than £10 million of goods.[29] On the face of it, its interests were aligned with Howard's. At each of the annual Cooperative Congresses held between 1900 and 1909, pro-Garden City speakers urged that the movement's factories and housing be re-directed to Letchworth, but the individual societies valued their independence, and wished to remain in their own localities. Thus the working-class cooperative initiative was lost, and the balance tilted permanently towards the

[27] *The Times* 2 October 1905.
[28] Ebenezer Howard, *To-morrow: A Peaceful Path to Real Reform* (London, 1898) p. 86.
[29] Fishman, *Urban Utopias* p. 65, citing *The Thirty-Sixth Annual Co-operative Congress* (Manchester, 1904) pp. 63, 65, 83.

capitalist interests and investors who comprised most of the directors of First Garden City.[30] Without the ability to provide good quality housing for working families, the Garden City movement risked losing much of its point, and the authorities in Letchworth spent much of the next decade grappling with plans for economically viable housing schemes. Howard tended to blame all of the shortcomings encountered at Letchworth on the lack of cooperative enterprise.

By 1905, the Garden City had ceased to be merely an idea in the minds of its founders and had developed sufficiently for people to begin to judge it against whatever they thought it had initially promised. H.G. Wells, who was very well known as a novelist, journalist, and social commentator, turned his critical fire on Ebenezer Howard in the first of a series of articles on 'Utopianisms' that he wrote for the *Daily Mail*.[31] Howard, whom he described as 'a simpler man than Plato' (the originator of the concept of utopia) had taken a pair of compasses and drawn a number of concentric circles. As such, Howard was the author of an important thought experiment; he had made people who had never thought about housing think about it for the first time. These were the people who had just assumed that cities grew, and were as uncontrollable as the weather. 'The manifest artificiality of these circles ended all of that for them' and the simplicity of the concept was accessible to even the dullest mind. But it seemed that for Wells, all that became tawdry as it was translated into a town bisected with a railway line, with cheap cottages, an asphalt works and a mineral water manufacturer. He thought that business and industry should remain in London, and workers should commute: 'When I hear the words Garden City now, I think of bitumen and nasty fizzy stuff in glass bottles and vans – mineral water vans! Moreover, I understand they have erected a gas works – Victorian, unbeautiful, obsolescent structures. My bright vision of beautiful homes among glowing gardens comes to me no more.'[32] How Wells thought the Garden City was to become economically viable without power or industry was unclear, and the piece had the air of quickly penned provocative journalism. Howard published a somewhat

[30] Fishman, *Urban Utopias* p. 65.

[31] *Daily Mail* 18 March 1905.

[32] *Daily Mail* 18 March 1905.

exasperated reply several days later, explaining that one of the major points in favour of Garden Cities was the proximity of employment, and the avoidance of commuting. The circularity of the town plan was not among its essential features. 'If, now we have descended to earth, our plan is not the best, it is at least infinitely better than none at all.'[33] What was essential was order and design, well-located factories and workshops, parks, public buildings, shops, and playing fields. A green belt separating the town from neighbouring settlements, and afford- able, well- located, low-density housing were also required.

For some residents, the low housing density, which had to remain below twelve units per acre, and the large tracts of empty space imparted 'an eerie sense of disconnectedness'.[34] It could be a challen- ging environment for Londoners who had uprooted themselves on the promise of a better life, and were accustomed to having friends, family, and facilities very close at hand. As one early resident put it: 'When I came out of that station, I thought, "Oh, what a place to come to, I'm being buried alive here." There was nothing here. We stood there, and on that side was all fields.'[35] Early Letchworth had something of the atmosphere of a bleak frontier town, which was exacerbated by the absence of the normal structures of local govern- ment, which were not developed until after the First World War. In common with many other towns, the railway line had the effect of scoring a social divide through the landscape, In Letchworth, the 'right' side of the tracks was to the south, and the 'wrong' side was to the north, where many of the factories and light industry were eventually located. In the absence of an Urban District Council, the First Garden City Company exercised control over almost all aspects of civic life, including the colours which people painted their houses.[36]

[33] *Daily Mail* 22 March 1905.

[34] Meacham, *Regaining Paradise* p. 105.

[35] Maureen Maddren, *Letchworth Recollections: A Unique Record of Life in The First Garden City as Remembered by some of its Earliest Citizens 1903–1939* (Baldock, 1995) p. 16.

[36] Maddren, *Letchworth Recollections* p. 11. For those influenced by Parker and Unwin, the expression of collective will, rather than individual whim, in decisions regarding the colour of external paint was considered very important. Neighbours agreeing to paint a row of houses in the same colour was a sign that society was improving; not doing so was a sign of social disintegration. Parker and Unwin, *Art of Building a Home* p. 108.

Although many early Letchworthians believed that they had been attracted to the town by the relative lack of social stratification, in fact very different communities existed in separate neighbourhoods. The golf club was one of the first institutions to open, in the Spring of 1905, in the grounds of the ancient manor house of Letchworth Hall, which was turned into a hotel.[37] Meanwhile, 400 unemployed men had been brought down from London to build the roads and were accommodated in a 'temporary barrack' and in an old brewery in Baldock. *The Times* reported on both developments in the same article.[38]

The most powerful person was the estate manager, who from early in 1906 was W.H. Gaunt, a man who seemed unsympathetic to both the theoretical concept of the Garden City, and to the proclivities of some of its early devotees. He denounced as subversive those residents who opted to challenge the norms of conventional Edwardian dress, although his reasons for doing so were logical, namely that anything which appeared weird or eccentric was likely to prove a barrier to the investment which the town so badly needed. He had previously managed an industrial estate near Manchester, and he was not perhaps the most obvious candidate for such an influential post at Letchworth. He kept his eyes on the balance sheet, and his major priority was to attract new residents and business owners, rather than frighten them away.[39] His arrival coincided with the first wave of Letchworth pioneers stepping back. Ralph Neville resigned as chairman on being appointed a high court judge, but kept a close eye on developments, and became president of the Garden Cities and Town Planning Association around 1912. Raymond Unwin moved from Letchworth in 1906, in order to work on Henrietta Barnett's Hampstead Garden Suburb, although he maintained his professional relationship with Parker, who remained in Letchworth. Unwin's uncompromising prioritization of the aesthetic created friction with Gaunt, who failed to

[37] GCC LBM4051.5.43.

[38] *Times* 17 April 1905. The road builders were mainly sponsored by the Lord Mayor's Mansion House scheme.

[39] Robert Beevers, *The Garden City Utopia: A Critical Biography of Ebenezer Howard* (Houndsmill, 1988) p. 126. A more sympathetic picture of Gaunt emerges from Meacham, *Regaining Paradise* pp. 107–8.

understand why he insisted on consistency in the use of expensive
building materials. Unwin also fell out with Thomas Adams, who
defended the right of smallholders to erect unsightly sheds. These
quarrels with Gaunt and Adams were one reason why Unwin left.
The next to leave was Thomas Adams himself, who, like Neville and
Unwin, had worked hard to bring the Garden City to life, and was
genuinely committed to its vision. Adams was the only person who
had had a serious plan for tackling the dilapidated state of the
agricultural land on the estate. He wanted to encourage smallholders,
finance the purchase of equipment and land improvement measures,
and develop a training farm, which could have developed into an
agricultural college.[40] Howard, who only ever seems to have thought
of the estate's agricultural belt as a resource for feeding the town at its
centre, showed little support for Adams, and none of the other
directors appeared to be interested. Perhaps Adams' plan reawakened
in Howard painful memories of his own failures as a farmer in
Nebraska thirty-five years earlier, and, having lived in cities in the
intervening decades, he found that he could not get to grips with the
issues affecting the agricultural land on which Letchworth was built.
Frustrated by the lack of support, Adams published his ideas in *The
Garden City and Agriculture* (1905), and in October 1906 began to work as
a planning consultant, the first such person in Britain to be employed
in this field.[41] As Robert Beevers remarked, the directors of First
Garden City, now chaired by the uninspiring Aneurin Williams,
could think no further than each month's balance sheet, and they
mostly visited Letchworth very rarely. They had become little different from the private absentee landlords that they claimed to have
replaced.[42]

Cooperative housekeeping

Buffeted by economic challenges and the loss of some of its key
thinkers and strategists, Letchworth could at this point have slid into

[40] Beevers, *Garden City Utopia* pp. 126–9.
[41] Michael Simpson, 'Thomas Adams, 1871–1940' *Oxford Dictionary of National
Biography* (Oxford, 2004).
[42] Beevers, *Garden City Utopia* p. 128.

being little more than a slowly developing suburbia, like so many of the new towns that would come after it. But it did not do this. It began to be a magnet for artistic and creative people, whose activities created the well-publicized bohemian culture for which the town became known. Nor did all of Letchworth's remaining leading residents abandon the practical idealism which had marked out the beginnings of their project. Howard, building on the ideas of Raymond Unwin, set about energetically promoting a scheme for cooperative housekeeping, something which had featured prominently in late nineteenth-century utopian thinking and activity.[43] He was, as we have seen, influenced by the literary examples, the best known of which was in Edward Bellamy's *Looking Backward 2000–1887* and, through friends such as Bruce Wallace, he was familiar with some of the practical experiments.[44] His personal enthusiasm had been evident back in 1885, when he tried unsuccessfully to persuade Lizzie to abandon her prejudice 'in favour of separate houses' and consider renting a property large enough for their extended family of nine, in which 'one kitchen fire would serve for both families' and 'a joint of meat would not have to stay about for days'.[45]

In his chapter on 'Co-operation in Building' in *The Art of Building a Home*, Raymond Unwin had made proposals for cooperative schemes for both working- and middle-class residents. The basic plan was for purpose built small individual housing units and shared communal space, designed in quadrangles, with the residents' garden in the square in the centre. In the working-class scheme, he envisaged that 'instead of thirty or forty housewives preparing thirty or forty little scrap dinners, heating a like number of ovens, boiling thrice the number of pans and cleaning them all up again' two or three would be retained as cooks, producing better and cheaper meals for all. The

[43] See Lynn F. Pearson, 'Ideal homes: Women and cooperative housing in Victorian times' *Ekistics* 52, 310 (1985) pp. 62–4; Helen Meller, 'Planning theory and women's role in the city' *Urban History Yearbook* 17 (1990) pp. 85–98; Iain Borden, 'Social space and cooperative housekeeping in the English garden city' *Journal of Architectural and Planning Research* 16, 3 (1999) pp. 242–57.

[44] One of the longest surviving was Whiteway, in the Cotswolds, with which Wallace had links. See Nellie Shaw, *Whiteway: A Colony in the Cotswolds* (1935) and Joy Thacker, *Whiteway Colony: The Social History of a Tolstoyan Community* (1993).

[45] HALS DE/FJO/I3 4 March 1885.

meals would be served in a common room, which would be generously proportioned and comfortable; in the evening, residents would gather around the fire, for reading, writing and conversation, as well as for sharing their meal. A communal laundry would mean that bulky coppers and mangles could be removed from living spaces, and there would be an avoidance of steam and drying clothes.[46] Unwin's middle-class scheme, in contrast, was mainly intended to solve 'the great servant difficulty', by which he meant the difficulty in finding reliable domestic workers who could cook and clean, but would also discretely disappear into the background when living in close proximity to their employers, and not gossip about them. Unwin envisaged the provision of serviced accommodation and high-quality meals, provided by servants who would live in pleasant conditions on site, but away from the tenants. The privacy of residents in their individual living quarters would be assured, and they would be saved from anxieties about maintenance, and other household matters. Their time would be free to enjoy the higher things in life, and there would be conviviality in the shared spaces. Airy, tasteful rooms, with cosy inglenooks and other typical Arts and Crafts features, would be available for entertaining friends, and for socializing with other residents. Meals could be taken in common or delivered to the private apartment. Unwin declared that 'such an establishment could readily be built and worked on co-operative lines, giving many of the advantages of hotel life without entailing its disadvantages or costliness.'[47]

Unwin's ideas were taken up more widely. H.G. Wells penned another of his 'Utopia' articles for the *Daily Mail*, in which he encouraged the idea of a number of families living 'in association' with a common kitchen, dining room, nursery and library, arguing that this would be particularly beneficial for reducing the labour expected of women, as well as expense. He encouraged 'the Garden City people at Letchworth' to consider it, while pouring cold water on the possibility that it might work for working class people: 'I doubt if one could get average working men's wives or clerk's wives into such a place; they would be suspicious of each other, they would quarrel and refuse to

---

[46] Parker and Unwin, *Art of Building a Home* p. 104.
[47] Parker and Unwin, *Art of Building a Home* p. 105.

speak, and do all sorts of nervous, silly, unbred things. But there are a
lot of people in any class above the average.'[48] These sorts of 'unpre-
tending sociable people' might be able to make the experiment work,
and Wells thought it might even be made to pay. It was for these
genteel folk, of the type also envisaged in the second of Unwin's
proposals, that Letchworth's two co-operative housing developments
were designed. Homesgarth, the one in which Howard lived, has
received most attention. Less well known but more successful was
Meadow Way Green, for single women.[49] It was designed by Court-
ney M. Crickmer, partly funded by two of Howard's friends, Ruth
Pym and S.E. Dewe, and built by the Howard Cottage Society in
1914. The women took it in turns to shop and devise a menu, and the
meals were prepared by a cook, and eaten communally.[50] The scheme
was extended to twenty-three housing units in 1924 and was still
operating successfully in its original form, over thirty years after it
first opened.[51]

Howard enthusiastically described his vision for Homesgarth in an
illustrated article in the *Daily Mail* in the summer of 1906.[52] Plans had
been drawn up by the equally enthusiastic architect Harold Clapham
Lander, a Quaker and a Fabian socialist; he had delivered a paper
about cooperative housing at the Bournville conference, and would
become a prominent Garden City architect.[53] Lander's illustrations,
the first captioned 'a set of co-operative houses with communal
kitchen' depicts how an Arts and Crafts architect might have designed
an Oxbridge college: there are the characteristic sloping roofs and
gables, a covered walkway which was to be called a 'cloister', a clock-
tower, a tennis court and a flower garden with sundial and pergola.
An arrow pointed down from the sky with the word 'Kitchen', to

[48] *Daily Mail* 25 May 1905.

[49] Photo at GCC LBM385.

[50] Josh Tidy, *A–Z of Letchworth Garden City* (Stroud, 2018) pp. 58–9. Meadow
Way Green has been retained as social housing, whereas the apartments in
Homesgarth, which became known as Sollershott Hall, were sold off after the
First World War, and the communal space, with the exception of the garden, was
lost. For Crickmer, see Tidy and Flack, *Arts and Crafts* p. 36.

[51] C.B. Purdom, *The Building of Satellite Towns* (London, 1949) pp. 63–4.

[52] *Daily Mail* 18 August 1906.

[53] Meacham, *Regaining Paradise* pp. 117–19.

emphasize the communal nature of the catering. A smaller illustration, a 'detailed view of one of the co-operative houses' conveys the impression of a rustic cottage, and the accompanying diagram indicates that in addition to the public garden, there would also be individual private gardens for each resident. Howard's article explained the proposal: the aim was to 'secure the maximum of privacy and economy with the minimum of inconvenience' and 'to provide a home of comparative comfort and beauty for those numerous folk of the middle class who have a hard struggle for existence on a meagre income'. Twenty-four homes would be arranged in a rectangle, in the style of a college quad. On one of the sides there would be the common kitchen and dining room, administrative offices, storage for boxes and bicycles and a telephone. Servants would provide hot meals and appear when needed to attend to cleaning and laundry, enjoying better than average terms of service and living quarters. Accommodation for residents would be offered in flats or houses with one, two or three bedrooms, and the all-inclusive rentals would range from £30 to £40 a year. The Garden City Association was, and remained, nervous about Howard's plan, fearing, with some justification, that it would be seen as too radical and challenging to the accepted conventions of domestic life. He was initially careful to present it in cautiously conservative terms, stressing that it was primarily a means for solving the servant problem, and for permitting people with limited incomes to live more economically, but it became evident that he also saw it as an important measure for liberating women to be creative and economically active, as well as less tired.

Homesgarth was opened in November 1910, by Lady Aberdeen, a well-known philanthropist, feminist, and housing campaigner. Her speech implied that the housing development was about liberating women from domestic drudgery, which presumably raised a few eyebrows amongst some of the GCA's directors. The opening of Homesgarth, she declared, marked the death of two long cherished prejudices, the first being 'that every woman was a born housekeeper' and the second that 'it is part of a good housewife's duty to work under difficult conditions'.[54] The originally planned twenty-four housing

----

[54] *Daily Mail* 24 November 1910.

units had been scaled back to sixteen, and only eight were completed at the time of the opening, although the ambition was to build thirty-two. The rents ranged from £40 to £62, and all meals and refreshments were extra, with a three-course dinner available for a shilling. Howard moved into one of the smallest flats during the second half of 1911 and remained there until he moved to Welwyn.

It was irritation at another of H.G. Wells's articles, this time poking fun at cooperative housekeeping, that prompted Howard to write in defence of the life at Homesgarth in 1913. He was clearly finding Wells's periodic interventions tiresome: 'Wells is, as all the world knows, a very clever man, and brimful of noble and quite practical ideas, which, however, he has not the least skill in putting into practice, or inducing others to do so.'[55] Howard's article described the happy community at Homesgarth, their comfortable accommodation, and the spacious public rooms.[56] There was central heating, and a telephone connection to the administrative building in each home. The way of life was ideal for those aspiring to elegance and flexibility:

> The elasticity of the scheme is an important feature. Thus one can invite a number of friends to dinner, though one has not a cook – one can, if one desires it, have meals brought into one's own house for payment of a small extra charge – or one can shut up one's house and go away for a month or so without feeling responsible for the comfort and safety of a maid or maids left at home ... All the dwellings are let and the tenants like the place immensely; for, on the one hand, it admits to complete privacy – greater than can obtain where you keep servants in your own home – while on the other hand it affords easy opportunities for social intercourse when you wish to avail yourself of them.[57]

[55] *Daily Mail* 27 March 1913.

[56] Photographs of Homesgarth give a good sense of how it was. See especially GCC LBM4052.47.50, LBM4052.47.44, and LBM4052.47.32.

[57] *Daily Mail* 27 March 1913. Lucy Carr Shaw, the sister of George Bernard Shaw, wrote to Howard after reading this article, saying that 'one of your £64 houses presents itself to me as a paradise after the turmoil of private housekeeping' and asking if there was any chance of a similar scheme to Homesgarth being developed nearer to London, as she was 'an inveterate theatre goer'. HALS DE/Ho/F25/58 Shaw to Howard, 3 April 1913.

Howard seems to have been describing a lifestyle somewhat more aspirational than the one that he was actually living. His absence of servants in the 1911 Census suggests that he had had no maids to worry about when he went away. When important visitors came to the Garden City, they tended to be entertained in the homes of other leading citizens with more conventional domestic arrangements, such as Garden City director Howard Pearsall, who lived in the elegant Parker and Unwin house known as Crabby Corner, and provided lunch when a journalist from the *Daily Mail* came to interview Howard in 1911.[58] Another sentence in Howard's article also seems to jar with the truth. Describing the private garden which each tenant cultivated he wrote, 'I see my wife (saved from housekeeping worries) is at work in hers now.' Yet he was almost certainly seeing her only in some mystical or metaphorical sense, for the evidence from Howard's children and from Osborn is that Howard lived in Homesgarth alone, the marriage with Edith having broken down. Perhaps the issue of moving to Homesgarth had been a trigger. Ben had long dreamed of living in a shared housing scheme, but it seems most unlikely that Edith, who was known to keep her distance from others, would have wanted to try the experiment.

A contributor to the *Letchworth Recollections* oral history project confirmed the picture of Howard at this time as a kindly, sociable, but somewhat lonely figure:

> My first introduction to Ebenezer Howard was when I was quite a small child and that was through the friendship of my father with him. My father was headmaster of St Ippolyts School and very often came into Letchworth and met Ebenezer Howard. A card would drop through the front door saying, 'I am coming for the weekend, from Ebenezer Howard,' and he would be there on the doorstep the next morning. We got quite used to these visits. He nearly always had sweets in his pocket and was quite happy with small children. So that's really where we got our first introduction to him. In those days he was on his own quite a lot and he didn't really spend his time for too long in one place as his work took him quite long distances away ... Although he only had a little tiny flat he gave us all a party at Homesgarth which is now Sollershott Hall. The party was in the main hall and all the flats

were left open with a bowl of sweets on the table in one, a book to read in another one, probably a picture book for the smaller children and we all had a most lovely tea helped by two other gentlemen who were retired and lived in one of the flats.[59]

Homesgarth did not permit resident children, and this vignette suggests that it may have developed something of the atmosphere of a community for older single people, congenial to those who would have equally happily resided in a college in nearby Cambridge. Borden has pointed out the many resonances between Homesgarth and Oxbridge architecture.[60] But, behind the traditional façade lurked a more radical agenda. Unencumbered by housekeeping, 'ordinary' women were now free to follow their own interests and activities. Indeed, Lady Aberdeen had made this clear in her speech at the opening. Although the *Daily Mail* was happy, at least until the outbreak of the First World War, to promote Garden City activities in a very positive light, it also made space for the views of those who were worried that 'cooperative housekeeping' was a form of socialism that would undermine the family, with cooperative childcare being a particular risk. A week before it published Howard's article, it ran a humorous article under the headline 'Our Co-operative Housekeeping' debunking the idea and illustrating it with two cartoons. The first showed the nursemaid in a shared nursery being berated by mothers and wondering if she was 'expected to obey one mistress or half a dozen'. The second showed two men studiously ignoring each other as they sat smoking and reading their newspapers: 'Picture the joy of the average male on learning that he is to have the privilege of sharing his "snuggery" with a fellow man!'[61] The message was clearly that 'normal' married people would not tolerate such unnatural domestic arrangements.

Howard's usually careful attempts to clothe his radical sensibilities for middle-class consumption in the *Mail* slipped on several later occasions, revealing that he had become something of a feminist. His article entitled 'A New Outlet for Woman's Energy' was a full-throttle defence of the right of mothers to engage in paid employment outside the home (albeit with part-time hours) with their children properly cared for in crèches. Women had suffered enough from the repression of their

[59] Maddren, *Letchworth Recollections* pp. 45–6.
[60] Borden, 'Social space and cooperative housekeeping' pp. 246–9.
[61] *Daily Mail* 18 March 1913.

talents, he claimed.[62] Then he gave another interview to the *Mail*, at a time when the Meadow Way Green women's housing project, and another artisans' housing scheme which did not come to fruition, were being discussed. He provided the familiar arguments about economies of scale, and then outlined the new features of the scheme envisaged for artisan families: a twelfth of an acre of land would be provided for each family to raise produce which could be sold, as well as consumed, women would take it in turns to cook, and a crèche would be provided. 'If the mothers were relieved of a large part of their housework, they could devote themselves to more profitable employments.'[63] This provoked consternation. A fortnight later, the paper reported that the Letchworth Trades Council had written to Howard, protesting against the suggestions in recent articles that 'his scheme of co-operative houses for working people would liberate women for work in the hygienic factories in the Garden City. They consider the scheme likely to introduce more married women to factories.'[64] But he stuck to his guns, defending his views about working mothers and crèches at a public meeting in Letchworth, and then in the local paper. Indeed, he went further than he had previously, suggesting that a day-time crèche might be an ideal place for an infant, and a lot safer than being under the feet of a harassed mother, as she worked in her kitchen.[65] After he had laid out his ideas in *To-morrow*, there is relatively little evidence of development in Ebenezer Howard's thought, which makes his open proclamation of feminist sympathies in the years immediately before the First World War particularly interesting.

The growing industrial town

The Liberal landslide election victory in early 1906 yielded forty-seven Members of Parliament who were members of the Garden City Association, or shareholders in First Garden City, or both. In early July, arrangements were made for members of both Houses of

[62] Ebenezer Howard, 'A New Outlet for Woman's Energy' *Garden Cities and Town Planning Magazine* June 1913 pp. 152–9.

[63] *Daily Mail* 15 August 1913.

[64] *Daily Mail* 1 September 1913.

[65] Meacham, *Regaining Paradise* pp. 120–1.

Parliament to visit Letchworth, and about 150 of them did so.[66] Garden City ideas had now entered mainstream politics, as had the concept of town planning and the government's responsibility to be actively involved in it. The Town Planning Act of 1909 would be the first milestone. But the change in political fortunes made no immediate difference to First Garden City Ltd, which continued to struggle with its precarious finances, spending more than its income (which it justified on the basis that the value of the Letchworth estate had increased significantly) and giving up its London office in order to save money. From the original share offer of £300,000, £168,240 still remained unsold in 1906, and these shares were now remarketed for sale at five pounds each.[67] Having failed to think seriously about developing agriculture, the directors decided to focus on factories and working-class housing, in an attempt to both secure the town's economic future, and prevent it from sliding completely into being a middle-class commuter settlement for aspirants to 'alternative' lifestyles. The company were responsible for providing roads, water, and other public services, and laid out the building plots, which were leased. It relied on small builders being attracted to the town, but it discouraged speculative builders from developing large housing schemes. A significant number of Letchworth's more prosperous residents took advantage of the Small Dwellings Acquisition Act, 1899 to become owner occupiers.[68] Meanwhile, several public utility housing societies were founded, which built workers' cottages that could be let at reasonable rents.

The first eight businesses were typical of the range of economic activity that early Letchworth would sustain, and all had acquired premises by 1906. Light engineering would predominate; Heatly-Gresham Engineering built the town's first factory, in which they manufactured parts for the rail industry.[69] Printing and publishing companies were already active with the Garden City Press,[70] and

[66] *Daily Mail* 6 July 1906.

[67] *The Times* 14 June 1906.

[68] Purdom, *Satellite Towns* pp. 60–1.

[69] See GCC LBM868.57 and LBM868.54 for photos of the Heatly-Gresham factory interior.

[70] See GCC LBM4081.2.34.4 and LBM4081.2.34.3 for photos of the Garden City Press interior.

J.M. Dent, who relocated from London, and became famous for their 'Everyman Library' of classic texts. Vickers and Field Asphalt and Idris Mineral Water arrived early; these were the two businesses reviled by H.G. Wells. The other early arrivals were G. Ewart, geyser manufacturers, whose advertising celebrated the benefits of instant hot water, and Stanard & Co, who manufactured photographic paper. There was also the Garden City Embroidery Company, a firm which led the way in the creative and textile sector which would thrive in the town.[71] There were, in 1906 over 1,600 residents of whom 400 were classified as artisans and labourers. A further 600 workers lived in the surrounding villages, of whom 300 were said to want to move into Letchworth.[72] In response to the shortage of workers' housing First Garden City Ltd set up a subsidiary company, Letchworth Cottages & Buildings Ltd, financed by its own share issue, and borrowing from the Public Works Loan Commissioners, under the Housing of the Working Class Act, 1890. Just over one hundred workers' cottages were constructed between 1907 and 1909, which eased the housing shortage in Letchworth, lessening the need for workers to cycle in from outlying villages.[73] By the outbreak of the War, the number of public housing cottages had risen to 1,060.[74]

After a slow start, some big names began to relocate to the town, the largest of whom was W.H. Smith, who moved their mechanized bookbinding department from London in 1907, bringing over 300 workers, many of whom were women.[75] Spirella, the corset manufacturers, arrived in 1912, and became one of the town's major employers of mainly female labour. They established all-encompassing welfare provision for their workers which went well beyond what was usually provided by the best of the large twentieth-century factory employers. There were medical staff in attendance, a lending library, a bicycle repair man, gym classes and baths and showers which could be taken in company time, in addition to the usual social activities found in large firms of the period. Spirella's 'Factory of Beauty' was

---

[71] See GCC 2010.44 for a photo of the Embroidery Company.
[72] *The Times* 14 June 1906.
[73] *The Times* 1 February 1907 and 19 October 1909.
[74] Purdom, *Satellite Towns* p. 67.
[75] Beevers, *Garden City Utopia* p. 130.

designed in the Arts and Crafts style by Cecil Hignett, and the corsets manufactured were technologically advanced, using the latest techniques with sprung aluminium, and ensuring a level of comfort for the wearer which had not existed with the traditional steel or whale bone stays.[76] By 1913, it was estimated that of the total population of about 8,000, around half were either working in local industries, or dependent on those who were.[77] First Garden City's attraction of industry was now a clear success, and in the following year the company was finally able to pay a dividend to its long suffering investors.[78] For the first time, it could afford to build its own factory, a three storey building capable of being divided into nine self-contained units.[79]

The 'founder and Garden City pioneer'

By about 1907, Howard had become a nationally and increasingly also an internationally known figure, a champion of healthy living, and of the nascent environmentalist sensibility, and he was seen as the natural leader of much of the Garden City's life. The first decade of the twentieth century was marked by a growing interest in pageants and celebrations which combined historical, folkloric, and communal elements.[80] Howard was very active in promoting two major annual festivals in Letchworth, the May Day Revels and Arbor Day. Both

[76] Tidy, *A–Z of Letchworth* pp. 79–80. See GCC LBM4093.7.41 for a photo of the Spirella factory.

[77] Beevers, *Garden City Utopia* p. 130, citing Purdom, *The Garden City* p. 177.

[78] *The Times* 17 February 1914.

[79] Beevers, *Garden City Utopia* p. 129.

[80] Pageants of the early twentieth century have been the subject of a significant amount of recent research, much of it the result of an AHRC funded project *The Redress of the Past: Historical Pageants in Britain 1905–2016*. See especially Angela Bartie, Linda Fleming, Mark Freeman, Alexander Hutton, and Paul Readman (eds.) *Restaging the Past: Historical Pageants, Culture and Society in Modern Britain* (London, 2020) and http://www.historicalpageants.ac.uk. See also the earlier work on the topic by Paul Readman, especially Readman, 'The Place of the Past in English Culture *c*.1890–1914' *Past and Present* 186 (2005) pp. 147–99 and Ayako Yoshino, *Pageant Fever: Local History and Consumerism in Edwardian England* (Tokyo, 2011). By 1907, there was talk of 'pageant mania' and 'pageantitis' in the press. See Michael Shallcross, 'The Pomp of Obliteration: G.K. Chesterton and the Edwardian Pageant Revival' p. 89, in Bartie, Fleming et al, *Restaging the Past*.

emphasized the rural aspects of the Garden City, with one looking backwards into England's imagined past, and the other looking forwards to Letchworth becoming a town with beautiful trees and mature woodlands. Interest in celebrating the English May Day had been gradually reviving since the 1840s, and had accelerated in popularity from the 1880s, with Anglican clergy often taking an early role in its re-establishment.[81] It was ideally suited for adoption as a major festival in the calendar of the Garden City, combining as it did the celebration of Spring and new life, with a type of pastoral nationalism seen in the evocation of 'Merrie England' and, by the Edwardian period, also including the veneration of workers and socialist ideals. Indeed, the rather generalized evocation of the English past implicit in May Day was much better suited to a new community, lacking historical traditions on which to draw, than staging a pageant would have been, although there were undoubtedly Letchworth citizens who would have thrown themselves enthusiastically into pageanting.[82] The sentiments expressed at the first May Day held by the Oxford branch of the Independent Labour Party, in 1906, the same year that the festival began in Letchworth, would have also captured the general mood in Letchworth:

> The idea of a May-day festival took us a long way back, to the days when men and women led simpler and more natural lives, when the air was purer and the food was unadulterated, when the people had a pride and pleasure in their work and felt glad to be alive ... [The purpose of their meeting was] to see established a Merrie England – full of freedom-loving men and women, with noble aspirations, and a country full of happy, contented, healthy children.[83]

[81] Roy Judge, 'May Day and Merrie England' *Folklore* 102, 2 (1991) pp. 131–48. For an account of May Day in Cheltenham in 1892, see W.H.D. Rouse, 'May-Day in Cheltenham' *Folklore* 4,1 (1893) pp. 50–4.

[82] Keith Johnson, writing about the pageants of Edwardian Yorkshire, noted that 'all were concerned with portraying versions of a shared past.' All were staged in towns with significant histories, including York, Pickering, Scarborough, Thirsk, and Whitby. Keith Johnson, 'Historical Pageants in Yorkshire before the First World War' in Bartie, Fleming et al, *Restaging the Past* p. 36.

[83] *Oxford Chronicle,* 4 May 1906, cited by Judge, 'May Day' p. 141.

May Day also provided a less jingoistic alternative to Empire Day, which had begun to gather pace as a public holiday on 24 May from about 1904. May Day in Letchworth included all the traditional features: processions, maypole dancing, a May queen, and a May fair, but it also developed additional aspects, including an arts and crafts exhibition, musical competitions, a horse and pony display, and a large amount of dressing up.[84] The lengthy and carefully choreographed procession, the centrepiece of which was the parading of the 'Four Square Our City' town banner, and the little girls in white scattering petals seemed like a secular echo of the rituals of a Corpus Christi procession (which could not be legally held in public in England until later in the twentieth century).

Arbor Day was something which Howard probably remembered from his time in Nebraska. The Nebraskan Julius Sterling Morton had been the first person to initiate an annual festival of tree planting, and give it this name, at the time that Howard was resident in the state in 1872. The Letchworth Arbor Day was held at the end of February, beginning in 1908. With its emphasis on a procession of children in costume, and of adults processing with spades, with singing, speeches, and community involvement, it was rather like a winter counterpart to the May Day Revels.[85] The focus was on the very practical task of planting trees. Howard presided over the proceedings, and each child was given a certificate after they had planted their tree.[86] Then the children sang 'The Planting Song' which had been composed by a Letchworth resident, Harold Hare.[87] In some years, a 'celebrity' tree

[84] Tidy, *A–Z of Letchworth* pp. 56–7; Maddren, *Letchworth Recollections* pp. 114–17. The May Day Revels remained an important fixture in the town's calendar until 1966. There are many photos of early May Day celebrations in the Garden City Collection. I particularly like LBM1966.331 and LBM1966.388. The enthusiasm for maypole dancing seems to have spread in Hertfordshire's primary schools, and was still regarded as an important part of the curriculum in the 1970s. I remember the energy that was put into teaching maypole dances in my Hertfordshire primary, and the conspicuous humiliation which came from being the child that became confused in the dance, and messed up the pattern of the ribbons.

[85] See GCC LBM1953.20.17 and LBM1953.20.18 for photos of Arbor Day 1913.

[86] See GCC LBM1960.7.

[87] Tidy, *A–Z of Letchworth* p. 8.

planter would also be present and would make a speech. In 1908, it was John Cockburn, the founder of Australia's Arbor Day, and in 1909, it was the novelist Rider Haggard.[88] Having served as a member of the Royal Commission on Afforestation, Haggard had become convinced that the 'race would fail' unless the British were restored to the land and lived in forests, becoming self-sufficient in timber. After the tree planting, he elaborated on this theme in a public lecture at the Mrs Howard Memorial Hall. He claimed that if nine million acres were afforested, in eighty years' time they would be worth five hundred million pounds, yielding an annual profit of eighteen million. Unemployment would be solved with forestry, he suggested, but the life he described sounded positively medieval; men would work in the woods, while their wives and children looked after cattle in small holdings in forest clearings. It was a very long way from the life envisaged for the garden citizens, and if Ebenezer Howard felt somewhat bemused listening to this lecture, he could at least have consoled himself with the thought that earlier in the day three thousand Scotch firs had been planted in Letchworth, and some sycamores.[89]

Howard's support was now solicited for numerous causes. Arbor days in other towns were one example. When the schoolchildren of Blackley in central Manchester had their arbor day, planting twenty-four trees and showing off the spring blooms that they had grown from bulbs, a highlight was a letter read out that had been sent by 'Mr Ebenezer Howard, the pioneer of the garden city movement from Letchworth'. He congratulated the children and urged them to 'go on planting trees and flowers.'[90] When new garden suburb schemes were opened, he would usually be present on the platform and make a speech, and if he was not present, he would be reverentially referred to in other people's speeches as 'the garden city pioneer'.[91] His thoughts were picked up and reported in the national press, as when he suggested that as a memorial to Edward VII, a new Garden City

[88] GCC LBM2361.
[89] *Sunday Times* 28 February 1909 and *The Times* 1 March 1909.
[90] *Manchester Courier* 26 March 1909.
[91] *Manchester Courier* 9 August 1909, reporting the opening of Oldham Garden Suburb; *The Times* 22 April 1912, reporting the cutting of the first sod at Knebworth Garden Village.

called 'King Edwardstown' should be constructed.[92] Almost every article in the journal *Garden Cities and Town Planning* began by making respectful references to him.

But fame did not bring Howard wealth. He continued his regular employment as a shorthand writer, occasionally entering speed writing competitions, which not only gave him and his cause some publicity, but also held out the possibility of a cash prize.[93] He devoted the rest of his time to the promotion of Garden Cities at home and abroad, as international branches of the GCA began to open all over the world. His internationalist outlook was reflected in his enthusiasm for Esperanto, which, like shorthand, he regarded as another useful modern communication tool to be mastered fully. Esperanto fitted perfectly with his optimism about the possibility for brotherhood and mutual understanding; like many others of his generation, he believed that Esperanto would foster world peace, and be the language of the future; a counterweight to the British exceptionalism which pervaded some sections of Edwardian society. There were plenty of Esperantists in Letchworth, giving Howard good opportunities to practice the language. He became president of the town's Esperanto Society, and a member of the Universal Esperanto Association.[94] In 1907, the third World Congress of Esperantists was held in Cambridge, in the presence of L.L. Zamenhof, who had developed the language in the 1880s. Fourteen hundred delegates attended from twenty-three countries, five hundred of whom opted for an excursion to Letchworth by special train. 'They were received by Mr Ebenezer Howard, who spoke of the affinity between Garden City and Esperanto ideals.' He told them that the Garden City aimed at doing something very similar to what Esperanto aimed at doing in the sphere of languages.[95] Having not had the opportunity to study European languages earlier in life, as he began to travel abroad more frequently he found Esperanto useful, and Esperantists congenial and receptive. He was attending an Esperantist conference when war

---

[92] *Sunday Times* 14 August 1910.

[93] In 1907 he was one of fifteen contestants to enter 'the great shorthand contest' at Olympia, but he did not win. *Exeter and Plymouth Gazette*, 19 July 1907.

[94] Tidy, *A–Z of Letchworth* p. 31.

[95] *Daily Telegraph* 14 August 1907.

broke out in 1914, and only managed to get back to Britain with some difficulty.

As the twentieth century entered its second decade, Howard's reputation reached its height, and he began to be honoured as a modern visionary. Visitors came from all over the world to meet him and to see Letchworth, including a party of senior politicians from Australia and New Zealand, and numerous delegations from Europe.[96] In 1911, the *Daily Mail* published a highly laudatory profile of him, declaring that he belonged to 'a new school of political philosophers ... a dreamer of dreams, but as deadly practical as the managing director of any great business.' The journalist described him as simple and entirely unaffected, with a fresh colour and bright eye, taking no credit for his success, and looking for no reward. The journalist claimed of *Garden Cities of To-morrow* that 'no book in the whole range of literature, other than a religious one, ever produced such momentous results in so short a time.' The 'innumerable' garden suburbs that were being developed in the United Kingdom and across the world were all 'enduring monuments to his far-sighted genius as a social reformer'. Furthermore, Letchworth was now 'easily the most healthy town in Europe' with an infant mortality rate of 54.5 per 100,000 in 1910.[97] In a journalistic over simplification, the article attributed all of this to Howard.

In 1912, the Garden Cities and Town Planning Association, the successor organization to the GCA, gave a dinner in his honour at the Holborn restaurant. Eight hundred guests attended and Earl Grey presided, making a speech which repeated the idea of Howard as a 'dreamer of dreams'. The GCTPA wanted to honour the founding

[96] For example, a group from Budapest, in 1909. The Anzac delegation visited in 1913 and included a former prime minister of New Zealand and the serving premier of Victoria. They were welcomed by Howard, who conducted a tour of the town, and a party of fifty dined at the Letchworth Hall Hotel, at the invitation of Cecil Harmsworth. In the absence of Harmsworth due to ill health, Howard presided. There was much celebration of the fact that Australia's new capital, Canberra, was to be laid out along 'town planning lines'. This is an interesting early substitution of the phrase 'garden city lines' for 'town planning lines'. *The Times* 21 April 1913.

[97] *Daily Mail* 6 June 1911. For comparison, the infant mortality rate in London in 1910 was recorded as 107 in London, and 68 in Worthing.

father it had not always found easy to work with, and to celebrate the fact that Letchworth's finances had now 'turned a corner'. Aneurin Williams, chairman of the GCTPA, declared that 'the time was long overdue when Mr Howard ought to receive some public recognition of his services'. Howard was presented with an oil portrait of himself by Gerald Spencer Pryse, which showed him seated and looking out at the artist, dressed in a characteristically shabby brown jacket, his hands resting on a plan on the table in front of him.[98] In the following year, he was granted a modest civil list pension of £75 per annum. It was a public acknowledgement of his poverty – most of the other recipients on the list were the widows of notable men who now found themselves in straightened circumstances. An exception was Arthur Symons, the *fin de siècle* poet and literary critic, who had suffered a severe mental breakdown and was deemed in need of £120 per annum, which was the largest pension on the list.[99]

Shabby, unworldly, and single-minded: Ebenezer Howard was increasingly cast in the role of the old man who was a dreamer of dreams.[100] In 1912, he was sixty-two, and had another sixteen years to live, but he was probably at the height of his fame and reputation. He received little further official recognition until the award of an OBE in 1924, and then a knighthood in 1927, a few months before his death. He responded to the knighthood by ordering new stationary: 'Sir Ebenezer Howard, OBE, JP' and he admitted to one of his friends that the honour had 'probably given effect to my own subconscious wishes.'[101] But for most of the second half of his life he was generally known simply as 'Mr Ebenezer Howard, the founder of the Garden City movement'.

---

[98] *Daily Mail* 20 March 1912; *The Times* 20 March 1912. The painting was partly paid for by Lord Lever. HALS DE/Ho/F25/45, Lever to Howard, 26 June 1912. GCC 870.

[99] *Daily Mail* 3 July 1913.

[100] Consciously or unconsciously evoking Joel 2:28.

[101] HALS DE/Ho/F25/23.

6

The Spiritual Life of the First Garden City 1904–1918

A blank canvas?

In London, the city from which a significant proportion of the first generation of Letchworth residents came, there were many different forms of religious expression and allegiance.[1] The building of Letchworth offered a rare opportunity to test what would happen when pre-existing religious commitments and instincts were planted in the uncultivated Hertfordshire soil. Would there be an abundant propagation of varieties, or would one strain emerge to dominate the rest? Or would religion turn out to be tricky to re-root, and wither away, with the new residents showing limited interest in investing in new churches or devoting time to religious activities? Letchworth, as a place conducive to religious freedom and the unfettered expression of ideas, was a particularly apt location to test the resilience and flavour of early twentieth-century religiosity under these new conditions. There were no equivalents of the Quaker Cadburys or the Congregationalist W.H. Lever, who sought to influence the religious

---

[1] W.M. Jacob, *Religious Vitality in Victorian London* (Oxford, 2021). See also Hugh McLeod, *Piety and Poverty: Working Class Religion in Berlin, London and New York 1870–1914* (New York and London, 1996) pp. 32–3. McLeod makes the point that this religious vitality distinguishes London from the majority of continental capitals. His table on p. 33 provides useful data about the percentage of church attendance amongst the estimated population in different areas of metropolitan London in 1902–3, precisely the areas from which many Letchworth residents came.

Ebenezer Howard: Inventor of the Garden City. Frances Knight, Oxford University Press.
© Frances Knight 2023. DOI: 10.1093/oso/9780198790815.003.0007

life of Bournville and Port Sunlight.[2] Later in the twentieth century, the rapid relocation of thousands of people to the new towns would become a familiar trend, but in the century's first decade, it was not something that Britain had witnessed before.[3] This chapter examines what happened to the religion that the people brought with them, and how the dynamics of the community which emerged shaped its religious life during the period that Ebenezer Howard was resident in Letchworth. How did established religious traditions change, particularly when they were mixed with the optimism that characterized the early Garden City, and the desire of its first residents to create the best possible world? To what extent did the religious impulses that had shaped them in the *fin de siècle* period fall away under the challenges of a new town and a new century?[4]

Letchworth during the years that Howard lived there, and later on, into the 1920s and 1930s, was a place of extensive and varied spiritual activity. It had not, of course, been a completely blank canvas in 1904, when the Garden City Association acquired the estate. It contained three tiny and ancient Anglican parish churches: St Nicholas, Norton, All Saints, Willian and St Mary the Virgin, in the hamlet that would become known as 'old Letchworth'. A full range of Nonconformist

[2] Each working day at the Cadburys factory began with prayers, often conducted by the brothers themselves, and they built a Quaker meeting house. Lever built the church in Port Sunlight for his workers. It was initially non-denominational, but later Lever vested it with the Congregational Union.

[3] After the New Towns Act for England became law in 1946, twenty-eight new towns were built with an estimated population of 2.6 million by 2001. Peter Hall and Colin Ward, *Sociable Cities: The 21st-Century Reinvention of the Garden City* 2nd edition (London and New York, 2014) pp. 45–56.

[4] This idea was suggested by Michael Ledger-Lomas, in his review of my book, *Victorian Christianity at the Fin de Siècle*. Although his review was balanced and generous, he found my definition of Christianity as a 'religious culture' rather too amorphous and thought that the concept of fin de siècle Christianity was 'evanescent'. Whilst I completely agree that the concept outlined in the book, fin de siècle Christianity was specific to its time and place, aspects of it mutated in interesting ways in the early years of the twentieth century, and I think there is evidence for this in Letchworth. Michael Ledger-Lomas, '*Victorian Christianity at the Fin de Siècle: the Culture of English Religion in a Decadent Age* by Frances Knight' *History* 102, 4 (2017) pp. 324–6.

chapels were to be found in nearby Baldock, and in Hitchin.[5] The ancient parish churches provided places of worship for the Anglicans who moved to the Garden City, and by around 1908, they were described as 'crowded out by the new-comers'[6] something which would have been relatively easily achieved, in view of their very small seating capacities. To address this problem, a new Anglican 'mission church', St Michael's in Norton Way, opened early in 1908, which in keeping with the prevailing ethos of the period developed something of an Anglo-Catholic character. But there is relatively little evidence that Anglicans played a large part shaping the religious or cultural life of early Letchworth, and the 'central church of the town', which Raymond Unwin had planned for the south end of the town square, was never built.[7] The non-Anglican religious bodies in early Letchworth can be broadly categorized into three groups. First, the free church people with evangelical sympathies; secondly the non-evangelical but broadly Christian people, who were often also open to exploring ideas derived from Spiritualism, Theosophy and other faiths, as well as what were then perceived as radical lifestyle choices, such as vegetarianism and simple living; and thirdly, the Roman Catholics.

The evangelical free churches

Many of the first generation of Letchworth's most prominent residents were from a similar religious background to Howard himself, and several members of the Rectory Road Congregational Church moved

[5] Judith Burg, *Religion in Hertfordshire 1847–1851* (Hertford, 1995) gives an indication of the variety which already existed in those towns in 1851. Hitchin had places of worship for two separate group of Independents, three separate Baptists congregations, Wesleyan Methodists and Quakers. Baldock had Wesleyan and Primitive Methodist chapels, an Independent meeting house, and a Friends meeting house.

[6] Undated article in the *Fortnightly Review* cited in Clyde Binfield, 'Garden City Religion: The Free Churches of Letchworth and Welwyn' *The Chapels Society Journal* 2016, 2 pp. 58–91.

[7] The illustration in Raymond Unwin, *Town Planning in Practice: An Introduction to the Art of Designing Cities and Suburbs* (Second edition, 1911) p. 227 shows the plan for an apsidal church with transepts that he had intended for this central site, and which seemed intended for Anglican use, although he did not state this explicitly.

with him to Letchworth.[8] As we have seen, he had spent a great deal of time publicizing his ideas at public meetings in the nonconformist chapels of London and trying to sell shares in the project to his friends and acquaintances. Early Letchworth pioneers, including Howard, gravitated towards the Letchworth Free Church, although a significant number moved on, as other places of worship became available. But in the earliest days, the support for the Free Church from leading citizens such as Charles Purdom, the estate accountant, who was the church's first secretary, and Thomas Adams, the estate manager, and the church's first chairman, helped to get it off the ground.[9] Howard and the well-known Baptist F.B. Meyer, at that date president of the National Free Church Council, jointly laid the foundation stone in August 1905, and in October, it became the first place of worship to open in the first Garden City. In the short term, it was obvious that nonconformists of all backgrounds either had to worship together, trek off to neighbouring villages, or abandon the habit. The original building, just fifty feet by twenty, and initially described as the 'Mission Hall (Unsectarian)' was timber and built by the congregation themselves.[10] R.J. Campbell, who had succeeded Joseph Parker at the City Temple, and was at this point a major star in the free church firmament, preached at the opening.[11] The building rapidly became too small. It was extended in 1908 and 1909, and then entirely rebuilt, to a design by Barry Parker, in 1924. An appeal that was launched to raise funds for the new building made much of its ecumenical

---

[8] Membership records for the church reveal the names of several families who are described as having 'moved to Letchworth'. Hackney Archives D/E/233 uncatalogued records for Rectory Road United Reformed Church, Stoke Newington. They included James Branch, and a family called King. A contributor to the *Letchworth Recollections* oral history project who had been born in Letchworth in 1915 noted that her parents had moved there in 1906, having met Howard in London, because he lectured at the Congregational church that they attended. Maureen Maddren, *Letchworth Recollections: A Unique Record of Life in The First Garden City as Remembered by some of its Earliest Citizens 1903–1939* (Baldock, 1995) p. 13.

[9] GCC LBM 4073.3.27.

[10] Photos of the first free church are at GCC LBM2301, 1966.327 and 1963.51.13.7.

[11] Binfield, 'Garden City Religion' p. 68. He provides a detailed account of Letchworth Free Church, which I have drawn on here.

credentials and gives some insight into the church community in the early 1920s. The famous Congregationalist, Sydney Berry, minister of Carrs Lane, Birmingham endorsed the appeal by observing that 'Amongst the many churches that one visits during the course of a year, there is no more delightful experience than to find oneself among the free churchmen of Letchworth. There is a splendid congregation on a week-night and the atmosphere is most responsive.' R.C. Gillie, a Presbyterian minister in London, added: 'I have known the Letchworth Free Church for a number of years. Every time I have spoken or preached there I have been impressed by the spirit of fellowship and the ardour and strength of its religious outlook. It has proved abundantly that a Union Church need not forfeit either spirituality or serviceability to the kingdom of God, owing to its devotion to Christian unity.'[12] The appeal was also endorsed by Herbert Marnham, an ex-president of the Baptist Union. The money was raised, and the new Free Church was large, light, and spacious. It has been described as a 'Neo-Georgian meeting-house, more New England than Puritan England' and 'attractively unorthodox'.[13] It had the potential for accommodating 850 worshippers, and by the 1930s, its membership was in excess of 500.[14]

Despite the positive comments from Gillie about the congregation's devotion to Christian unity, some of the difficulties that it experienced in its early years probably stemmed from its arrival too early on the ecumenical scene. Others related to how it positioned itself in relation to the central tenets of Nonconformist Christianity. There was ready agreement that 'sectarianism' and the acrimonious or fossilized religious conflicts of the past should not be transported into the theologically pristine Garden City, but it was less clear how those who had been nurtured in different Protestant traditions, in different parts of Britain, were going to work together. The stated aim was 'to provide a place of worship as the centre for Religious work and teaching on lines which will be acceptable to residents in Garden City who have been or are Members of the Nonconformist Churches comprised in the

---

[12] GCC LBM4073.3.3.

[13] Binfield discussed the rebuilding in detail, 'Garden City Religion' pp. 69–72.

[14] Photos of the interior of Parker's new free church are at GCC LBM4312.31.1 and LBM4312.30.1.

National Council of Evangelical Free Churches, as well as others who desire to join in a united Religious service'.[15] Those seeking membership were asked to subscribe to a four point statement of faith: belief in God, recognition of the Holy Spirit, belief in Jesus Christ as the saviour and redeemer, and acceptance of the authority of his teachings, and finally, a willingness to live in a spirit of peace and Christian charity with all.[16] Arrangements were made with local Baptist ministers, for believers' baptism for those who wanted it, and for a class meeting, for those Methodists who wanted that. Four elders were elected annually, each with a district, and each assisted by three district visitors. When it came to calling its first minister, however, the church looked towards Congregationalism. Initially, two young men from Mansfield College Oxford were invited to Letchworth to preach with a view to the pastorate, but neither were found quite satisfactory, and the choice turned to R.W. Jackson, a fifty-one-year-old who had been a Methodist schoolmaster before becoming a Congregational minister. He must have brought an understanding of both traditions, although presumably also a sense of having favoured one, and rejected the other.[17] Thereafter, Congregational ministers alternated with Baptists, until the Baptists broke away and formed their own congregation in the early 1930s.

Denominational differences were difficult to leave behind. A.E. Stark, who succeeded Purdom as church secretary, commented that although the first generation of church members had 'hoped to see such a broadening out of religious ideas as would make it possible to reach an agreed form of religious service in which all could join' there was in fact 'a sharp division of opinion . . . as to the form in which religion should find public expression among the members of the new community at Garden City'.[18] Those favouring a more evangelical ethos remained at the Free Church, whilst those with more ethical or free thinking sympathies moved to the other Christian fellowships that were soon available, and in particular to the Society of Friends, and or

[15] GCC LBM 4073.3.27.

[16] GCC LBM 4073.3.270.

[17] Binfield, 'Garden City Religion' pp. 68–9.

[18] A.E. Stark, 'The Story of the Free Church' *Letchworth Free Church Magazine* 5, 4 April 1935 pp. 37–8. Cited in Binfield, 'Garden City Religion' p. 69.

to Bruce Wallace's Alpha Union, with its Sunday evening services at the Mrs Howard Hall, and its loosely associated Garden City Adult School. A significant number of the original members of the Free Church distanced themselves from it without formally leaving it behind. Bruce Wallace always remained on the register of Congregational ministers, despite having founded his own organizations – the Brotherhood church in the 1890s, with branches in Southgate and Croydon – and then the Alpha Union in Letchworth. Dugald MacFadyen, Howard's first biographer, and another Congregational minister, found the preaching at the Free Church intellectually unsatisfying, and began to worship among the Quakers, although his wife and children remained prominent members at the Free Church. Another product of the Congregational manse, Clifford Fleming Williams the artist son of Charles Fleming Williams, the influential minister at Rectory Road, became interested in Theosophy, and taught at St Christopher's, the school established by Theosophists in Letchworth in 1915. Annie Lawrence, who built the Cloisters as a study centre for religion, psychology, and social science, was also originally associated with the Free Church, as well as with the Quakers and Unitarianism. Ebenezer Howard himself, although he remained associated with the Free Church (it would eventually be the venue for his funeral) attended the Adult School meetings held in the Howard Hall on Sunday morning, and the Sunday evening meetings at the Hall. Although it retained the allegiance of a significant number of Letchworth's prominent residents, the de facto departure of so many of the Free Church's free spirits meant that the church moved more towards the more conservative end of a liberal evangelical spectrum.[19]

Speaking to a journalist in 1908, Howard announced that:

> We have solved the religious difficulty. We have the Church of England, the Society of Friends, the Roman Catholics, the Nonconformists, who dropping sectarianism meet at their Free Church, the Salvation Army, the worshippers at the Cloisters, and I suppose every denomination that so surprised Voltaire. But they have a wonderful unity, and through our Letchworth Guild of Health (sic) all charity in money or kind is administered.[20]

---

[19] Binfield, 'Garden City Religion' p. 76.
[20] *Millgate Monthly* interview with Howard, Sept 1908. GCC LBM 3004.26.

He was evidently papering over the cracks of divisions within the Free Church, although perhaps at this date they were not as obvious as they would shortly become. As the great advocate of cooperation and harmonious living, Howard was inevitably unwilling to acknowledge any evidence of religious division, even though he himself appears to have become disenchanted with the Free Church. It was apparent that the religious 'difficulty' was already seeding a variety of highly varied Christian communities, although 'unity' was undoubtedly a major objective for many of them.

Howard's reference to the decision not to proliferate philanthropic enterprises along denominational lines is significant. The journalist had evidently misheard him, for it was in fact the Guild of Help, not Health, that had been set up on ecumenical lines in 1907. The Guild was the major source of what in the nineteenth century would have been termed 'parish relief', although its funds came from a number of sources: collections raised at places of worship, fundraising events, and donations from larger employers, notably W.H. Smith, the Arden Press and the Garden City Press. The Roman Catholic priest, Adrian Fortescue, donated the money he made from his lecturing activities. The executive committee comprised clergy identified as Anglican, Roman Catholic, Congregational and Baptist, which made the Guild of Help a remarkably ecumenical endeavour for the Edwardian period.[21] The money raised, £144.7.2, in the year ending June 1909, was spent on weekly allowances, loans, milk, meat and groceries, boots, medicine and school dinners, as well as the overheads

---

[21] GCC LBM3056.37.7. The Anglican clergy were F.N. Heazell, rector of Letchworth, and J.H. Bailey, vicar of Norton, the Congregationalist was R.W. Jackson, minister of Letchworth Free Church, the Baptist was H. Perkins and the Roman Catholic was A. Fortescue, parish priest of Letchworth. It is possible that there were other free church ministers, listed simply, like Perkins, as 'Mr'. In addition to nine men on the executive committee, there were six women, and it was from mainly among these women that the 'District Heads' were drawn. It was these women who were responsible for organizing the welfare relief, assisted by a team of 'friendly helpers' who sought to befriend the families who were allocated to them. See also GCC LBM3056.37.6, for the 'Constitution and Administration of the Letchworth Guild of Help' which provides detailed information on how the charity operated in its early years.

associated with running the charity.[22] A photograph from 1909 shows the Guild's banner being paraded on May Day: the banner depicts a eucharistic cup, and above that, a larger, stronger hand grasping a smaller one, possibly a child's, in a gesture of Christian-inspired help.[23] The fact that welfare relief on this scale was required in a town where almost every working age man and many women were in employment is evidence of inadequate wages and higher than average living costs. To this extent, the existence of the Guild of Help was a sign of the failure of Letchworth as originally conceived; children were arriving at school wet, cold and hungry.[24]

The spiritual journey of Charles Purdom, who was a leading light in the first three decades of the Garden City movement, is an intriguing example of just how far a Garden City nonconformist could travel in the space of a lifetime. He described himself as 'brought up an Independent of the kind that made Cromwell's armies'.[25] As one of the earliest to move to the Letchworth estate, and 'still in my nonconformist phase' he initially attended the Congregational and Baptist churches in Hitchin.[26] He claimed to have been the first person to conduct a nonconformist service in a private house in Letchworth, and from this the Free Church grew, of which he was briefly church secretary. But he became rapidly disillusioned: 'the evangelical element among the members, rigid and backward looking, was strong, and I could not reconcile it with the idea of the new community, so I left them, and joined the free and unconventional Sunday Evening Meeting at its first meeting in the new Howard Hall in 1906.'[27] There he remained, until after the First World War. He was also one of the most regular Sunday morning lecturers at the Garden City Adult School, speaking on philosophical, literary or theological topics. In 1912, he married a Roman Catholic; it was the first marriage to be celebrated in Letchworth's new Catholic church. The brevity of the ceremony

[22] GCC LBM3056.37.1.

[23] GCC 2009.81.7.

[24] Standish Meacham, *Regaining Paradise: Englishness and the Early Garden City Movement* (New Haven and London, 1999) pp. 133–4.

[25] C.B. Purdom, *Life Over Again: An Essay in Autobiography* (London, 1951) 6.

[26] Purdom, *Life Over Again* 42.

[27] Purdom, *Life Over Again* 55.

astonished many of those attending, because as a 'mixed' marriage, the religious content was pared to the minimum. Purdom seriously considered converting to Catholicism when he returned from the War in 1918, and spent a year being instructed, but he declined to go ahead on the grounds that he found the Church too political and worldly.[28] Whilst on a retreat in 1931, he met Meher Baba, an Indian silent mystic who was visiting Britain. Meher Baba's mission was to 're-vitalize all religions' by teaching people to seek an elevated state of consciousness, and he had a global following during the middle decades of the twentieth century. Purdom remained a disciple of Baba for the rest of his life, and published five books expounding his life and message.[29] It is probably significant that only two of these were listed in the extensive publications section of his *Who's Who* entry, and both titles were edited in a way that would have made them appear to a casual mid twentieth-century reader as being books about Jesus Christ, not Meher Baba: the titles were shortened to *The Perfect Master* and *The God-Man*.[30] After Howard himself and Frederic Osborn, Purdom was perhaps the most significant figure in the history of the Garden City movement, but his devotion to an Indian mystic may have been seen as rather too unorthodox, and costly, in terms of his reputation and career. Lewis Mumford, writing to Osborn in 1963, commented that 'Purdom is a strange man ... Fate has not, I think, dealt quite as kindly with his career as it has with mine; yet perhaps he hoped for more than I did, and thus was doubly disappointed'.[31] It is striking that someone who had been extremely active in both the Garden City movement and the theatre world, as well as in

[28] Purdom, *Life Over Again* 250–1.

[29] Purdom was the author of *The Perfect Master: Shri Meher Baba* (1937); *Meher Baba by his Eastern and Western Disciples (1939); Three Incredible Weeks with Meher Baba* (1954); *God to Man and Man to God: The Discourses of Meher Baba* (1955); *The God-Man: The Life, Journeys and Work of Meher Baba with an Interpretation of his Silence and Spiritual Teaching* (1964). A brief film clip of Purdom and Baba in 1932 may be found on You Tube: 'Meher Baba Interview 1932 Newsreel'. For his short account of his friendship with Baba, see Purdom, *Life Over Again* 253–66.

[30] *Who Was Who* entry for Charles Benjamin Purdom.

[31] Michael R. Hughes (ed.), *The Letters of Lewis Mumford and Frederic J. Osborn: A Transatlantic Dialogue 1938–70* (Bath, 1971) p. 345.

various government ministries during the Second World War, did not receive a single obituary in a national newspaper.[32]

The resurgence of Methodism in Letchworth dealt a significant blow to the early ideal of the united Free Church. A Wesleyan Methodist mission church was established in Norton village in 1908. Ebenezer Howard spoke at the opening, trying to navigate around the rocks which were threatening to dash the ecumenical project. He told the Wesleyans that their new mission was heartily welcome: 'We are thankful that you have put your spade into the soil and we beg you to cultivate it.' His speech provides a rare insight into his thoughts about the Churches at this point. He had, he claimed, never shared the views of those who

> Have thought that the ideal of the Garden City should be one church, in which all should join in the same service ... We are differently constituted; we are in different stages of growth – the most advanced intellectually being sometimes least advanced spiritually; we have different needs – to some, ritual is really helpful and illuminating; to others, it is a veil: to some, a new presentation of truth is helpful, with others, nothing moves the heart and senses as do the old phrases. This is true, and perhaps will always be true. Uniformity would be nothing short of hypocrisy. The great art of life which above all things it is necessary to acquire is the production of harmony through diversity; and as we are conscious that no power can create this harmony but the Spirit of Love shed abroad in our hearts, so in full confidence that the Church which you are now establishing will stand as an emblem of love and fellowship, we hail your coming with glad and thankful hearts.[33]

The Norton Wesleyan Methodist mission was originally supported by the Free Church, but they withdrew in 1910, a year after the Wesleyans, who had established their 'Central' Methodist society in the town, took it over. The Wesleyans built a substantial church in Pixmore Way in 1914.[34] An extremely ambitious Primitive Methodist church, the largest and most expensive in Hertfordshire, as well as the last one

---

[32] Purdom wrote extensively on town planning and is probably best remembered as the author of *The Building of Satellite Towns* (Letchworth, 1925, with a new edition in 1949).

[33] HALS DE/Ho/F3/23.

[34] Photo at GCC 2017.29.

built by that denomination in the county, was also opened in 1914.[35] This setting up in rivalry suggested just how far apart the sister denominations of Methodism felt themselves to be. A leaflet appealing for funds for the building of the Primitive chapel emphasized that it would be catering for the expanding number of factory workers.[36]

The carefully contrived ecumenical project of early Letchworth could evidently not withstand either the growth in population, or the persistent belief that different classes of people would require different styles of religious life, despite the cherished belief of some members of the Free Church that they were a relatively classless community. As indicated by Howard's interview, the Salvation Army were already present by 1908, and other less ecumenically minded Christian groups gradually established themselves, although not in the earliest years. An Elim chapel, the first in Hertfordshire, opened in 1923, and there was some disquiet at the Free Church, when Percy Bichener, who had led their Christian Endeavour group, switched his allegiance to it.[37] The Plymouth Brethren and the Mormons also arrived a little later into the century.

The Pleasant Sunday Afternoon (PSA) movement, which by the early twentieth century was becoming better known as the Brotherhood movement, founded its Letchworth branch in 1908. The 'Pleasant Sunday Afternoon' title seems to have been dropped after the inaugural meeting, and within a short time it became known as the Letchworth Brotherhood Literary and Debating Society.[38] It was a spin-out from the Free Church, and for many years the President was

[35] David Noble, 'Primitive Methodism in Hertfordshire from 1838–1932' University of Hertfordshire PhD, 2021. Photo at GCC LBM4073.6.107.

[36] GCC LBM 4073.6.3.

[37] Binfield, 'Garden City Religion' p. 76.

[38] The Basingstoke PSA similarly rebranded itself as the Basingstoke Brotherhood. See Roger Ottewill, 'The Men's Own Brotherhood Movement in Basingstoke' (2018) https://www.victoriacountyhistory.ac.uk/explore/items/men%E2%80%99s-own-brotherhood-movement-basingstoke-1899-1929 accessed 13 August 2021. See also Roger Ottewill, 'Churches and Adult Education in the Edwardian Era: Learning from the Experiences of Hampshire Congregationalists' in Morwenna Ludlow, Charlotte Methuen, and Andrew Spicer (eds.) *Churches and Education: Studies in Church History* 55 (2019) 494–510 for more on the general context on educational activities of Congregational churches at this period.

A.E. Stark, who was also the Free Church secretary. The original aim of the PSA, which had grown rapidly from its origins in West Bromwich in 1875, was to reach working men with meetings that were 'brief, bright and brotherly'.[39] The movement's early twentieth-century values chimed well with the wider culture of Letchworth: in 1912, it stated that its aim was 'nothing less than to teach a "democratic religion" leading to a "practical Christianity" full of love and good works.'[40] Roger Ottewill suggests that for Congregational churches, conscious as they were of their bias towards the middle classes, the PSA and Brotherhood movement represented a particular effort to widen their social appeal to male artisans. Despite its identification as a man's organization, its regular open meetings welcomed women, and sometimes women were used as speakers and musicians at meetings that were intended for men. Ottewill notes that in Hampshire at a time when it was 'extremely rare for women to occupy the pulpits in Congregational churches, it was not unknown for them to give addresses at Brotherhood meetings'.[41] It seems likely that this was also true in Letchworth, which was always in the vanguard of female equality; by 1928, the Letchworth Brotherhood had a female Vice-President.[42] Although the ubiquitous Bruce Wallace had been the speaker at the opening meeting of the Letchworth PSA and Brotherhood, the movement was separate from his London-based Brotherhood churches, and from his *Brotherhood* newspaper; 'brotherhood' was a concept that emerged from multiple directions in Edwardian Letchworth. In the 1930s, funds were available to build the Brotherhood Hall near the town square, which hosted a weekday programme of musical events, debates, talks and activities.

[39] David Killingray, 'The Pleasant Sunday Afternoon Movement: Revival in the West Midlands 1875–90?' in Kate Cooper and Jeremy Gregory (eds.) *Revival and Resurgence in Christian History: Studies in Church History* 44 (2008) 262–74.

[40] Frederick DeLand Leete, *Christian Brotherhoods* (Cincinnati, 1912) 272, cited by Roger Ottewill, '"Brief, Bright and Brotherly": Assessing the Relationship Between the Men's Own Brotherhood Movement and Congregationalism in Edwardian Hampshire', *The Journal of the United Reformed Church History Society*, Vol 10(3), 2018 158–71.

[41] Ottewill, '"Brief, Bright and Brotherly"' 163, 169–70.

[42] A programme for the Letchworth Brotherhood Literary and Debating Society which survives from 1930 includes several female speakers and musicians.

The Brotherhood was described as 'vigorous' in 1941, and the hall still exists.[43]

Non-evangelical free churches, and esoteric and free-thought traditions

Another major strand of Letchworth's religion emphasized spiritual exploration, the avoidance of binding doctrinal or creedal formulations, and a belief, stated with varying levels of fervency, in humanity's ability to redeem itself. Political radicalism was its natural, although not always entirely congenial, partner. Several women were prominent in developing these ideas, indicating that Letchworth was a fertile environment for female religious entrepreneurs. The Quakers were well established in north Hertfordshire, and Juliet Reckitt, the daughter of the wealthy Hull industrialist James Reckitt who manufactured cleaning products, built the Letchworth Quaker meeting house, Howgills, which was opened in 1907. It was based on a famous seventeenth-century Quaker meeting house, Brigflatts, near Sedbergh. Although internally very similar to the Cumbrian meeting house, externally it fitted with Letchworth's Arts and Crafts style, and was designed by the local architects Bennett and Bidwell.[44] It incorporated a flat in which Juliet Reckitt resided. Quakers were prominent in Letchworth, including Bidwell himself, his fellow architect Thomas Geoffry Lucas, and as we have seen, some who had arrived in the town as Congregationalists.

Annie Lawrence was another independent woman with significant wealth who had identified Letchworth as the place where she could make her contribution to religious life. The prominent suffragette couple Frederick and Emmeline Pethick-Lawrence were her brother and sister-in-law. As noted earlier, her name appeared on early membership records at the Free Church, and although she is sometimes described as having been a Quaker, she was almost certainly brought up as a Unitarian.[45] Denominational labels had little meaning when

---

[43] GCC LBM4073.1.13. Photo at 2016.242.94.

[44] Photos of Howgills are at GCC LBM4337 and LBM4052.50.46.

[45] Chris McNab, *St Christopher School: A Short History* (Oxford, 2014) p. 12 suggests that she was a Quaker, an idea repeated on various websites. Her brother was brought up as a Unitarian, hence my suggestion that this was an early

applied to Annie Lawrence. She spent the vast sum of £20,000 building the Cloisters, a public amenity next to which she lived. Its flamboyant design had apparently come to her in a dream.[46] The centrepiece was the Cloister Garth, a large oval hall, with a colonnade supported by columns of green Swedish marble which was open on one side to the fresh air. The architect, W.H. Cowlishaw incorporated many symbolic decorative and design features, which added to the overall sense of the building's uniqueness. Lawrence had done social work amongst the London poor, and as a result had become convinced of the benefits of healthy lives lived as much as possible in the open air. She had originally intended the Cloisters as an outdoor school, but during its construction she decided to switch her focus to adult education, with the result that the Cloisters became well known for its courses on philosophy and religion, weaving and other arts and crafts, and science and outdoor living. Annie Lawrence became a highly respected Letchworth figure. She had the first swimming pool in the town, and encouraged the public to use it, rewarding every child who learned to swim in the pool with the gift of a fountain pen. She also hosted musical and dramatic perform-ances at the Cloisters, installed an organ and employed an organist.

Lawrence's social and cultural activities were underpinned by her religious views. She opened the Cloisters with a ceremony in January 1907, in which she dedicated the building 'To the unity, eternal reality ... wherein sin and pain and death are not, and all contradic-tions reconciled ... confident that, through progressive recognition of this unity, mankind will ascend to a full, harmonious and joyful expression of life, in soul, body and social organisation.'[47] Her belief in harmony was put into practice with activities organized around her concept of the Dual Day, in which work and play, study and recre-ation, practical and theoretical work, and material and spiritual

---

formative influence on her as well. Brian Harrison, 'Frederick William Pethick-Lawrence, Baron Pethick-Lawrence, 1871–1961', *Oxford Dictionary of National Biography* (Oxford, 2004).

[46] Photos of the Cloisters are at GCC 1966.376 and 1966.369.

[47] http://www.utopia-britannica.org.uk/pages/Cloisters.htm, accessed 19 March 2021.

activities were paired in the interests of achieving a healthy balance.[48] Lectures and discussions took place in the open air environment of the Cloister Garth, and by night, residents slept in hammocks that were let down from the ceiling at bedtime. These unorthodox sleeping arrangements, in which men and women were separated only by a curtain, led to regular comment. David Garnett, a nephew of the architect Cowlishaw, described his stay:

> One slept in a canvas cot sleeping a couple of feet off the floor, sheltered from rain or snow but in the open. In the morning, one hauled up one's bed, either had a hot bath or a plunge in the swimming pool, collected a breakfast, which was eaten sitting raised up behind a vast slab of rose-coloured alabaster . . . Those breakfasting at the table looked like a painting of the last supper.[49]

About eighteen guests could be accommodated in this way.

Bruce Wallace, the maverick Congregational minister, moved the activities of the Alpha Union to the Cloisters and was given the title 'director of studies'. He had founded the Alpha Union in Letchworth in 1905, after receiving a bequest of £3,000 for this specific purpose from Antony S. Swinton, who had been one of the founders of the Land Nationalization Society. The Alpha saw itself as an educational union, founded on the belief, strongly endorsed by Lawrence, that humanity was essentially spiritual and progressive, and that a common life could be formed around the principles of faith, optimism, and anti-materialism. It saw itself not as an alternative to existing churches, but as a means of quickening and reviving them, and it made its appeal chiefly to young people disillusioned by the narrow doctrines espoused in the nonconformist traditions in which they had been raised. An enthusiastic member of the Union, W. Ravenscroft Hughes, was helpfully explicit about the kinds of people attracted to it. They included

[48] Annie Lawrence, *A Dual Day: From a Paper Read at the Adult School Letchworth, November 1913* (Letchworth, 1913) and Josh Tidy, *A–Z of Letchworth Garden City* (Stroud, 2018) pp. 50–1.

[49] Tidy, *A–Z of Letchworth* p. 20. The photograph at GCC LBM4041.2.75 conveys this sense of the dining arrangements echoing an artistic representation of the Last Supper.

Some who have been attracted by the glamor of eastern thought; others who have found no help in circles of evangelical thought, which seems to them to belong to a past age; others again who have felt a salvation not out of personal sin, but rather into earnest social life that is striving toward a new birth for society; there is again a large group of over seventy ministers and clerics (largely from 'new theology' circles) whose progressive sympathies have drawn them into the Union.[50]

The Alpha Union claimed to have a membership of between 700 and 800 in 1909, although it was reluctant to circulate its membership list publicly. Its activities included taking over the publication of the monthly magazine *The Brotherhood* which Wallace had been producing for years, and the development of a library at Letchworth, which specialized in the subjects which interested its members, such as religion, psychology, ethics, Theosophy, mysticism, and child development.[51] It was, however, best known for its summer schools which began in 1906. It ambitiously held three during the summer of 1908, in the contrasting surroundings of Montreux[52] on Lake Geneva, Aberystwyth (a town also filled with intellectually curious nonconformists) and Letchworth. Thereafter, and no doubt for reasons of economy and convenience, the Cloisters in Letchworth became the established summer school venue.

Hughes's reference to 'new theology circles' is interesting. This particular 'new theology' stemmed from R.J. Campbell, who had published a book with that title in 1907. The book was hastily written and took issue rather unskilfully with aspects of traditional Protestant doctrine. It proved enormously controversial, exposing fault lines that

[50] W.R. Hughes, 'An Experiment in Social and Religious Education without Creed Limitations – the Alpha Union' *International Journal of Ethics* 19, 3 (April 1909) pp. 362–70.

[51] GCC LBM2394 provides the supplementary catalogue of the Alpha Union Library as it was in May 1911. The breadth of the library's religion holdings is reflected in the separate entries for Athanasius, R.J. Campbell, H.S. Holland, George Tyrell, and A.S. Peake, amongst others.

[52] The well-known former Congregational minister John Hunter was at Montreux, speaking on 'Inspiration'. Hunter was evidently interested in Campbell's New Theology, although this is somewhat played down in the biography by his son, who had become an Anglican in his early twenties, and later became the bishop of Sheffield. L.S. Hunter, *John Hunter, D.D. A Life* (London, 1922) p. 225.

had existed within English Nonconformity for decades.[53] Since taking over from Joseph Parker in 1903, Campbell had developed the City Temple – the 'cathedral of Nonconformity' – as a stronghold for liberal Christianity, and a refuge for 'men of culture and independence of character, who had given up organized Christianity as hopeless, but are glad to find that they can satisfy their desire for religious fellowship without having to affirm what their knowledge of the universe denies'.[54] He boasted that under his influence 'liberal Christianity is now a spiritual movement whose manifestations are comparable to the great religious revivals of the past' and that he had supporters throughout the world. Large numbers of people were, he claimed, shunning 'practical materialism on the one hand, and an antiquated dogmatic theology on the other' in order to follow his teachings.[55] The League of Progressive Thought and Social Service (the Progressive League) was set up in 1908 to progress Campbell's ideas in England and Wales. There was a natural overlap between the Progressive League and the Alpha Union.

The Alpha Union summer schools are probably the best documented aspect of religion in early Letchworth, although they only ever involved small numbers, and drew in participants from far beyond the town. Vegetarian catering was provided by Letchworth's Food Reform and Simple Life Hotel, and delegates were warned that none should come to the Cloisters 'but such as are prepared for the simple life'. In addition to the eighteen or twenty who could be accommodated in the hammocks, 'under shelter, but practically in the open air' others were welcome to pitch their tents.[56] Analysis of the surviving summer school programmes for the years from 1906 to 1911 suggests that there were two distinct tendencies within the Union, with some members wishing to see the summer school focussed

[53] Keith Robbins, 'Reginald John Campbell, 1867–1956' *Oxford Dictionary of National Biography* (Oxford, 2004).

[54] R.J. Campbell, *The New Theology* (Popular edition, 1909) p. vii. See also Keith Robbins, 'The Spiritual Pilgrimage of R.J. Campbell', *Journal of Ecclesiastical History* 30,2 (1979).

[55] Campbell, *New Theology* p. 2. See also Alan Argent, *The Transformation of Congregationalism, 1900–2000* (Nottingham, 2013) pp. 51–78.

[56] GCC LBM3056.1.1 and LBM2391.

on social, political and economic questions, and others wishing to concentrate on religious and spiritual exploration. Bruce Wallace frequently lectured himself, or invited guest lecturers, with Eastern religion explored alongside Christianity. A four-part syllabus advertised for 1907 on 'Meditation' began with a lecture on 'Oriental systems of meditation: Vedanta and Yoga' and was followed by one on 'Early Christian Systems: Christ's doctrine of Prayer, and the monks of the Desert'. The third lecture continued with a Christian standpoint: 'Catholic contemplative Prayer, and Quietism' and the final lecture was entitled 'Meditation and Philosophy: A Pathway to Reality'.[57] A highlight of the 1907 summer school was doubtless the appearance of R.J. Campbell himself, who delivered a sermon. Howard was present, and he would have been interested to hear Campbell, not least because of his links with Joseph Parker.[58] In the following year, presumably in an attempt to keep both wings of the movement happy, Wallace arranged a 'Beta' conference, with a focus on social and political ideas (including Howard on 'Garden Cities') whilst the Alpha conference had a series of lectures on 'The Bearing of Recent Psychical Research on Religion' from John W. Graham, of Dalton Hall, Manchester, followed by a series of lectures on biblical figures from J. Stitt Wilson, including 'Jesus, the Hero of the Common People' and 'Moses, the Greatest of Labour Leaders.'[59] Given Howard's interest in Spiritualism, we may assume that he would have been an eager participant at Graham's lectures.

In 1909, Wallace seemed to be making more of an attempt to pull the two-week programme towards mainstream Christianity, with guest lectures from, amongst others, Letchworth's resident Roman Catholic intellectual Adrian Fortescue, the Anglican J.N. Figgis, who had recently joined the Community of the Resurrection in Mirfield, and the Wesleyan Methodist leader S.E. Keeble. There was also a 'devotional meeting' at ten o'clock every morning, which had not

[57] GCC LBM4041.2.58.

[58] A photograph of the Alpha Union summer school in August 1907 shows a group including Bruce Wallace, Annie Lawrence, Ebenezer Howard, and very unusually, his second wife Edith; they had only been married for five months at this date. GCC 554.1980.

[59] GCC LBM4041.2.73.

appeared on the programmes of earlier summer schools, and visits to some of Letchworth's creative industries – the W.H. Smith printing works, the tapestry weavers, the embroiderers, and the potters at the Iceni lead-free pottery.[60] The summer schools continued in this vein until 1911. That year saw the usual mixture of lectures on psychical research, spiritual awakening, and socialism, with three female speakers for the first time, including two very big names: the Theosophist Annie Besant, and the famous American suffragist and women's rights campaigner, Clara Bewick Colby. On Sundays, delegates were directed to worship in the Howard Hall, which was led by a Quaker, after which there was 'a brief Communion Service', which was seemingly a new innovation at an Alpha Union summer school.[61] By the time Bruce Wallace moved to Glastonbury, in 1912, he had done his best to ensure that summer school participants had had their consciousnesses expanded in multiple directions. They had met Hindus and Baha'is, and had pondered the different traditions of Christianity, as well as Spiritualism, reincarnation, spiritual healing, and a galaxy of socialist and economic ideas.

Theosophical ideas featured prominently at the Alpha Union, which was unsurprising in view of Wallace's interests, Lawrence's sympathies, and the presence of a sizeable Theosophical community in the town. After significant fundraising, the Theosophists opened the Garden City Theosophical School (also known as Arundale School) next door to the Cloisters in 1915.[62] In the previous year, the Theosophist leader Annie Besant had opened the Vasanta Hall in Gernon Walk. Hope Rea, who had moved to Letchworth in 1907, was active in both the Theosophical School, and the Vasanta Hall, and she was also a regular speaker at the Garden City Adult School. Emblazoned on the wall of the Vasanta Hall was the Theosophist mantra 'There is no religion higher than truth' and on the platform there were photographs of a woman or women, probably including Besant, but in other respects it looked much like any other small chapel.[63] The building was later taken over by Letchworth's Spiritualists. Another off-shoot

[60] GCC LBM4041.2.61.
[61] GCC LBM2391.
[62] McNab, *St Christopher School* pp. 7–15.
[63] A photo of the Vasanta Hall is at GCC LBM70.132.

of the Theosophists was the Liberal Catholic church of St Alban, built on the corner of Meadow Way and Norton Way South, and opened in 1923, with many Theosophists amongst its early supporters. Constructed in the style of a small rural church, it would have been easy for the uninitiated to assume that it was either a Roman Catholic or an Anglican place of worship.[64] In common with other Old Catholics, its clergy traced their orders from the Old Catholic Church of Utrecht.

The Garden City Adult School

How did Ebenezer Howard spend his Sundays? Although he remained officially moored in Congregationalism through association with the Letchworth Free Church, he was, as we have seen throughout this study, keenly interested in spiritual exploration. Sometimes he attended the Friends' meeting at Howgills, and he was as happy to preside at a Spiritualist meeting as he had been at the opening of the Wesleyan mission.[65] His gravitation towards the Sunday morning meetings of the Garden City Adult School, and the Sunday evening meetings founded by Bruce Wallace, both held at the Howard Hall, was unsurprising. The Adult School was one of Letchworth's earliest organizations, established just a month after the opening of the Free Church, in November 1905, and initially for men only. It advertised itself 'for fellowship, and the mutual study of Social, Religious, and other questions.' There was an order of service devised by Bruce Wallace, 'not unlike those compiled by Dr John Hunter, which was said at each meeting, no matter who the speaker was, and a hymn book was used.' According to Purdom, the meeting had no membership, only attenders, who were of all religions or none.[66] Presumably this militated against its being seen as mutating into an independent

---

[64] A photo of the Liberal Catholic church is at GCC LBM70.180.

[65] The information about his attendance at Quaker and Spiritualist meetings in Letchworth came from Arthur Bradshaw, a Letchworth Quaker, who supplied reminiscences to St John Catchpool in 1928. Howard was, said Bradshaw, 'willing to help any good cause'. HALS DE/X/1053/S8/11.

[66] Purdom, *Life Over Again* pp. 55–6. John Hunter's *Devotional Services in Nonconformist Chapels* was widely used in Congregational circles.

congregation. Without a membership, there was no need for assent to any formalized statement of faith.

The Adult School had clearly been influenced by the Adult School movement, although it was never affiliated to the National Council of Adult School Unions (NCASU).[67] The Secretary's fourth annual report, in 1909, explained the situation:

> Our relationship to the Adult School Movement has never been quite definite. Although we are in accord with their main objects, we have never become affiliated to the Union, and our constitution and practice differ from other Adult Schools. We have developed our own lines. Thus the readings at first were exclusively from the Bible, taken according to the Adult School Lesson Sheets; but afterwards we extended the scope to include all serious literature. . . . We have never adopted an exclusively religious basis, or indeed any exclusive basis at all. We have started and continued non-sectarian and non-partisan. Everybody is welcome, and all have equal rights to hearing and of being heard.[68]

In 1906, the Adult School moved to the Howard Hall, where it met for the next twenty-eight years. Its meetings were at a sufficiently early hour – nine o'clock and concluded by ten thirty – to permit the possibility of later attendance at a place of worship, although there is no evidence that Howard did this. Being in the Hall itself, dedicated to the memory of his beloved first wife, may have given him a special feeling of closeness to Lizzie, and no doubt it felt more congenial to him than any of the chapels.[69] It became the natural platform from which he could from time to time continue to expound his views, as he had once done in the nonconformist chapels of North London. He had stated in *To-morrow* that available public buildings should be used for worship in the years before churches could be built, and so he was, whether consciously or not, simply fulfilling a suggestion he had made in 1898 for the conduct of spiritual life in the early Garden City.

[67] For the National Adult School movement, see Mark Freeman, 'The Decline of the Adult School Movement Between the Wars' *History of Education* 39, 4 (2010) pp. 481–506.

[68] GCC LBM4047.1.92.

[69] A photo at GCC LBM4312.23 shows the hall in use at its opening in 1906.

Howard often took the chair at the Sunday morning meetings and was himself the speaker on at least ten occasions between 1906 and 1919.[70] The Adult School mixed in variable quantities discussion of religious, philosophical, literary, political, and social topics, resulting in a gentle form of Christian socialism, and reinforcing the atmosphere of progress and optimism that characterized Letchworth's Edwardian middle-class residents. As already noted, the Bible study was rapidly replaced with the 'serious' reading, which over the years extended from the fifteen minutes initially allocated, to a full forty-five minutes, and then contracted back to twenty minutes. The length of the reading determined the length of the address and discussion, as the business was concluded promptly after ninety minutes. Time was found for the singing of a hymn, probably at the mid-point between the reading and the talk. In some weeks the reading might be from the Bible, and in others from the Koran or the Bhagavad Gita, or from one of the modern authors revered by Garden City dwellers: Ruskin, Tolstoy, Darwin, William Morris, Tennyson, Emerson, and Whitman all featured regularly, and on one occasion Howard himself read from *Garden Cities of To-morrow*. There appeared to be no connection between the reading and the address, so a reading from G.K. Chesterton might be followed by a talk about Plato, or a reading from the New Testament with a talk about the 'Celtic Twilight'.[71] At a very early meeting on Sunday 3 December, 1905, a Mr Beckley spoke on 'The Practical Value of the Modern View of the Bible'[72] and over

[70] His first paper was on 23 September 1906, 'The Responsibility of the Masses for the Condition of the Classes'. GCC LBM4074.1.7. The other papers advertised in the syllabuses of the Adult School were 'Footpaths and Roads from the Old to the New Order', 14 June 1908, GCC LBM4074.1.15; 'Unity', 25 September 1910, GCC LBM4074.1.25; 'The Design Argument in the light of Evolution' 4 June 1911, GCC LBM4074.1.28; 'Co-Workers with God' Christmas Eve 1911, GCC LBM4074.1.30; 'Some Suggested Near Future Possibilities' 26 May 1912, GCC LBM4074.1.32; 'The Consumer in Revolt' 2 March 1913, GCC LBM4074.1.35; 'A Great Victory and a Lasting Peace' 14 January 1917, GCC LBM4074.1.51; 'God's Opportunity' 3 March 1918; GCC LBM4074.1.55; 'Can Optimism be Justified?' 7 September 1919, GCC LBM4074.1.61.

[71] Both examples from the syllabus published for the winter of 1917, GCC LBM4074.1.51.

[72] GCC LBM4052.59.6.

three Sundays in August 1906, the topics covered were 'The Ebbtide of Faith', 'Genius under Socialism' and 'Our Food Supply'.[73] The initial decision to limit membership of the Adult School to men was evidently rapidly regretted, and in September 1906 the School went co-educational, declaring 'All Men and Women [are] Cordially Invited – Free and Open Discussion' which remained its strapline thereafter. The year ended with the first of what would be a regular contingent of female speakers, when Miss Dally spoke on 'Women and Progress';[74] 1907 saw a total of nine Sundays in which women addressed the Adult School. The overlap of interests, and sometimes of speakers, between the Alpha Union and the Adult School was evident. Annie Lawrence, Bruce Wallace, Hope Rea and Frank Merry, the organist at the Cloisters, were among the regular speakers, as were various local architects, craftspeople, socialists, Theosophists and Quakers. Whether at the Cloisters or at the Howard Hall, audiences could expect a staple supply of papers with titles such as 'What is religion?' or 'Poverty: its cause and cure' or 'A Theory of Life'.

Only a few of Howard's addresses to the Adult School have survived, but 'Unity' (1910) and 'Co-workers with God' (1911) give an insight into Howard's approach to this audience. He blended mysticism with assumptions derived from Christianity, and the ideas about light that he had expounded decades earlier at the Holborn Literary Society. Those ideas, taken originally from the physicist John Tyndall, were evidently still important to him, even though they were now scientifically discredited. His horizon was panoramic, rather than parochial. The universe, he argued in 'Unity', 'is held together by a great purpose, a mighty love, an all-embracing wisdom' and Light (always with a capital L) 'is as it were the voice of God, telling His people more and more, even as they are able to see more of the wonders of the universe'. Just as the postal, telegraph and telephone systems bind the world together, 'so does Light, all pervading, universal Light, helps us to know God. For it is not that we discover God, but that He discovers himself, by this and other wondrous messengers'.

[73] GCC LBM4074.1.7.
[74] GCC LBM4074.1.9.

Disorder in the world arises from man's freewill, but he assured his audience that a time of order, peace, and unity was coming.[75] A similar message emerges in 'Co-workers with God': 'The Infinite Unity who is ever more revealing Himself to man calls upon us to be conscious co-workers with Him . . . to bring order into those fields of life and activity where disorder seems at present to reign supreme'. But God reveals himself to men and women on his own terms – and 'perhaps the chief of these revealing forces is Light – the mysterious power obeys laws and exercises influences which are the same here on this planet, and on the far away places'.[76] Perhaps some of the audience might have expected to hear that God revealed himself in Jesus, not in lumens, and it would be interesting to know how the discussion developed after his paper.

Howard delivered some other sermon-like material at the Howard Hall Sunday evening meetings, and at the 'Letchworth men's meeting' at a location unspecified, but quite possibly also at the Hall. The Sunday evening sermons at the Hall came from a variety of mainly local speakers,[77] and seem to have exemplified the 'do-it-yourself' strand in Garden City theology. On the evening of Howard's sermon on 'Tolerance' in April 1912, the congregation sang four hymns, and listened to Luke 18:9–14 (the pharisee and the publican) and an edited version of Romans 14:1–13 (about not judging the choices of others). These readings set up Howard's theme nicely, in which he began by presenting his early mentor the Congregational preacher Joseph Parker as a figure who had embodied 'the true spirit of tolerance'. He said that he regretted his own intolerance as a young man when he 'deliberately broke' with him. He went on to condemn the 'cold, cruel and unchristian reception' which the churches of the late nineteenth century had given to Darwin, Huxley, Tyndall, and Herbert Spencer, 'four great teachers and thinkers'. The notion that Christ would be dethroned by evolution was, he suggested, yet another example of intolerance. Equally, tolerance was needed in the political sphere, and he noted that the enmity which once fuelled religious controversy now appeared to have been transferred to the vilification and abuse of

[75] HALS DE/Ho/F3/14.
[76] HALS DE/Ho/F10/1-14.
[77] GCC LBM4073.1.13.

political opponents. The spirit of toleration was supremely illustrated
in the life and teaching of Christ. 'Nothing in the whole of Christ's life
and teaching, so endears him to me – so fully reveals him as a
supremely great Teacher – and has done so much (to use an old
phrase) to win me for Christ – as his conduct – his example in this
regard.'[78] It was a revealing insight into Howard's view of the man he
regarded as the great Teacher.

A second surviving sermon may have been for the Letchworth
Men's Adult School, which came into existence at some point during
the town's second decade, probably in response to growing numbers
of workingmen in the town, and the recognition that the highbrow
content at the Garden City Adult School was unlikely to meet their
needs. A Men's Adult School had also been established in Norton in
1910 to cater for the men living north of the railway line in the
industrializing Norton and Green Lanes districts; Howard had
chaired the initial fundraising meeting for Norton in April 1910.[79]
Mark Freeman has argued that Adult Schools of this type – typically
single sex, working class and affiliated to the NCASU – were increasing their religious content at this period, with the 'First Half Hour'
given over to Bible study and a mini-sermon.[80] It may have been for
such a gathering that Howard prepared a paper 'on religion' for the
'men's meeting' in May 1916.[81] He began with some somewhat
random biblical verses – Luke 4:18–19; Matthew 15:8; Luke 6.46,
and Isaiah 2:1–5. From the Isaiah text he developed his theme – a
prophecy of peace between nations – with a warning that it might
come very slowly, or 'far more rapidly than in our wildest moments we
dare to dream'. Two years of the world at war had not extinguished
Howard's sense of optimism about the human capacity to effect
change for the better, although it had shaken it. This sermon also
illustrates Howard's continuing attachment to the American Tran-
scendentalist poets. He referred to Emerson as 'one of the greatest
thinkers of the nineteenth century' and concluded by reading

---

[78] HALS DE/Ho/F10/26.
[79] GCC LBM4074.1.22.
[80] Freeman, 'Decline of Adult School Movement' p. 484.
[81] HALS DE/Ho/F3/17.

Longfellow's 'The Peace-Pipe', an allegory of peace established among warring tribes.

Letchworth's free thinking spiritual explorers, with whom Howard evidently felt very much at home, provide an interesting glimpse into one of the distinctive strands within Edwardian religion. Its members had nearly all been nurtured in nonconformity but were in various stages of rebellion against the theological orthodoxies with which they had been brought up. For them, religion no longer stopped at the boundaries of Protestant Christianity. There were the desert fathers and the medieval mystics to explore, and the living religions of the East, as well as new religious movements such a Spiritualism and Theosophy, and modern science and philosophy. Christian concepts provided these spiritual explorers with many of the significant features on their mental maps; religious ideas still very much mattered, but they had to be scrutinized by discussion and critical examination. The evangelical certainties of their youth now seemed to belong to a past age, rigid and unserviceable. There was a feeling, which Howard evidently shared, that if only men and women could make sense of all this knowledge and religious wisdom, joining the dots and making the connections, the path would be opened to finding the Truth behind everything, and from this Unity would emerge. This was the 'unity and eternal reality, where all contradictions are reconciled' which Annie Lawrence had invoked when she dedicated the Cloisters; this was humanity throwing off its illusions in order to become conscious of unity with the divine. It was a frequent theme in the papers delivered by Bruce Wallace, and it was evoked by the 'Unity of the Universe, a great all-pervading reality' that Howard had described in one of his addresses at the Adult School. He had also hinted at it when he told a journalist in 1908 that 'wonderful unity' was the particular feature of Letchworth religion.

Optimism, unity, and the belief in cosmic and human interconnectedness were much more fragile than Howard and his friends were ever willing to believe. The institutions they created were part of a strand of the English Protestant Nonconformist tradition that would gently become extinct. The Alpha Union did not survive in Letchworth after the departure of Bruce Wallace. Annie Lawrence lived on at the Cloisters, but the religious discussions gave way to the teaching of craft skills. Letchworthians continued to enjoy her swimming pool and musical recitals until the building was requisitioned by the army in 1940. The Garden City Adult School closed due to falling numbers in 1934. Its syllabus had changed somewhat in the 1920s. Although there were still talks on 'The meaning of life', 'The decline of the West' and 'The Religion of the Spirit' there were less ambitious talks from speakers describing their holidays in the Tyrol or Provence or Snow-donia, or 'Gardens in Literature'. The big philosophical and theo-logical debates of the early years were less frequently timetabled. We must remember, of course, that even in its pre-War heyday, the numbers actively involved in Letchworth's progressive intellectual movements had never been large. It seems that the Garden City Adult School never had an attendance that exceeded double figures, and the Cloisters could not accommodate more than about twenty residents at any one time. Meanwhile, Letchworth was growing very rapidly as a light industrial town. The 1911 census reveals its streets filled with builders, print workers and corset makers. These were the Letchworth residents for whom the Methodists churches were built, and for whom the Men's Adult Schools catered. But compared with the supporters of the Garden City Adult School, the Alpha Union, and the Cloisters, much less can be reconstructed about their spiritual lives.

Adrian Fortescue and Roman Catholicism

Until late in 1907, Roman Catholics in Letchworth who wanted to attend Mass would have needed to find their way to Hitchin, where a church had opened in 1902. But by late in 1907, there were forty-seven adult Catholics and fifty-four children in the town, and the Archdiocese of Westminster decided that it was time to station a priest in the Garden City. Their choice fell on Dr Adrian Fortescue. He was thirty-three and had recently returned from a year travelling in the Levant. Independently wealthy, he was a scholar of very considerable theological, liturgical, linguistic, musical, and artistic abilities. His travels in Greece and the Middle East, and studies in Beirut, had provided the groundwork for several of the academic projects he undertook in his presbytery in Letchworth. As he arrived in Letch-worth, he was completing work on *The Greek Fathers* (1908) a lively text intended for the Catholic laity and embellished with his first-hand observations of the places described. He was a priest whose inclinations were largely scholarly, but the evidence suggests that he was painstaking with his parish work.[82] Although he privately hoped to become a professor, he was expected to work wherever his diocesan superiors sent him.[83] Fortescue played an active part in Letchworth life, and the town provided him with various opportunities which he might not have found elsewhere. His linguistic and literary abilities were in demand: from 1910 until his death, he ran an annual class on Dante in Italian, and he also taught a German class. 'Nothing delighted him more than to debate any linguistic subject, and he reduced advocates of Esperanto, among them Ebenezer Howard, to despair.'[84] His aesthetic sensibilities and artistic skills made it easy for him to mix with Letchworth's artists and makers. Shortly after his ordination, Fortescue had enrolled in a calligraphy course at the London County Council's Central School of Arts and Crafts, together with his friend Douglas Cockerell, who became the leading exponent of high-quality bookbinding.[85] The course developed his distinctive calligraphy, which was much in demand for letterheads and notices. He also developed a skill in designing heraldic arms, something which endeared him to the bishops who requested his services.[86] Cockerell, and his bindery, moved to Letchworth in 1907, meaning that Fortescue had friends in the town from the moment of his arrival.[87] Another early Letchworth friend was the artist Mary Crickmer, wife of the architect Courtenay Crickmer who designed extensively for the Garden City movement, and had moved to Letchworth in 1907.

[82] Purdom, *Life Over Again* pp. 244–53 provides an interesting first-hand account of Fortescue at Letchworth.

[83] He was eventually appointed Professor of Church History at the nearby diocesan seminary, St Edmund's Ware, in 1919.

[84] Purdom, *Life Over Again* p. 246.

[85] Aidan Nichols, *The Latin Clerk: The Life, Work and Travels of Adrian Fortescue* (Cambridge, 2011) p. 30.

[86] Nichols, *Latin Clerk* pp. 38–9.

[87] On Cockerell, see Alan Crawford, 'Douglas Bennett Cockerell, 1870–1945' *Oxford Dictionary of National Biography* (Oxford, 2004). Cockerell re-bound the *Codex Sinaiticus* for the British Museum in 1935, and his bindery, managed by his son, continued in existence until 1987. The Cockerells also taught book binding skills to young people at the Cloisters.

Fortescue had been at school with her brother-in-law, and his letters to her reveal a close friendship of disarming frankness; he confided to her his private unhappiness at what he saw as the Church's lack of recognition of his academic abilities, and his frustration and loneliness at being stuck in Letchworth when he would rather be in European sunshine: 'I have to sit in a poky room by a stupid fire all alone; with fog and damp and the *petite bourgeoisie anglaise* outside.'[88] But for all of its dampness and Englishness, Letchworth did offer some compensations. Cambridge and London were easily accessible by rail, and he had plenty of time to pursue his academic interests.

In common with Letchworth's other religious organizations, the initial venue for Roman Catholic worship was the 'sheds', the wooden buildings which housed the town's first public amenities, as well as some of the labourers who had been brought in from London. Fortescue was predictably horrified at having to say Mass in a shed, and set about building his church, an opportunity which allowed him to design and furnish the building with enormous care, and gave full reign to his theological and aesthetic sensibilities.[89] He shared the beliefs of his Anglican contemporary Percy Dearmer that the values of the Arts and Crafts movements should be thoroughly infused into the churches.[90] Fixtures and fittings should be tasteful, well-made and ethically produced. His new church was opened in the summer of 1908, with Fortescue singing the responses to the Byzantine liturgy in Greek and Arabic, which must have been another intriguing moment in Letchworth's early religious history.[91] At the lunch which followed in the Letchworth Hall Hotel, the visiting bishop told those assembled that 'Dr Fortescue is worthy of a Chair in a University, but like the humble violet, he bloomed and shed his fragrance in Letchworth.'[92] It seems unlikely that he appreciated the flowery simile. His church is now the parish hall.

[88] Nichols, *Latin Clerk* pp. 151–4.

[89] Nichols, *Latin Clerk* pp. 144–8.

[90] On Dearmer, see Frances Knight, *Victorian Christianity at the Fin de Siècle: The Culture of English Religion in a Decadent Age* (London, 2015) pp. 215–25.

[91] Photos of St Hugh's Catholic Church can be found at GCC LBM4073.11.21, LBM4073.11.20 and LBM4073.11.19.

[92] Nichols, *Latin Clerk* p. 147, as quoted from the *Letchworth Citizen* newspaper.

Fortescue spent the rest of his relatively short life in Letchworth, dying in 1923 at the age of forty-nine. Relationships with parishioners were sometimes fraught. He had an 'impatience with stupidity', and his remarks could be unwittingly cruel, but according to one of the members of the church choir, Edith Cowell, he was 'a far better [parish priest] than many who think they understood him suspect'.[93] Academically productive and locally active, he embraced the true spirit of a garden citizen:

> His services were at the disposal of everyone. I doubt if anyone who asked him to give a lecture or translate a letter, or clear up a difficulty, went away disappointed. If the book club wanted a Dante lecture, or the dramatic society wanted help in their costumes for *Everyman*, or the golf club wanted an illuminated address, they all knew their way to the presbytery, and Dr Fortescue always found time somehow to do what they wanted.[94]

The Catholic population was very small 'a mere handful of ordinary people' according to Cowell. Prominent among them were the Newdigates, who owned the Arden Press, and brought a number of Catholic employees to Letchworth, Antonia Purdom, and Cowell herself, who translated Italian and sang.

Fortescue had many contacts in the wider community and become much better known among the local Protestant population than would have been usual for a Catholic priest at this date. He does not seem to have regarded them as an alien tribe. When preaching for the Feast of the English Martyrs, he would remind the congregation that Protestants had also died for their faith.[95] His close friends Mary Crickmer and Douglas Cockerell do not appear to have been Catholics, and he was keen not to employ a Catholic housekeeper. He asked Mary Crickmer for help in finding a suitable non-Catholic who was neither 'absolutely decrepit' nor 'a fair young thing'; he was hoping for a 'decent cook of the kind called plain but not too infernally

---

[93] Edith Cowell, 'Adrian Fortescue' *Blackfriars* IV 41 (1923) pp. 1029–34.
[94] Cowell, 'Fortescue' p. 1034.
[95] Cowell, 'Fortescue' p. 1032.

plain'. One of his housekeepers was a Baptist.[96] Fortescue admired the Dante scholar and Unitarian minister Philip Wicksteed. When praising the brilliance of a lecture that Wicksteed had delivered at Letchworth whilst giving the vote of thanks, Fortescue defended Wicksteed's theological opinions as his own affair (some in the audience had evidently questioned them) and noted that 'it was a strange experience to hear one's own theology – St Thomas – explained with an insight, an accurate knowledge and a sympathy that a Catholic professor might envy'.[97] Although Fortescue engaged in theological controversies with various Anglicans (and W.E. Orchard) he seems only to have entered debate when the Anglicans had seemed to him very muddled or ignorant.[98] He appeared to be on good terms with the other clergy in the town, and probably found the Free Church ministers preferable to the Anglo-Catholics, who walked around in cassocks, trying to look like Roman Catholic clergy.[99] As previously noted, he supported financially the ecumenical Guild of Help, and when the Fabian Sidney Webb came to lecture on 'Unemployment and Destitution' Ebenezer Howard was in the chair, and 'support' was provided by a list of clergy headed by Fortescue.[100] He avoided politics, but evidently felt socially engaged. His funeral, conducted by Cardinal Bourne, was particularly well attended, and the photographic evidence attests to the length of the cortege, as it slowly made its way to the town cemetery.[101] Fortescue's work and reputation lived on, and in Letchworth he became a 'personality' remembered decades after his death.[102]

[96] Courtenay Crickmer was a life-long Anglican, and Mary may have been too. On the housekeeper, Maddren, *Letchworth Recollections* p. 47.

[97] GCC LBM2838.16.

[98] Nichols, *Latin Clerk* pp. 233–63.

[99] Fortescue stuck to wearing a Norfolk suit and straw hat. He considered that the 'extreme high Anglican is as remote from us as any other Protestant'. Cowell, 'Fortescue' p. 1034 and Nichols, *Latin Clerk* p. 261.

[100] GCC LBM4074.14.11.

[101] Photos of his funeral procession are at GCC 2010.75.1, 2010.75.2. The next funeral on that scale was almost certainly that of Ebenezer Howard himself.

[102] For example, he featured in a local newspaper cutting from 1953, describing a meeting in which various women had reminisced about the early days of the town. 'Dr Fortescue' featured alongside 'Mr Howard' and 'Miss Annie Lawrence'. GCC LBM.4067.103.

Letchworth and the War

The outbreak of the War affected Letchworth's communities in various ways. For Fortescue, it meant the arrival of around 2,000 Belgian refugees. He noted their presence at midnight Mass at Christmas 1914 and was rude about them in a letter to Mary Crickmer: 'The town suffers from the Belgies all round. They are all drunk and fight among themselves in the street.'[103] Nevertheless, he set about using English, French and Flemish when preaching on the major feasts, and in his church notices.[104] Three of the most prominent Belgian refugees, Jacques and Georges Kryn and Raoul Lahy, founded a munitions factory in the town, and many of the Belgians were involved in munitions manufacture. The rest of the resident male population of military service age were divided between those who were prepared to enlist or be conscripted, and those who registered as conscientious objectors. The pacifist, socialist, internationalist mindset that had been fostered in Letchworth, together with the historic strength of the Quakers in north Hertfordshire, resulted in the Hitchin district having the highest rate of conscientious objection in the whole of the country.[105]

For this reason, Letchworth developed a reputation for harbouring wartime shirkers and found itself vilified by *The Daily Mail*, the newspaper which had played such an important part in publicizing and promoting it in its early days. During 1916, after conscription was introduced, the paper became fixated on hunting down conscientious objectors. A particularly vitriolic article, entitled 'Garden City Weeds: Raking Them Out' claimed that up until September of that year, only thirty per cent of eligible men in north Hertfordshire had been in the army, and the 'black spot' had been diagnosed as Letchworth. 'The first Garden City, like the First Garden, possessed a very vigorous, virulent Serpent crawling about in the hygienic raiment of the Conscientious Objector.' It then made detailed claims about the ways in which Letchworth men had attempted to persuade the military service tribunal to grant them exemptions and noted that some were in

---

[103] Nichols, *Latin Clerk* p. 159.
[104] Cowell, 'Fortescue' p. 1030.
[105] Tidy, *A–Z of Letchworth* pp. 22–4.

prison. Although by no means all conscientious objectors objected on religious grounds, some were using religious arguments. The *Mail* reported that a new military representative on the Hitchin rural tribunal was 'an old barrister of ready, quick wit, and a profound student of the Old Testament, he has met the Conscientious Brotherhood on their own battleground, and they are nearly all turned down now.'[106] Norman McFadyen, the town's medical officer, wrote to the paper to deplore the tone of the article, stating that there were only twenty or thirty conscientious objectors in the town, and none were in prison. He claimed that the Garden City was making an 'exceedingly honourable' contribution to the war effort, and singled out the munitions workers, who were able to be particularly productive because of their healthy housing conditions.[107] But the *Mail* would not let the topic rest, reporting a few days later that 'a ninth conscientious objector' from Letchworth had been handed over to the military in the space of a week.[108] Whatever the precise figure, there were undoubtedly some high profile individuals with pacifist sympathies in the town, including Herbert Morison, Frederic Osborn and Howard himself.

A glimpse of the tensions between the pacifist and non-pacifist sections of the community can be seen in the unlikely context of a struggle for control of the Howard Hall, in March 1917. The Hall was managed by an elected committee of six, something which in less fraught times would presumably have attracted only limited local interest. The *Mail* reported that six pacifist candidates were standing for election, in an attempt to depose the existing hall committee, who had refused to allow it to be used as a platform for Ramsay McDonald, and for other peace meetings, including those organized by Howard. Despite the support of the Letchworth Trade and Labour Council, the pacifists were described as 'routed', with 5,044 votes cast for the 'win-the-war' candidates and 3,841 for the pacifists.[109] This ban on the Howard Hall being used for peace activities greatly disturbed Howard, and as a protest, he removed his portrait from

[106] *Daily Mail* 17 November 1916.
[107] *Daily Mail* 20 November 1916.
[108] *Daily Mail* 27 November 1916.
[109] *Daily Mail* 26 March 1917.

the Hall to the Skittles Inn. His estranged wife Edith, who was living in a caravan in a vacant building plot in the Quadrant, near the centre of the town, caused him further difficulty by announcing her strong opposition to pacifists.[110] Around this time Howard resigned his membership of the Liberal Party, and threw in his lot with the Independent Labour Party and McDonald, whom he greatly admired.

Ebenezer Howard's initial response to the War had been to think that it could be stopped if he was given the opportunity to drop pacifist literature over Germany. He outlined his plan to Bernard Shaw, H.G. Wells, the Cadburys, and possibly other of his influential associates. He wrote to Shaw shortly after War broke out:

> A few days ago I suddenly awoke with the thought of Peace Propaganda working by entirely new means – that of aeroplanes. I calculate that from an aeroplane capable of carrying three men besides the aviator, but carrying one, there might be taken 3 cwt [i.e. 336 pounds] of printed matter, and as every pound might easily represent four thousand messages, there will be a total of one million two hundred thousand messages. These would spread themselves over a very wide area whose length might be hundreds of miles and my present idea would be to travel southward from some point, say in Belgium, till one reached Switzerland, travelling of course at a very great height, and again at night I woke up with the thought that I must myself go up in such an aeroplane and deliver a special message carefully prepared.[111]

Howard enclosed the message which he intended to deliver from the air. It began 'A Friendly Message to the German People' and was framed as an appeal from the 'heart and conscience of the people of England' to the 'heart and conscience of the people of Germany'. The war was not wanted, he told them, and it was preposterous that people of goodwill, unconsulted, could be plunged into mutual slaughter by the hasty decision of rulers 'who lord it over them'. Arbitration at the Hague was the only solution, because for civilized nations, war ought to be now morally impossible. He concluded by urging the Germans to 'throw off the tyranny of militarism. Down with every government that chooses an appeal to force, rather than an appeal to reason! Let

[110] HALS DE/X/1053/S8/11.
[111] HALS DE/Ho/F25/57 Howard to Shaw, 15 August 1914.

the workers of all nations unite in mutual service. Let humanity and civilisation triumph over brutality and barbarism.'[112] Shaw wrote back, telling him that the idea was 'entirely impractical' and that he should 'sit quietly at home'.[113]

It was a curious incident, and his decision to communicate the idea to some of the most prominent men of his day reveals Howard's naivety, even allowing for the heightened emotions brought about by the outbreak of war. But it fitted the pattern of his earlier epiphanies. These include his account of his return to Christian faith after his second lecture on Spiritualism in 1880, his insistence on the British publication of Bellamy's *Looking Backwards* in 1888, the restoration of his speech after three mute days before the launch of *To-morrow* in 1898, and his sense that that book had come to him as a revelation from a mysterious source, which he only became able to communicate after he had obtained the forgiveness of his friend. By this point in Howard's story, we should not be surprised that he had woken from this dream about dropping peace messages over Germany, and interpreted it as a call to action, in the manner of an Old Testament seer.

He could not follow Shaw's advice to 'sit quietly at home', not least because he needed to keep commuting to London to earn enough to support himself and his estranged wife in separate households. He continued to make speeches in Letchworth, and to campaign for a negotiated peace. He was also turning his attention to planning for the post-War world. He had never intended that Letchworth should be a single example of a Garden City. As originally conceived, his plan for 'slumless, smokeless cities' was for groups of communities, set apart from each other, independent but interconnected. If this part of *Garden Cities of To-morrow* was ever to be realized, he knew that he needed to take the initiative, and build a second Garden City.

---

[112] Two different versions of this message survive. The version sent to Shaw is at HALS DE/Ho/F25/57. A slightly later version can be viewed at GCC LBM41.2. This version may have been reworked, and toned down, by Bruce Wallace. The earlier version sent to Shaw refers to war as the product of 'despotic rulers' who are the enemies of the German people. It tells the German people that they have the power to stop the War, if they demand an Armistice and a free constitution.

[113] Robert Beevers, *Garden City Utopia: A Critical Biography of Ebenezer Howard* (London, 1988) p. 150.

7

Howard and Welwyn – the Second Garden City 1919–1928

The Garden City relaunched

Ebenezer Howard was sixty-eight when the First World War ended, and he had another ten years to live. He was past the peak of his fame, which had occurred around 1912, and was less in demand for public speaking and committees. Some of his views, on matters ranging from public crèches to aerial drops of peace literature on Germany, had caused him to be politely regarded as 'eccentric' in some circles, but it is an intriguing feature of his ability to find common ground with others that he had generally been able to argue for radical ideas, such as vegetarianism and cooperative housekeeping, without frightening off supporters of more conservative temperaments. He remained a very well-known figure in British society, was celebrated internationally by town planners and those concerned with post-war reconstruction, and he remained a committed internationalist. The War had dented, but not destroyed, his relentlessly optimistic views on unaided human efforts to find the way to live in peace and unity,[1] and he viewed the prospect of post-war government intervention with a sense of impatience. His disillusionment with Letchworth had grown steadily, and privately he believed that the experiment had gone wrong due to slow growth, financial difficulties and community tensions. While Europeans had been engaging in mutual slaughter, he had witnessed Letchworth being turned into a munitions town, with bitter

---

[1] In his paper 'on religion' at the men's meeting in 1916 Howard had repeated some of his thoughts on peace and prophecy, but the message felt disjointed, and he took refuge in a lengthy reading from Longfellow. HALS DE/Ho/F3/17.

Ebenezer Howard: Inventor of the Garden City. Frances Knight, Oxford University Press.
© Frances Knight 2023. DOI: 10.1093/oso/9780198790815.003.0008

arguments over the use of the Howard Hall for peace meetings. Even Homesgarth, the much-heralded cooperative housing scheme in which he had lived since 1911, had been converted into conventional private rentals in 1916, and had lost its communal life. Howard wanted to build a second Garden City, starting anew on another pristine plot of land, and he knew that time was not on his side.

A second Garden City was not an impossibility. The War had given a new urgency to the housing issue, and a distinct boost to the Garden City movement. 1917 had been a crucial year. In July, a new and wide-ranging government ministry for Reconstruction headed by Christopher Addison had been set up, and within it a specialist housing panel with Lord Salisbury, who until 1917 had been president of the Garden City and Town Planning Association (GCTPA) as its chairman.[2] It was widely accepted that significant injections of government money would be needed for new housing, and that schemes could no longer be left to business entrepreneurs. Meanwhile, two of Howard's closest younger disciples, Frederic Osborn and C.B. Purdom, were actively 'refreshing' the Garden City debate. Purdom, who had enlisted in the army, published a pamphlet entitled *Garden Cities after the War*. He claimed in his memoir that this pamphlet had had no influence on anyone besides Howard, who astounded him by walking unannounced into the camp near Chatham where he had been stationed on his return from France. They went into Chatham, and Howard, in an excitable mood, urged that he and Purdom should work together.[3] Osborn, meanwhile, was spending 1917 in the reading room of the British Museum, studying the history of community projects. As a conscientious objector, and apparently on the advice of Purdom, he had come to the conclusion that 'the best way to hide was to be conspicuously visible'. He was in almost daily contact with Howard, who was still working in London as a shorthand writer.[4] Howard and Purdom urged Osborn to use his time in the library to develop Purdom's pamphlet. The result was *New Towns after the War*,

---

[2] Dennis Hardy, *From Garden Cities to New Towns: Campaigning for town and country planning, 1899–1946* (London, 1991) pp. 120–1.

[3] C.B. Purdom, *Life Over Again: An Essay in Autobiography* (London, 1951) p. 60.

[4] Michael R. Hughes, (ed.) *The Letters of Lewis Mumford and Frederic J. Osborn* (Bath, 1971) p. 447.

published in 1918 under the authorship of an anonymous group of 'New Townsmen', a strategy which was designed to avoid drawing attention to Osborn. The 'New Townsmen' were Howard, Purdom, Osborn and W.G. Taylor, who was a director of Dent, one of the Letchworth-based publishing firms, and the publisher of the work. The group formed themselves into the 'National Garden Cities Committee', a short-lived pressure group within the GCTPA, with an address in the Strand.

Osborn's prose was fluent, and unlike Howard in *To-morrow*, he was less prone to becoming bogged down in detail and speculation. He reworked the familiar themes of the defects of both the city and the countryside, offering his readers the Garden City, but perfected in the light of experience at Letchworth. He stated that the development of post-war Garden Cities would be centrally directed by government and much faster than Letchworth had been, but he was careful to re-emphasize some of the key elements in the original scheme. There would be local autonomy and individual freedom in matters of design. 'There is no need for the new cities to be tied to the apron-strings of a grandmotherly Government department.'[5] Perhaps under pressure from Howard, he even revived the co-operative housing idea, something which, as we have seen, had encountered difficulties at Letchworth. The ambitious plan was for one hundred Garden Cities to be built at a cost of around 500,000,000 pounds over a five-year period.[6] But in case this level of state intervention and expenditure seemed mind boggling, Osborn was careful to emphasize, as Howard had always done, that other funding streams were likely to be available, and that as millions of new homes were going to have be built anyway, they might as well be planned, rather than entirely left to the haphazard vicissitudes of private enterprise. The eighty-four-page pamphlet read like a new edition of *To-morrow* updated and abbreviated for a busy wartime readership.[7] Thirty years later, Osborn reflected that

[5] New Townsmen, *New Towns after the War: An Argument for Garden Cities* (London, 1918) p. 53.

[6] New Townsmen, *New Towns* p. 56.

[7] Robert Beevers provides a longer discussion of the pamphlet and its significance. Robert Beevers, *The Garden City Utopia: A Critical Biography of Ebenezer Howard* (London, 1988) pp. 151–7.

although as a policy document *New Towns After the War* was 'very complete and convincing', its economic and political arguments had been 'undeveloped and thin'.[8]

Since reconstruction and housing were central to the national debate, the GCTPA was well positioned to make the interventions necessary to ensure that new Garden Cities were kept at the top of the agenda. But Howard was impatient, and he still believed in private enterprise rather than state intervention. He told Osborn, who was thirty-four at the time, that 'if you wait for the Government to do it, you will be as old as Methuselah before they start. The only way to get anything done is to do it yourself.'[9] Dennis Hardy captures the scene well: 'There was Howard, pacing the fields of Hertfordshire as if these were still the golden days of an Edwardian summer. The world had changed since the pioneers had broken the soil at Letchworth . . . But Howard, the gentle idealist, loyal to the cause but somehow oblivious to the dictates of history, simply went off and did it his way.'[10] What he did was to go to an auction and bid for the land on which to build Welwyn Garden City, without either securing the formal support of the GCTPA, or the necessary funding. The decision would have seemed reckless to most rational observers. But Howard, although showing signs of nervous agitation lest he should fail at the auction, appeared relatively untroubled by the magnitude of the financial commitment he was taking on. He was having another of his spiritual epiphanies, recollecting some eight years later his conviction that 'there was a beneficent Power behind us'.[11]

On his regular commutes from Letchworth to London King's Cross, and from the elevated position of the Digswell viaduct, he had spotted acres of beautiful undeveloped land in the valley below.

[8] Hughes, *Letters of Mumford and Osborn* p. 162.

[9] Hardy, *From Garden Cities to New Towns* p. 150, citing F.J. Osborn, *Genesis of Welwyn Garden City: Some Jubilee Memories* (London, 1970) p. 8. The same quotation is found in Beevers, *Garden City Utopia* p. 160, citing a different work by Osborn. Methuselah is recorded as being the oldest person in the Bible, having lived for 969 years, Gen.5:27.

[10] Hardy, *From Garden Cities to New Towns* p. 150.

[11] Howard writing to J.R. Farquharson, 10 January 1927, cited in Dugald MacFadyen, *Sir Ebenezer Howard and the Town Planning Movement* (Manchester, 1933) p. 122.

This he believed was the site for the Second Garden City. It was about twenty-two miles from London and twelve from Letchworth. The railway line ran close by, and so did the Great North Road. Howard assumed it was part of Lord Salisbury's Hatfield estate. If this was the case, then ownership rested with one of the grandee patrons of the Garden City movement. It seemed to Howard that the forces under the control of the beneficent Power were coming into perfect alignment. He suggested that Purdom and Osborn should accompany him on a Saturday in late 1918, so that they could explore the site further. The three men alighted at Hatfield station, and walked north towards Peartree Farm, and across what became the golf course at Stanborough. Purdom described their strenuous day in detail, including his irritation when Howard and Osborn declined refreshment at the Bull in Stanborough, because they were teetotallers, and beer was the only drink available. Lunch had to wait until they had made their way back to Hatfield.[12] But all three judged the day a success. Osborn and Purdom went home and assumed that they would bring the site to the attention of the relevant authorities at the appropriate time.

Howard, however, was not prepared to wait, and had one final burst of autonomous entrepreneurship to unleash. Without any consultation, he wrote to Lord Salisbury, telling him that he 'would greatly aid in the solution of many difficult problems' if he would consent to the sale of land north of Hatfield. He assured the fourth marquess that he shared his belief in private enterprise, adding rather mystically that private enterprise could put 'into operation spiritual forces which have not yet reached far enough down among the constituent elements of Society to permit the things being done by the State which in a democratic country implies that the Nation is ready for them'. Salisbury was clearly taken by surprise, replying that he had no thoughts of such a thing, although he might consider selling land south of Hatfield. Howard pressed again: 'There are strong and sufficient reasons for greatly preferring, for the purpose I have in mind, the land to the North...' Unsurprisingly, Salisbury was annoyed by this unorthodox attempt to pressurize him into a sale, firing back that although Howard might be 'a very notable example

amongst the pioneers of the movement' he had no intention of
discussing the matter further until a firm business proposal came
forward from the GCTPA itself.[13]

There the matter might have rested, but at the very same moment
that Howard was corresponding with Salisbury, he noticed that Lord
Desborough had advertised the sale by auction of his Panshanger
estate. It encompassed a large part of the land that Howard was
interested in, which was not, in fact, owned by Salisbury. This was
Howard's *kairos*, his urgent moment of decision and action. He had
only a few days to raise the money for the deposit which would allow
him to bid at the auction, an action that he believed would release the
spiritual forces that would enable a second Garden City to arise in the
Lea valley around Digswell. If he failed, he would lose the chance
forever, and the land would fall into other hands. Howard was thrown
into a state of extreme emotional agitation. He immediately travelled
to London, and met with Richard Reiss, the chairman of the GCTPA
in a café close to King's Cross. A friendly Norwegian who observed
the scene commented that Howard appeared more 'agitated than
I have ever seen an Englishman'.[14] Having persuaded Reiss that
they must immediately raise £5,000, Howard jumped into a cab,
and began to canvass his wealthy friends in the City of London. By
the following Friday, the day of the sale, Howard was still £200 short
of his target, but in a further extraordinary turn of events, the auc-
tioneer, Norman Savill, who had taken a liking to Howard when he
went to speak to him about his intention to bid, unexpectedly put up
the money himself. Howard emerged from the auction as the owner of
a prime fifteen-hundred-acre Hertfordshire shooting estate, and with
an outstanding debt of over £50,000. He was clearly in a state of
shock. Norman McFadyen, the Letchworth medical officer, noted that
'He was in an extraordinary state, trembling all over with a fine
tremor that was quite beyond his control, and in a cold sweat all
over.'[15] He was met by Purdom and Osborn, who were both severely

---

[13] The correspondence took place between 30 April and 23 May 1919.
Excerpts are reproduced in Hardy, *From Garden Cities to New Towns* pp. 151–3.
The originals are in the Osborn papers.
[14] Beevers, *Garden City Utopia* p. 163.
[15] Beevers, *Garden City Utopia* p. 163.

shaken by what Howard had done. Purdom was particularly horrified, having made it perfectly plain that he did not want to see another inadequately funded Garden City, on the same lines as Letchworth.[16] The fallout continued, as Purdom recalled:

> On the following Sunday, Howard was due to give a religious address to the Theosophical Society at Letchworth, but instead gave an impassioned talk on the second garden city, on the site purchased the previous Friday, and on the imminent purchase of land from Salisbury to complete the scheme. His plans were reported in the London press ... Howard went at once to Salisbury, who was furious, refused to see him, and said he would have nothing further to do with him or his hare-brained scheme. That was the position when Second Garden City Limited was formed in the following October. Desborough was by no means pleased on finding that his land had been purchased for so socialistic a purpose as a garden city, and would have been pleased to cancel the contracts, but sold a bit more land at Sherrards Wood. When the company was formed, Howard saw Salisbury again, who finally agreed to the sale of a minimum area of his land, 689 acres, at a price of £40,000, but on onerous conditions, including a right of pre-emption in the event of land not being used for a garden city. The right of pre-emption was to embarrass the undertaking for years to come.[17]

There was also the question of to how manage the public relations. Within weeks of the land purchase, Osborn and Purdom had decided that it would have to be presented to the public as part of a new strategy being enacted by the GCTPA, and not the hare-brained scheme of an individual who appeared to have taken leave of his senses. The new town at Welwyn would need to be presented in the context of the post-war plan to solve London's housing crisis with a ring of 'satellite towns', and, abandoning the plan for 'one hundred new towns' which they had published in 1918, they both set to work to turn Welwyn Garden City into a reality.

Just as at Letchworth in 1903, the first step was to set up a company and a board of directors. The directors of the Second Garden City Pioneer Company included J.R. Farquharson and R.L. Reiss, who

[16] Purdom, *Life Over Again* pp. 65–6.
[17] Purdom, *Life Over Again* pp. 67–8.

had found the deposit and who would lose their money if the balance could not be paid, and others who had links with Letchworth, the construction industry, or interests in health or economics. Sir Theodore G. Chambers, a chartered surveyor with experience of estate management, and a Tory who had been knighted for his services to promoting National Savings during the War, became chairman. He had come to the attention of Howard after writing an article on the repopulation of rural districts, and he was known to be deeply concerned about living conditions in London. Chambers remained chairman until the Company was wound up when Welwyn was redesignated as a New Town after the Second World War, while simultaneously retaining its Garden City status. Chambers provided the Garden City with wise leadership and continuity, living there for the whole of his twenty-eight years at the helm. He was able to use his personal influence with the chairman of the Midland Bank, who provided an immediate overdraft of £100,000 and was consistently sympathetic towards the difficulties which ensued with servicing this debt.

Howard and Osborn tried to enlist the Labour politician Ramsay MacDonald, entertaining the future prime minister to a 'frugal lunch' in a teashop, but he declined on the grounds that his appointment might be too controversial. He recommended another Labour politician, J.R. Clynes, but he too declined because his sponsoring trade union believed that its members should not become directors of capitalist enterprises.[18] Howard's combination of socialist pacifism with staunch belief in private enterprise presumably meant that he deployed different arguments when trying to attract the support of Lord Salisbury, on the one hand, and Ramsay McDonald, on the other, and this was a skill that he had always had. He had framed the introduction to *To-morrow* with supportive quotations from Liberal and Conservative politicians, trades union leaders, and clergy. Part of Howard's success came from his instinct for drawing in others with arguments that they would find appealing. He spent the early months of 1920 writing to everyone that he could possibly think of, canvassing their support for Welwyn. Some of the eminent men

[18] Hardy, *From Garden Cities to New Towns* pp. 153–4.

who had supported early Letchworth – including George and Edward Cadbury, Jesse Boot and Lord Lever, wrote back to say that they were either too elderly or financially committed to help out this time.[19]

In the event, the Welwyn Garden City Company had to rely, much as Letchworth had twenty years earlier, on the leadership of wealthy entrepreneurs and professional men. The changed political context produced some important differences, however. The Company was soon able to take advantage of loans that were briefly available from the Public Works Loan Board, which had been set up under the Housing Act of 1921. It was at times an uneasy transition from the mentality of private finance to public works, but it was necessary for the town to succeed. Hertfordshire County Council, and the district council, gradually took over services in Welwyn in the manner that was becoming established elsewhere.[20]

The early promotion of Welwyn came from the *Daily Mail*, a newspaper which, as we have seen, had long been supportive of the Garden City movement, even if it had disliked Letchworth's conscientious objectors. Since 1908, the *Mail* had sponsored the Ideal Home Exhibition at Olympia. In 1920, it decided to take its support for post-war housing and modern domesticity further with the sponsorship of an 'Ideal Village' near Welwyn. The Garden City Company leased the newspaper 6.3 acres of land on which were built forty-three exhibition houses, and a temporary station was set up. It was slightly reminiscent of the 'Cheap Cottages Exhibition' in Letchworth in 1905. The paper's idyllic description of the turf cutting ceremony, when the sun shone, the scent of new mown hay filled the air and nightingales sang at midday, was clearly intended to encourage Ideal Home regulars to venture out to this picturesque part of Hertfordshire.[21] The 'Ideal Village' and the Garden City were separate developments, but inevitably they became linked in the public mind, to the extent that Welwyn in its early years was known in some quarters as

---

[19] A selection of these replies to Howard's requests are preserved in HALS DE/Ho/F25.
[20] MacFadyen, *Howard* pp. 126–35.
[21] *Daily Mail* 10 June 1920.

Daily Mail town, and the assumption was made that the newspaper was sponsoring the Garden City.[22]

Welwyn's development

Howard, Purdom and Osborn, who had all been resident in Letchworth, threw in their lot with the new Garden City and moved to Welwyn, once again embracing life in a frontier town, with its muddy lanes, and handlamps and a station made out of railway sleepers.[23] Howard moved towards the end of 1920, the year in which he finally retired as a shorthand writer, setting up home with his eldest daughter, Kathleen Rawlinson and her family. The house was in Handside Lane, one of the first fifty houses built by a public utility company, to take advantage of the Housing Act of 1919. It was in effect a council house, which was let to the family at a subsidized rent.[24] After a few years he was able to move to a pleasant semi-detached and centrally located house at 5 Guessens Road. The house was purchased for him by his friend the wealthy socialist James Leakey, who had been chairman of the board of the Spirella corset factory in Letchworth.[25] Edith Howard, after more than a decade of living apart from her husband, also moved into the house in Guessens Road. What prompted the reconciliation, if that is what it was, is unclear, and it was against the advice of Kathleen. Perhaps it was an awareness of their increasing frailty, as Howard was now in his seventies, and Edith Howard, in her late fifties, suffered poor mental health. It may also have been financial difficulties associated with continuing to fund two separate establishments after Howard's retirement. Osborn moved to 16 Guessens Road, and Sir Theodore Chambers lived in a considerably larger detached house at 9 Guessens Road. From 1922, Purdom

[22] C.B. Purdom's *The Building of Satellite Towns: A Contribution to the Study of Town Development and Regional Planning* (New edition, London, 1949) p. 193 and Purdom, *Life Over Again* p. 71.

[23] This description of Welwyn Garden City in its 'pioneer' days comes from Theodore G. Chambers' foreword to Purdom, *Satellite Towns* p. x.

[24] Photos of the early housing in Handside Lane can be seen at GCC LBM4015.128 and LBM4070.4.

[25] Beevers, *Garden City Utopia* p. 168.

resided at Digswell Lodge, an elegant seventeenth-century property around which the new Garden City developed. Howard, Osborn and Purdom lived in Welwyn until the end of their lives.[26]

Welwyn's transition from an agricultural estate to a Garden City was rapid. In twelve years, it went from an estate of just under 2400 acres, with five farmhouses, labourers' cottages, and a mansion (Digswell House) to a town of 2,500 houses and some forty industries, with the public services and infrastructure suitable for a population of 9,000. Although he was on the board of directors, Howard was less involved with Welwyn's day-to-day development than he had been at Letchworth. He did, however, make one significant early intervention. He had been dissatisfied with the way in which shopping had developed in Letchworth, and decided that a single store would better meet the needs of the residents than the usual cluster of small shopkeepers offering different products and services, operating in an unregulated market. The unplanned proliferation of small shops in Letchworth had resulted, Howard thought, in both useless duplication and the non-availability of certain products. Operating in the same unilateral spirit that had taken him to the Panshanger auction, at a very early date before the Second Garden City even had a board to consider the matter, he invited H. Gordon Selfridge to open a department store in the new town, and when Selfridge turned the idea down, he approached the St Albans Co-operative Society, who were similarly negative. If Welwyn was to have a department store, clearly the Welwyn Garden City Company would have to operate it themselves, by setting up a subsidiary company. The Welwyn Stores Ltd, with its duty of providing shopping facilities for the town, opened for business in October 1921.[27] No other shops were permitted, and this monopolistic shopping arrangement continued even as the town grew. It was clearly unusual, provoking quite a lot of negative comment. The obvious fear was that lack of competition would lead to inflated prices, but Purdom claimed that staff were sent out to check on prices in other Hertfordshire towns, and prices at the Stores were lowered, if

[26] Howard died in 1928, Purdom in 1965 and Osborn in 1978.

[27] Purdom, *Satellite Towns* pp. 256–74 devotes a chapter to Welwyn's shopping. He was managing director of the Stores, and his wife Antonia worked there as a demonstrator.

they were found to be higher than in the surrounding area. The arrangement was defended on the grounds that it provided the best possible retail facility in a town that was initially tiny, but then rapidly growing, and that it allowed profits to be fed back into the Company, and then into the Garden City itself.

The architect appointed to build Welwyn Garden City was the young French Canadian, Louis de Soissons. His plan took account of Howard's original diagrams, with roads fanning out in a radial pattern, and the Parkway designed as a central green promenade, with the civic buildings grouped around it. There was zoning of industrial areas, and an agricultural belt encircling the town. The architectural style adopted was neo-Georgian, creating a very different character from Arts and Crafts Letchworth. Indeed, the contrasts served to illustrate that the essentials of the Garden City vision could be interpreted in completely different architectural styles. De Soissons exercised a powerful influence, similar to that which Parker and Unwin had had at Letchworth. As well as laying out the plan, he designed many of the public buildings, factories and houses. Plans for new buildings drawn up by other architects had to be approved by his office. Some of the Letchworth architects also designed for Welwyn, including Crickmer, Bennett and Bidwell, Clapham Lander and Parker. De Soissons moved to the town in 1922 and stayed in its vicinity for the rest of his life, exercising close supervision over the project as it developed.

The balance between 'garden' and 'city' was better achieved in Welwyn than in Letchworth. The neo-Georgian atmosphere made the town seem rather more urban than Letchworth, although there were of course plenty of features which highlighted the importance of green space. There were spacious gardens, neighbourhood greens, grass verges, playing fields and enormous amounts of tree planting in streets and parks. The town was easy to walk around and navigate. The Great North Road (designated as the A1 in 1921) formed the town's western boundary, and the Great Northern Railway ran through the centre, with stations in old Welwyn (Welwyn North) and Hatfield. Some inconvenience arose from the absence of a Garden City station on the mainline until 1926; the temporary station, made out of railway sleepers, had been opened on the branch line, which linked Hertford in the east, and Dunstable, in the west.

But after the opening of the mainline station, communications, particularly with London, were excellent. Welwyn Garden City fulfilled perfectly its designation as 'London's first satellite town'.[28]

Religious developments followed a pattern familiar from Letchworth, although the Church of England, perhaps galvanized by the proximity of the prominent Anglican Lord Salisbury, seemed more active than it had been in Letchworth. In 1920, the newly appointed bishop of St Albans, Michael Furze, wrote to Howard to wish him success with his new venture, expressing the hope that the Church of England would play 'a not unworthy part in the making of the new Garden City'.[29] It was perhaps a tacit admission that it had not been on the front foot in Letchworth, which Furze had recently visited. The existing Church of England parishes in the Welwyn area included the ancient parish of Digswell, and St Mary Magdalene to the south, whose church had been built by the Salisbury family in the 1880s. But it suited the *Daily Mail* to suggest that religion had arrived with the Garden City, headlining an item in the Spring of 1921 'First Wedding and First Christening: Welwyn Garden City's History Begins'. The wedding had actually taken place in Highbury in North London, but the bridegroom, Stuart Yuill, was the Company's cost accountant, and the couple moved into 'one of the very first houses' on the Monday after their wedding. The christening was more significant, combining as it did the baptism of 'the first little citizen' Marie Evelyn Setter in a silver rose bowl given to the baby by Sir Theodore and Lady Chambers, with what the paper described as 'the christening of Welwyn . . . the first religious service to be held at the Garden City'. This was probably more accurately the first service to be conducted by Anglican clergy after the decision had been made to establish a new parish for the Garden City, and to appoint a curate. The new curate, J.B. Hunt, was present, as was the archdeacon of St Albans, who gave the address.[30] The hall of the new St Francis of Assisi parish was technically the first religious building to open in Welwyn Garden City

[28] Purdom, *Satellite Towns* pp. 181–360 provides a very detailed account of the development of Welwyn.
[29] HALS DE/Ho/F25/24.
[30] *Daily Mail* 22 April 1921.

in 1923, and a second new parish, in Peartree, was established some years later.[31]

A Congregational church opened shortly after the St Francis hall in 1923, and a Free Church was built in 1929. As at Letchworth, the original Free Church was too small, and by 1933 there were plans for building a larger one. The Quakers were prominent in early Welwyn, and by 1925 a Friends Meeting House had appeared. The Roman Catholics arrived early, and by 1926 had a church, rapidly followed by a convent school, in a prominent position in the Parkway. A Gospel Mission also had its own premises by 1933, and other religious groups hired public rooms for services. As at Letchworth, separate Baptist and Methodist churches appeared later, in 1937 and 1944, thus frustrating any earlier hopes of ecumenical union among the Free Churches.[32] Purdom recounted a strong feeling amongst the garden citizens against the 'nuisance' of bellringing, resulting in Roman Catholics, Anglicans and Free Churches agreeing to desist after protracted negotiations.

Howard's final years

After the War, Howard had been anxious to revive the work the International Garden Cities and Town Planning Association, of which he was President. It was at this date the only global organization concerned with the internationally important area of housing and planning.[33] A conference on 'Reconstruction' was held in Brussels in September 1919, and a plan was discussed for building an international Garden City in Belgium, as a peace symbol. In an early example of battlefield tourism, the British delegation of twenty-five, which included Barry Parker and Raymond Unwin, as well as Charles Purdom, toured the West Flanders Front. Howard made a characteristically eschatological speech, declaring that the old order was passing away, and plans must be made for the new order of a combined industrial and rural life. The new international Garden City would

---

[31] Purdom, *Satellite Towns,* p. 218.

[32] Purdom, *Satellite Towns* pp. 218–19; MacFadyen, *Howard* p. 138.

[33] Stanley Buder, *Visionaries and Planners: The Garden City Movement and the Modern Community* (New York and Oxford, 1990) p. 142.

be simultaneously a war memorial, and 'a model for all the world of the peaceful arts and the happier civic life that is to be'.[34] This Garden City did not materialize.

Although Howard remained a director of both the Letchworth and the Welwyn Garden City companies until his death, during his few remaining years of active life, he mainly devoted his energies to the international Garden City movement. In 1922, together with Chambers, he hosted 160 delegates from thirty-eight countries who came to inspect the *Daily Mail* ideal village, and he was on hand to propose a toast to the newspaper and to its proprietor Lord Northcliffe.[35] Howard gave lectures in various parts of Europe, presumably using Esperanto whenever possible, and in 1925 he made a final visit to the United States. It was the first time that he had been in the country that had been so influential in shaping his thinking since 1884, when he was an unknown Englishman hoping – and failing – to sell a typewriter modification to Remington. This time, sailing into New York he was leading a delegation of thirty other prominent British town planners and architects, all of them on their way to the conference of the International Federation of Town and Country Planning and Garden Cities (IFTCPGC).

Howard was met at the quayside by a reporter from the *New York Times*. The interview he gave was republished in the *Daily Mail*. Headlined 'Former U.S. Typist's Work for Britain: Originator of England's Garden Cities' it managed to give the impression that Howard, a 'one time Chicago stenographer' was an American. Howard was reported to have said 'I was restless because stenographers grow restless . . . They listen so much to the ideas of others that unless they think of something original for themselves they become mere phonograph records. I went to England and the idea came to me of a garden city . . .'[36] It was at this conference that Howard met Lewis Mumford. Mumford was a leading light in the newly formed Regional Planning Association of America. He became a public intellectual who incorporated many of Howard's ideas into his philosophical and practical perspectives on twentieth-century

[34] *Garden Cities and Town Planning Magazine* December 1919 pp. 239–40.
[35] *Daily Mail* 17 March 1922.
[36] *Daily Mail* 16 April 1925.

America. Mumford's thirty-year published correspondence with Frederic Osborn includes numerous reflections on Howard and his legacy. At the New York conference, together with the other members of the RPAA, they discussed plans to build an American Garden City for a population of twenty-five thousand on a site near New York City.[37] Howard stayed at the luxuriously grand Commodore Hotel on East 42nd Street, which had opened six years earlier, and had two thousand rooms. He watched cranes lifting into place the steel frames for the new sixty- to eighty-storey skyscrapers. What he thought about this is unfortunately not recorded.

Back home in Welwyn, Howard could be regularly seen out on the Broadway, a small, now rather stout elderly man, with wispy silver hair and a straggly moustache, dressed as ever in well-worn clothes, and a battered felt hat. He retained his friendly demeanour and was an unintimidating presence who was always sociable and lacking in self-importance.[38] To those who observed him at closer quarters, he could seem sometimes irrational and obsessive. His mind had returned to the mechanical devices which had taken up so much of his energy in the 1880s. He had always wanted to invent a machine that would write shorthand, and the result was a complex typewriter with ninety-six keys which he called 'The Phonoplayer'. In 1923 he took out patents on it in Britain, the United States and Germany, wrote a lengthy users' manual and offered free lessons and demonstrations. Tinkering with machines in his shed, which had long been his hobby, might have seemed a harmless diversion for the old man, but Howard's obsession with his Phonoplayer went far beyond that. He borrowed large amounts of money to invest in the project and accumulated nearly 3,000 pounds of debt, a vast sum for someone who had always had to live on a few hundred pounds a year. He became fixated with the idea that the Phonoplayer would make him at

[37] Buder, *Visionaries and Planners* p. 128.

[38] F.J. Osborn, 'Sir Ebenezer Howard: the evolution of his ideas' *Town Planning Review* 21, 3 (October 1950) p. 222. A photo of Howard in 1926, sitting for the sculptor Ivy Lloyd-Young is at GCC LBM4067.15. During the sittings, he entertained her with 'cheerful and witty conversation' and sometimes brought along some work to do in connection with his shorthand typewriter. HALS temporary catalogue reference Acc 3485.

least one million pounds, and that with this money it would be possible
to found a third Garden City. His son Cecil, himself an accomplished
shorthand writer, became increasingly exasperated. The whole point
of shorthand, he told his father repeatedly, was that it was fast, silent,
and simple. All that was needed was a notebook and pencil; it did not
require learning to use a noisy and cumbersome machine. Howard's
counterargument was that machine-written shorthand would be con-
sistent in appearance, and therefore much easier to read back. The
result of his investment in a project that made no money was that he
died with only £185 14s 1d, a fact which may have raised some
eyebrows when it was reported under the headline 'Garden city
founder's small estate'.[39] Cecil has the unpleasant task of writing a
formal report on the inadequacies of the machine for those who had
invested in it, and requesting that they release the debt.[40] It was the
kindness of his creditors that prevented Edith Howard from being left
in severe financial difficulty.[41] She was awarded a small pension from
the Welwyn Garden City company, and an even smaller civil list
pension of £75 a year in 1929.

As well as the Phonoplayer, Howard's thoughts turned to the
contemplation of his life beyond death, and the prospect of reunion
with Lizzie. His attendance at séances increased, something which was
perhaps also intensified after the death of his close friend the Spiritualist Cora Richmond in 1923. In his present life, he remained pain-
fully yoked to Edith. Some surviving pages of his diary for 1927 reveal
their miserable state. In August, they visited Birkenhead, and he noted
that 'the wife' chose the back bedroom. He felt very unwell and lame
and spent much of the holiday in bed. When they ventured out, 'the
wife [was] interested in shops' while he settled down in the 'new books
section' of the Birkenhead Central Library. He was much impressed
by a passage on page 277 in a new book written by the Anglican
theologian, Charles E. Raven.[42] Other names in the diary indicate

---

[39] GCC LBM 4067.126.

[40] HALS DE/Ho/F27/1/44.

[41] Beevers, *Garden City Utopia* pp. 178–80.

[42] Charles Raven, *The Creator Spirit: A Survey of Christian Doctrine in the Light of Biology, Psychology and Mysticism* Cambridge 1927. Page 277 contains several passages which Howard would have warmed to. They included the suggestion that

that he was also taking an interest in the work of the Anglican theologians G. Studdert Kennedy and Dick Sheppard, who also had a best-selling new book out in 1927, *The Impatience of a Parson*. In it, Sheppard argued that the churches had complicated something that was essentially simple, an interpretation of Christianity that would have appealed to Howard. By 1927 both Sheppard and Raven were known to be pacifists, and all three had radical leanings. They were just the kind of clergy that Howard would have been excited to discover.

The holiday in Birkenhead appeared to do nothing to ease his domestic tensions. On 22 October 1927, Howard wrote (in short-hand, which she could not read) 'I must think out a course of action towards my wife – a firm course, but a living course, one which I hope will bring down her pride and haughtiness'. A week later he went to London, to see a Mr Fenton, presumably a solicitor, about a separation from Edith, but once in London, he lost his nerve. 'When I came . . . to Mr Fenton . . . I decided not to proceed in the direction I had intended but to seek to get a substantial sum from [?] for my wife's home as some compensation [?].'[43] Perhaps this indicates that he was aware of the scale of the debt that he was in, and that he blamed Edith for it. The diary mentions 'money being spent very freely'. In the event, their marriage had only six more months to run, for Howard died on 1 May 1928. He had stomach cancer, a weakened chest, and a painful problem with his leg. Accounts of those last months suggest that Howard's death may have been hastened by

---

'the formative periods of Christian theology have been times of evangelistic and practical activity' and that 'action in partnership with others opens up to us new visions of our own limitations, wider worlds of sympathy and understanding'. He may also have liked Raven's comment that 'Anglicans cannot waste time on jealousies or precedents, but inevitably beckon to our partners in the other ship. It is obvious to every honest mind that the Church of England is not the only boat on the beach, and the ark outside which there is no salvation . . . These other boats are sea-worthy; and the shoal is in the bay'. See F.W. Dillistone, *Charles Raven: Naturalist, Historian and Theologian* (London, 1975) pp. 127–38 for more on *The Creator Spirit*.

[43] HALS DE/Ho/F19. Parts of the diary were transcribed from the original shorthand by F.J. Osborn, but the entries remain fragmentary and unclear.

Edith's neglect and mental instability. She blamed the Garden City movement for his illness and projected her hostility on to everyone associated with it. According to his daughter, she was completely unable to cook, and 'fed him on undercooked rice'. When concerned family and friends called, she shouted at them to go away. Some of them persisted. Osborn, a close friend and neighbour, was anxious to record the final reflections of the dying man. He managed to get into the house but remembered that Edith spent the whole of his visit shouting up the stairs, telling him to go. Another friend, the wife of Harold Craske, who had been company secretary at Letchworth, sent him 'a proper bed to die in' after she found the sick man languishing on an uncomfortable couch in the sitting room.[44] The Revd James Burns, minister of the Welwyn Garden City Free Church, also attended Howard during his last days. He may have received a more friendly reception from Edith, as he was her preferred choice to write her husband's biography.

Burns, and the other ministers of the Free Churches in both Welwyn and Letchworth led Howard's funeral service. For this occasion, the influences of Spiritualism and Theosophy faded into the background, and Free Church theology was once more in the ascendant as the religious context that would shape events. The funeral was a predictably large affair, held in both of the Garden Cities. Factories and shops closed, and people arrived two hours in advance to ensure a seat in church. The first part was held in the newly built Handside school hall in Welwyn. A solitary vase of white tulips stood on the draped school desk on the platform, and Howard's coffin was placed in front of the platform. James Burns led the service, with clergy of various denominations in attendance. The coffin was then taken to the Letchworth Free Church, where the service was conducted by the minister, Alexander Kerr, assisted by Burns. Kerr's funeral address blended David's lament for Abner 'here is a great man fallen' with Joel's prophecy of young men seeing visions and old men dreaming dreams. As a young man, Howard had seen visions, Kerr said, and his vision was to spend his life 'in the endeavour to secure decent housing conditions for the workers and their families'. It was inevitable that

[44] HALS DE/FJO/I35.

Blake's lines about 'building Jerusalem' would also be quoted. Kerr celebrated Sir Ebenezer as a 'staunch friend' of the Letchworth Free Church, who had attended the first service in its first building in 1905.

After the service, a cavalcade of fifty cars motored to the Letchworth cemetery, the route lined with people paying their respects. Enormous numbers of wreaths were sent, from many individuals and organizations ranging from the Institute of Shorthand Writers and the Royal Institution of British Architects to the Welwyn Garden City Labour Party and the Boy Scouts.[45] Burns led a memorial service at Handside school on the following Sunday morning. His address drew on the knowledge he had gained of Howard in old age at Welwyn, and he made the point that Howard had evidently repeated to him, as he had to Osborn, that the Garden City movement was designed to solve a spiritual, as much as an economic problem, and that Howard believed that it had arisen as the result of his being the recipient of divine inspiration, which empowered him to do the work. He compared Howard to General Booth, and Dr Barnardo.[46]

After his death, Edith made a bonfire in the garden, and burnt his books and many of his papers. This naturally infuriated Cecil Howard, for these items had been explicitly left to him, with 'all the rest of my estate' bequeathed to Edith.[47] Relations deteriorated further as they argued over who should write the biography of Ebenezer Howard. Four potential biographers were discussed. The first was Frederic Osborn, who had been collecting material for years, and knew a great deal about both Howard and his context; Howard

[45] GCC LBM4067.199. A contributor to Maureen Maddren, (ed.) *Letchworth Recollections* (Baldock, 1995) p. 66 remembered their father making wreaths for '36 hours straight off' when Howard died.

[46] There are several newspapers accounts of Howard's funeral arrangements available online from the Garden City Collection. This one comes from the *Welwyn Times* 11 May 1928.

[47] Howard had made a new will on 12 April 1928 (HALS DE/Ho/F26/1) just a few weeks before his death. The children evidently felt that their father had been pressurized into doing this by Edith. In the new will, all their father's possession were left to her. When she died, she left everything to J.J. Parkes Cole, who had been one of Howard's executors (together with Cecil and Edith). This meant that the children were denied the opportunity to inherit items of family furniture, or any of the remaining possessions of their father or mother.

himself had considered that 'he will be a very efficient writer of my life, especially in relation to the Garden City movement.'[48] The second was Egerton St John Pettifor Catchpool, a Quaker who was subwarden of Toynbee Hall, and who was about to become the first national secretary of the Youth Hostel Association. The third was George Bernard Shaw, who had known Howard since 1880, and lived nearby at Ayot St Lawrence. The fourth potential biographer was James Burns, the local Free Church minister. Howard had been known to favour either Osborn or Catchpool. Edith Howard hated Osborn, had been rude to Catchpool, and was evidently not impressed with the suggestion of approaching Britain's most eminent playwright. She vetoed all of the first three candidates, and insisted that it should be Burns, a suggestion which Cecil Howard evidently found extraordinary.[49] No biography by Burns, Osborn, Catchpool, or Shaw was ever published.

Shortly after her husband's death, Edith Howard took out a tenancy on Howard's former home, 359 Norton Way South, and moved back to Letchworth. In 1931, Cecil was still trying to persuade her to reimburse him from the estate for funeral and other expenses that he had incurred as his father's executor.[50] She tried to sell various of Howard's possessions, including the only existing prototype of the Phonoplayer, to raise money for the Spitfire fund in 1940. She died in the Three Counties Asylum in Arlesey, Bedfordshire 1941, and was buried in Letchworth cemetery next to Howard.

[48] HALS DE/Ho/F27/3.

[49] HALS DE/Ho/F27/3; HALS DE/Ho/F/27/2/11 29 August 1928 and HALS DE/Ho/F/27/2/12 31 August 1928.

[50] HALS DE/Ho/F27/1 Howard's funeral expenses were initially paid by the Welwyn Garden City Company. Cecil Howard reimbursed the Company, imagining that he in turn would be reimbursed from his father's estate. Edith obdurately refused to believe that this was a legitimate claim, and relations between the three executors – Cecil, Edith, J.J.P. Cole, and the solicitors trying to wind up the estate, remained fraught for years after his death.

Conclusion

Ebenezer Howard: A Spiritual Life

Ebenezer Howard's views on the spiritual life evolved to a far greater extent than his views on town planning and Garden Cities, which remained almost unchanged over a period of some thirty-five years. He found it unproblematic to incorporate new religious beliefs alongside the Congregationalism in which he had been raised. If he ever reflected in writing on his long-term relationship with Congregationalism, the text has not survived. Probably its culture was so much part of the air that he breathed that, unlike Spiritualism, he thought it unnecessary to defend or explain it. He was introduced to the faith by his father, and his early formation took place at the Poultry Chapel, in the heart of the City of London. The spirit world fascinated him from an early age, and he experimented with automatic writing with the son of the chapel deacon. When Joseph Parker arrived as the new minister, Howard was impressed, and took the initiative in proposing himself as his shorthand secretary, but then he broke away. The circumstances are unclear, although he regularly recounted the anecdote about Parker 'feeling his head' and telling him that he should be a preacher. It is not clear whether he retold the story with a sense of amusement, pride, discomfort, or something else. Years afterwards, he blamed the break on his own intolerance, stating in a sermon delivered in 1912 that unlike himself, Parker had embodied 'the true spirit of tolerance'.[1]

Some years of serious religious exploration in Chicago followed, during which he read widely, debated theological questions with his

---

[1] HALS DE/Ho/F10/26.

Ebenezer Howard: Inventor of the Garden City. Frances Knight, Oxford University Press.
© Frances Knight 2023. DOI: 10.1093/oso/9780198790815.003.0009

Quaker friend Alonzo Griffen, and attended various types of religious meetings. A very important encounter was with the famous Spiritualist Cora Richmond, who became a lifelong friend. His interest in Spiritualism deepened on his return to London, and his first experience of formal public speaking, at the Holborn Literary and Debating Society (the Zetetical Society) was on that topic. Howard was in formal church membership at Rectory Road, Stoke Newington in the 1890s, and it is quite possible that he attended other Congregational churches in London before the move to Stoke Newington. Plenty of people at this date were simultaneously adherents to Congregationalism and Spiritualism, the most famous of whom was W.T. Stead.[2] At Rectory Road, he was immensely in tune with the church's politically active minister, C. Fleming Williams, developing close friendships with him, and with some other ministers during this period, particularly J. Bruce Wallace. Meanwhile, the youthful evangelicalism of his wife Lizzie was giving way to a powerful belief in Spiritualism and spiritual healing, on which she increasingly relied as her health declined. She too was an active member of Rectory Road Congregational Church, speaking at women's meetings, and supporting the Hoxton mission. Having started their marriage with very different religious views, it is apparent that after about a decade their beliefs had converged. Both were energized by the blend of socially active North London Congregationalism and Spiritualism. Howard also drew on the radical strand in the English Dissenting tradition as one of the influences which shaped his views on land-ownership and equality.

The death of Lizzie in 1904, just as the Garden City project at Letchworth was beginning to get off the ground, was the personal tragedy from which he never really recovered. Howard lost his major source of advice and support; after her death, he sometimes said and did things which she might well have counselled against. His ill-judged second marriage created a permanent wedge between himself and his children. His Spiritualist beliefs meant that he hoped and expected to receive messages and guidance from his deceased first wife, but we

---

[2] Stewart J. Brown, *W.T. Stead: Nonconformist and Newspaper Prophet* (Oxford, 2019) pp. 135–64.

know very little about what messages he thought he had received. Undoubtedly, she remained very much in his mind, permanently memorialized in Letchworth's Mrs Howard Hall, in which he spent a great deal of his time, particularly on Sundays. He supported the Letchworth Free Church, as did virtually all of Letchworth's prominent residents in its early days. But although he had laid the foundation stone with the famous Baptist F.B. Meyer, he probably felt most at home in Bruce Wallace's Sunday evening meetings at the Howard Hall, and at the Sunday morning Garden City Adult School. The large contingent of Theosophists in Letchworth meant that he became interested in Theosophy. Bruce Wallace, who operated at the outer limits of avant-garde Congregationalism, was the catalyst for bringing these ideas together, at the Alpha Union at its meetings in the Howard Hall, and later at Annie Lawrence's outdoor adult education centre, the Cloisters.

Howard's Theosophist discoveries permitted him to be cheered by the prospect of reincarnation, which he thought would allow him to continue with his work, more or less unhindered by the inconvenience of death. In 1911, he summarized his thoughts in a letter to Cecil Harmsworth, who as well as being chairman of the Garden City Association and a Liberal politician, was a theology graduate with vaguely Protestant sympathies:

> I have quite made up my mind that soon after giving up this body I will come back again and make a fresh start in a new body, just as I believe the new Garden City must start with a new field. And I am told that although generally about 600 years elapse between one incarnation and another that at this extraordinary juncture of affairs special arrangements are made under which volunteers who have special work to do on this planet can return to Earth within a few years.[3]

The Theosophists believed that reincarnation normally only occurred after many centuries. Howard was clearly hoping to volunteer for a much more rapid re-birth.

What might have happened if Howard had followed Joseph Parker's advice, and become a preacher? Would he have been

---

[3] Howard to Harmsworth, 24 July 1911. The original letter is currently awaiting cataloguing at HALS, with the temporary reference Acc3485. I am grateful to Gary Moyle at HALS for locating it for me.

another R.J. Campbell, spinning out a 'new theology' at an Alpha Union summer school? Possibly, for as he told the journalist who interviewed him in New York in 1925, he had wanted to say 'something original' and not become like a repetitive phonograph record. It is not known what he thought about Campbell's later religious odyssey, which included reconversion to Anglicanism in 1915, but he would have disapproved of his support for the War. Howard does, however, seem to have been interested in Anglican theologians in the last months of his life, with diary references to Charles Raven, Geoffrey Studdert Kennedy and Dick Sheppard. Perhaps he was interested in them earlier, but it is impossible to tell.[4] The Church of England seems to have impinged on him very little. He had not of course needed to accept Parker's suggestion to become a professional preacher in order to preach. He gained his first preaching experience as a young man at the weirdly coincidentally named Ebenezer church, in Howard County, Nebraska. Later, he delivered sermon-like talks in London's Nonconformist churches, and in Letchworth, he was a fairly regular speaker at the Howard Hall.

Howard's cultural background was strikingly similar to that of his closest younger associates, Frederic Osborn and Charles Purdom. All three had emerged from London's small business class, beginning work as teenage office clerks, and relying quite substantially on informal and self-education. All three were also brought up as 'chapel': Howard, as we have seen, in Congregationalism, Osborn in Methodist Sunday schools where he got into trouble for questioning doctrine, and Purdom in the type of Independency which he claimed had 'made Cromwell armies'.[5] But the way in which they reacted to their nonconformist roots seems reflective of the different generations to which they belonged. Howard was born in 1850, Osborn in 1883 and Purdom in 1885. Howard, as we have seen, added ingredients from Spiritualism and Theosophy, but without really subtracting the older elements of his English Protestantism. He continued to be content with its basic structures, seen in his regular reliance on biblical quotations, and attendance at Sunday gatherings where there was

---

[4] All three theologians are noted in his diary for 1927. HALS DE/Ho/F19.

[5] C.B. Purdom, *Life Over Again: An Essay in Autobiography* (London, 1951) p. 6.

preaching, readings and singing. His Jesus was the supreme teacher and example, although possibly not as divine as Joseph Parker would have expected; his God was working in partnership with humanity, to bring about the new world order.

His two younger colleagues, in contrast, severed themselves completely from chapel culture. Osborn focussed his energies on politics and was open about his atheism. He was a life-long supporter of the Labour party and later became active in the British Humanist Association. In later life, he found the still pervasive Christian culture of mid twentieth-century England irksome, but also surprisingly useful. On the one hand, as he complained in a letter to his friend the American Lewis Mumford in March 1943: 'I am patted on the head by Archbishops, who smile at my declared atheism as a form of unconscious Christianity,'[6] but on the other, as he remarked a little over eighteen months later:

> One odd thing about the situation here is that I, as a lifelong, almost instinctive anti-clerical, find myself in alliance with the Anglican Bishops. Partly, I think, as the result of my own work, the Church here (which has influence far in excess of the numbers of its congregations), has clearly seen and stated the connection between house-planning and family idealism; and it is a valuable ally. It is all the more odd because there is no real chance of a revival of large-scale church-going. But people who don't accept the theology of the Church, and have no intention of deserting the prevailing agnosticism, do somehow accept the Bishops as guides in this sort of issue. And just now, for reasons difficult to explain, the Bishops are intelligent and wise. Both the Archbishops are strong supporters of our decentralisation policy.[7]

Purdom, although an original officer of the new Letchworth Free Church, seems to have abandoned his nonconformity within a few years of arrival in the town. He became a regular Sunday speaker at the Howard Hall, and married a Roman Catholic. Returning from

---

[6] Michael R. Hughes (ed.) *The Letters of Lewis Mumford and Frederic J. Osborn* (Bath, 1971) p. 35.

[7] Hughes, *Letters of Mumford and Osborn* pp. 63–4 Osborn's letter was written on 6 October 1944. The archbishops referred to were William Temple and Cyril Garbett. Temple died later that month.

the First World War he seriously considered conversion to Rome, but decided that it was too political and worldly. Then in the 1930s he became an ardent disciple of the Indian mystic, Meher Baba. He remained devoted to him for the rest of his life, publishing five books to expound his teachings.

The vignette of Howard on his deathbed in 1928, instructing Osborn, whom he assumed would be his biographer, to remember that 'the spiritual dimension' had been central to his life and work was the starting point for the present study. He had told him: 'I want it brought out in my life that my absolute belief in a future life was one of those influences which made me dare to do anything for the cause I had at heart.'[8] His renewed interest in séances and Spiritualism in his final years was noted in the previous chapter. His naturally forward-looking orientation became re-directed to looking forward to reunion with Lizzie, and to the possibility of rebirth on earth in a new body, although it is not clear how he thought both could be achieved. Howard's friends knew that his 'spiritual dimension' and belief in a future life was of the utmost importance to him, even if they could not share it. He had a warm friendship with James Leakey, the man who had generously provided him with a home in Guessens Road in Welwyn. They had become friends during Howard's solitary years at Homesgarth. There they had played chess regularly, spoken Esperanto, and shared their memories of London in the final decades of the nineteenth century. Leakey was, like Howard, a non-smoker and a vegetarian, but he did not share Howard's insistent belief in a future life: he reported that Howard had said to him 'whatever you may say, old Leakey, we shall meet again hereafter'.[9]

What was perceived as Howard's 'mystical turn' was the subject of a certain amount of satirical, although apparently affectionate, humour. There was a long-standing joke about the 'oneness of the one' which followed him from Letchworth to Welwyn, and was still being repeated by Osborn after his death. The phrase had originated in a pantomime in Letchworth, possibly written by Purdom, where it was

---

[8] HALS DE/Ho/F27/3 biographical notes dictated to AC Howard by Sir Ebenezer Howard in the presence of Lady Howard on Wednesday 11 April 1928.

[9] Dugald MacFadyen, *Sir Ebenezer Howard and the Town Planning Movement* (Manchester, 1933) p. 189.

intended to evoke Howard's concept of an ideal material and spiritual state in which all opposites would be reconciled and unity achieved.[10] The search for unity, as we have seen, was a central quest for Howard and for many others in Letchworth, and it was one which his close associates, like Osborn and Purdom, must have heard him elaborating upon on many occasions. Howard spoke often of the future, and always with a sense of optimism, and a belief in human improvement, with fraternal unity as the ultimate goal. Lewis Mumford, who was more sympathetic to religion than Osborn, also remembered the nonconformist values which had shaped Howard. Writing in 1945 he commented: 'Heaven help England when the nonconformist streak that Howard represented, with a sort of quaker (sic) gentleness and humility, disappears'.[11] Personal understatement was certainly one of Howard's virtues. Osborn commented in 1950 that there was nothing cult-like about Howard or the Garden City movement: 'He had no fanatical devotees who hung on or pondered his words and obeyed his dictates.'[12]

Howard has often been remembered as the archetypal 'little man' fighting against all the odds to defeat vested interests and reactionary forces and battling for the rights of ordinary people to enjoy decent housing in pleasant surroundings. This picture of him was already well established before his death, and it was rapidly magnified in the immediate aftermath. Bernard Shaw, writing a much-quoted letter of condolence to Howard's son Cecil, memorably described him as 'one of those heroic simpletons who do big things whilst our prominent worldlings are explaining why they are Utopian and impossible. And it is of course they who will make money out of his work'.[13] 'Simpleton' would be offensively derogatory when applied to most people, but Shaw seems to have meant it as a reference to Howard's

---

[10] Robert Beevers, *Garden City Utopia: A Critical Biography of Ebenezer Howard* (London, 1988) p. 173. Osborn recounts a humorous depiction of Howard at the Welwyn pageant in 1923, when an actor played him walking about in a characteristically distracted manner, with the lines 'For though his thoughts are in the skies/ His feet are on the ground.' Howard laughed, along with the rest of the audience. F.J. Osborn, 'Sir Ebenezer Howard: the evolution of his ideas' *Town Planning Review* 21, 3 (October 1950) p. 222.

[11] Hughes, *The Letters of Mumford and Osborn* p. 106.

[12] Osborn, 'Howard' p. 222.

[13] HALS DE/Ho/F22/2 Bernard Shaw to Cecil Howard, 25 May 1928.

unassuming nature, and single mindedness. The newspapers published laudatory obituaries, proclaiming, correctly, that Howard was not only 'the Father of Garden Cities' but 'the Father of Town Planning'.[14] The journal of the GCTPA was particularly fulsome, to the point of sycophantic extravagance in the eyes of the Association's historian, who commented perceptively that within the town planning community, he was mourned 'not so much in the sense of a political as that of a spiritual leader'.[15] Perhaps that is why, even among those who would baulk at the idea of a 'spiritual leader' Howard is remembered still.

James Burns's funeral orations emphasized Howard's humility and selflessness, and his spiritual motivations which had clearly been widely observed. Dugald MacFadyen's popular memoir, which appeared five years after his death, cast Ebenezer Howard as

> A people's hero. Thousands knew him by sight or name, and to them all he was the same – the genial, kindly, eager, spectacled figure – slightly stooping and much occupied with what was going on inside his busy brain – never the autocrat even of a breakfast table – never too busy to speak kindly to an acquaintance, never inclined to rest on his oars or parade his laurels, thinking of workers, unemployed, strugglers, sick, needy folk, and planning to help them if he could, instinctively brave and cautious, cheerful and contented in the present but ambitious and forward looking for the future, not putting this on as a pose, but speaking and acting because he was himself like that.[16]

It was the language of secular sainthood. There was even a sort of glamour attached to his uncomplaining acceptance of poverty: 'Until almost the end Ebenezer Howard was occupied day in and day out in the drudgery of a grinding and ill-paid profession.'[17] This was not something that could said of most of his associates, who tended to be wealthy and successful in the professions or business. Howard matched the criteria for impoverished, saintly humility, in a way that other important figures in the Garden City movement, such as

[14] Dennis Hardy, *From Garden Cities to New Towns: Campaigning for town and country planning, 1899–1946* (London, 1991) p. 212.

[15] Hardy, *From Garden Cities to New Towns* p. 213.

[16] MacFadyen, pp. 193–4.

[17] MacFadyen, *Howard* p. 195.

Ralph Neville, or Thomas Adams, or Cecil Harmsworth, or Theodore Chambers did not.

In the century since his death, Howard has proved to be a very durable hero, the human face who has come to symbolize the efforts of what in fact was a numerous cast of planners, architects, entrepreneurs, craftspeople, clergy, activists, professional and businesspeople who created the two original Garden Cities. Howard has been memorialized in many forms, with plaques, medals, annual lectures, and busts, and in the buildings, boulevards, and the shopping centre that bears his name. The most recent is a striking and beautifully executed seven-foot bronze statue by Ben Twiston-Davies, which was unveiled in Howardsgate in the centre of Welwyn Garden City in 2021.[18] The final stanza of Blake's Jerusalem is inscribed at the base:

> I will not cease from Mental Fight,
> Nor shall my sword sleep in my hand:
> Til we have built Jerusalem,
> In England's green and pleasant land.

Howard holds a spade which artfully strikes through the word 'sword', in a subtle tribute to the pacifism of the man who built the Garden City.

---

[18] See http://www.bentwistondavies.com/ebenezer-howard

Select Bibliography

Archives

Hackney Archives
Uncatalogued records for Rectory Road United Reformed Church, Stoke Newington
Hertfordshire Archives and Local Studies
HALS/DE/Ho Ebenezer Howard papers
HALS/DE/FJO Frederic J. Osborn papers
Garden City Collection, Letchworth
Miscellaneous printed items and photographs, including GCA Annual Reports, and early material relating to Alpha Union, Garden City Adult School, Letchworth Free Church, Letchworth Guild of Help, Methodism, May Day festivities, Arbor Day festivities. Some items may be viewed on-line.

On-line sources

Census records, multiple years
Dissenting Academies Online: Data Base and Encyclopaedia
W.T. Stead Resource Site

Newspapers

Bucks Herald
Cambridge Independent Press
Daily Mail
Daily News
Daily Telegraph
Derby Daily Telegraph
Exeter and Plymouth Gazette
Gloucester Citizen
Hull Daily Mail
Letchworth Citizen
Manchester Courier
Monthly Missionary Herald
Morning Chronicle
Morning Post
Review of Reviews

Sheffield Daily Telegraph
Sheffield Evening Telegraph
Sheffield Independent
Spectator
Sunday Times
The Times
Welwyn Times
Western Times

Reference works

Congregational Year Book
Oxford Dictionary of National Biography
Who Was Who

Printed sources

Adamson, William, *The Life of Joseph Parker, DD.* Glasgow, 1902.

Allwood, Ros, 'Innate Bohemians All: decorative artists in the early Garden City', *Journal of the Decorative Arts Society 1850–The Present* 41 (2017).

Argent, Alan, *The Transformation of Congregationalism 1900–2000*. Nottingham, 2013.

Armytage, W.H.G., *Heavens Below: Utopian Experiments in England 1560–1960*. London, 1961.

Bartie, Angela, Fleming, Linda, Freeman, Mark, Hutton, Alexander, and Readman, Paul (eds), *Restaging the Past: Historical Pageants, Culture and Society in Modern Britain*. London, 2020.

Beaumont, Matthew, *Utopia Ltd Ideologies of Social Dreaming in England 1870–1900*. Chicago, 2009.

Bebbington, D.W., *The Nonconformist Conscience: Chapel and Politics 1870–1914*. London, 1982.

Beevers, Robert, *The Garden City Utopia: A Critical Biography of Ebenezer Howard*. Houndsmill, 1988.

Bellamy, Edward, *Looking Backwards, 2000–1887* (1888). Edited and with an introduction by Matthew Beaumont, Oxford, 2007.

Binfield, Clyde, 'Garden City Religion: The Free Churches of Letchworth and Welwyn', *Chapels Society Journal* 2 (2016).

Booth, Charles, *The Life and Labour of the People in London: Third Series: Religious Influences Vol 1 London North of the Thames: The Outer Ring*. London, 1902.

Booth, William, *In Darkest England and the Way Out*. London, 1890.

Borden, Iain, 'Social Space and Cooperative Housekeeping in the English Garden City', *Journal of Architectural and Planning Research* 16,3 (1999).

Bowie, Duncan, *The Radical and Socialist Tradition in British Planning: From Puritan Colonies to Garden Cities*. London, 2017.

Brake, Laurel, *Print in Transition 1850–1910: Studies in Media and Book History*. Houndsmill, 2001.

Brown, Stewart J., *W.T. Stead: Nonconformist and Newspaper Prophet*. Oxford, 2019.

Buchan, John, *Mr Standfast*. London, 1919.

Buder, Stanley, 'Ebenezer Howard: The Genesis of a Town Planning Movement', *Journal of the American Institute of Planners* 35,6 (1969).

Buder, Stanley, *Visionaries and Planners: The Garden City Movement and the Modern Community*. New York and Oxford, 1990.

Burg, Judith, *Religion in Hertfordshire 1847–1951*. Hertford, 1995.

Byrne, Georgina, *Modern Spiritualism and the Church of England, 1850–1939*. Woodbridge, 2010.

Campbell, R.J., *The New Theology* (1907). London, 1909.

Chandler, Michael, *The Life and Work of Henry Parry Liddon*. Leominster, 2000.

Cowell, Edith, 'Adrian Fortescue', *Blackfriars* IV,41 (1923).

Crawford, John, *The Church of Ireland in Victorian Dublin*. Dublin, 2005.

Dale, R.W. *The Laws of Christ for Common Life*. London, 1884.

Davies, C.M. *Heterodox London: Or Phases of Free Thought in the Metropolis* vol. 2. London, 1874.

Dickinson, H.T., *The Political Works of Thomas Spence*. Newcastle, 1982.

Dillistone, F.W., *Charles Raven: Naturalist, Historian and Theologian*. London, 1975.

Dyson, Erika White, ' "Gentleman Mountebanks" and Spiritualists: Legal, Media and Stage Contest between Magicians and Spirit Mediums in the United States and England', in T. Kontou and S. Willburn (eds), *The Ashgate Research Companion to Nineteenth-century Spiritualism and the Occult*. London and New York, 2012.

Ferguson, Christine, 'Recent Scholarship on Spiritualism and Science', in T. Kontou and S. Willburn (eds), *The Ashgate Research Companion to Nineteenth-century Spiritualism and the Occult*. London and New York, 2012.

Fishman, Robert, *Urban Utopias in the Twentieth Century: Ebenezer Howard, Frank Lloyd Wright and Le Corbusier*. New York, 1977.

Forsyth, P.T., *Religion in Recent Art: Being Expository Lectures on Rosetti, Burne-Jones, Watts, Holman Hunt and Wagner*. Manchester and London, 1889.

Fortescue, Adrian, *The Greek Fathers*. London, 1908.

Freeman, Mark, 'The Decline of the Adult School Movement Between the Wars', *History of Education* 39,4 (2010).

Gaustad, Edward S. and Barlow, Philip L., *New Historical Atlas of Religion in America*. Oxford, 2001.

Hall, Peter and Ward, Colin, *Sociable Cities: The 21st Century Reinvention of the Garden City*. 2nd edn London and New York, 2014.

Hardy, Dennis, *From Garden Cities to New Towns: Campaigning for Town and Country Planning, 1899–1946*. London, 1991.

Hine, R.L., *Relics of an Uncommon Attorney*. London, 1951.

Holden Pike, G., *Dr Parker and His Friends*. London, 1904.

Howard, Ebenezer, 'Spiritualism: A Paper Presented to the Holborn Literary and Debating Society', Medium and Daybreak XI, 16 April 1880.

Howard, Ebenezer, 'Garden Cities: by their Inventor', *Daily Mail*, 22 March 1905.

Howard, Ebenezer, 'Life in the Garden City by its Founder', *Daily Mail*, 25 July 1905.

Howard, Ebenezer, 'Co-operative Housekeeping', *Daily Mail*, 18 August 1906.

Howard, Ebenezer, 'Healthy Homes: A True Remedy for Social Ills', *Daily Mail*, 14 December 1906.

Howard, Ebenezer, 'A New Way of Housekeeping', *Daily Mail*, 27 March 1913.

Howard, Ebenezer, 'A New Outlet for Woman's Energy', *Garden Cities and Town Planning Magazine*, June 1913.

Howard, Ebenezer, 'Housekeeping Wholesale', *Daily Mail*, 15 August 1913.

Howard, Ebenezer, *Garden Cities of To-morrow* (1902). Edited with a Preface by F.J. Osborn and an Introductory Essay by Lewis Mumford. Abingdon, 1965.

Howard, Ebenezer, *To-morrow: A Peaceful Path to Real Reform* (1898). Original Edition and Commentary by Peter Hall, Dennis Hardy, and Colin Ward London, 2009.

Hughes, Michael R. (ed.), *The Letters of Lewis Mumford and Frederic J. Osborn: A Transatlantic Dialogue 1938–70*. Bath, 1971.

Hughes, W.R., 'An Experiment in Social and Religious Education without Credal Limitations – the Alpha Union', *International Journal of Ethics* 19,3 (1909).

Hunt, Tristram, *Building Jerusalem: The Rise and Fall of the Victorian City*. London, 2004.

Hunter, L.S., *John Hunter, DD: A Life*. London, 1922.

Jacob, W.M., *Religious Vitality in Victorian London*. Oxford, 2021.

Johnson, Dale A., *The Changing Shape of English Nonconformity 1825–1925*. Oxford, 1999.

Johnson, J.O. *Life and Letters of Henry Parry Liddon*. London, 1904.

Jones, Peter D'A, *The Christian Socialist Revival 1877–1914*. Princeton, 1968.

Judge, Roy, 'May Day and Merrie England', *Folklore*, 102,2 (1991).

Killingray, David, 'The Pleasant Sunday Afternoon Movement: Revival in the West Midlands 1875–90', in Kate Cooper and Jeremy Gregory (eds), *Revival and Resurgence in Christian History: Studies in Church History. 44*. Boydell, Woodbridge, 2008.

King, Andrew and Plunkett, John (eds), *Victorian Print Media: A Reader*. Oxford, 2005.

Knight, Frances, *Victorian Christianity at the Fin de Siècle: The Culture of English Religion in a Decadent Age*. London, 2015.

Knight, Frances, 'The Victorian City and the Christian Imagination: From Gothic City to Garden City', *Urban History* 48,1 (2021).

Kontou, Tatiana, and Willburn, Sarah (eds), *The Ashgate Research Companion to Nineteenth-century Spiritualism and the Occult*. London and New York, 2012.

Koven, Seth, *Slumming: Sexual and Social Politics in Victorian London*. Princeton, 2004.

Lamont, Peter, 'Spiritualism and the mid-Victorian Crisis of Evidence', *Historical Journal* 47,4 (2004).

Larsen, Timothy, *Crisis of Doubt: Honest Faith in Nineteenth-Century England*. Oxford, 2006.

Lawrence, Annie, *A Dual Day: From a Paper Read at the Adult School, Letchworth, November 1913*. Letchworth, 1913.

Ledger, Sally and Luckhurst, Roger (eds), *The Fin de Siècle: A Reader in Cultural History* c.*1880–1900*. Oxford, 2000.

Lewis, Brian, *'So Clean': Lord Leverhulme, Soap and Civilization*. Manchester, 2008.

Livingston, James C., *Religious Thought in the Victorian Age: Challenges and Reconceptions*. New York and London, 2006.

MacFadyen, Dugald, *Sir Ebenezer Howard and the Town Planning Movement*. Manchester, 1933.

MacKenzie, Norman and Jeanne, *The First Fabians*. London, 1977.

Maddren, Maureen, *Letchworth Recollections: A Unique Record of Life in the First Garden City as Remembered by some of its Earliest Citizens 1903–1939*. Baldock, 1995.

McLeod, Hugh, *Piety and Poverty: Working Class Religion in London, Berlin and New York 1870–1914*. New York and London, 1996.

McNab, Chris, *St Christopher School: A Short History*. Oxford, 2014.

Meacham, Standish, *Regaining Paradise: Englishness and the Early Garden City Movement*. New Haven and London, 1999.

Mearns, Andrew, *The Bitter Cry of Outcast London* (1883). Anthony S. Wohl (ed.), Leicester, 1970.

Meller, Helen, 'Planning Theory and Women's Role in the City', *Urban History Yearbook* 17 (1990).

Miller, Mervyn, *Letchworth Garden City*. Stroud, 1995.

More, Thomas, *Utopia* (1516). London, 1965.

Morris, William, *News from Nowhere and Other Writings* (1890). London, 1993.

Moss-Eccardt, John, *Ebenezer Howard: An Illustrated Life of Ebenezer Howard 1850–1928*. London, 1973.

'New Townsmen', *New Towns After the War: An Argument for Garden Cities*. London, 1918.

Nichols, Aidan, *The Latin Clerk: The Life, Work and Travels of Adrian Fortescue*. Cambridge, 2011.

Noakes, Richard, 'The Sciences of Spiritualism in Victorian Britain: Possibilities and Problems', in N. Bown, C. Burdett, and P. Thurschwell (eds), *The Victorian Supernatural*. Cambridge, 2004.

Noakes, Richard, 'Spiritualism, Science and the Supernatural in mid-Victorian Britain', in T. Kontou and S. Willburn (eds), *The Ashgate Research Companion to Nineteenth-century Spiritualism and the Occult*. London and New York, 2012.

Oppenheim, Janet, *The Other World: Spiritualism and Psychical Research in England 1850–1914*. Cambridge, 1985.

Osborn, Frederic J., 'Sir Ebenezer Howard: The Evolution of His Ideas', *Town Planning Review* 21,3 (1950).

Ottewill, Roger, ' "Brief, Bright and Brotherly": Assessing the Relationship between the Men's Own Brotherhood Movement and Congregationalism in Victorian Hampshire', *Journal of the United Reformed Church History Society* 10,3 (2018).

Ottewill, Roger, 'Churches and Adult Education in the Edwardian Era: Learning from the Experiences of Hampshire Congregationalists', in Morwenna Ludlow, Charlotte Methuen, and Andrew Spicer (eds), *Churches and Education: Studies in Church History 55* Cambridge, 2019.

Owen, Alex, *The Darkened Room: Women, Power and Spiritualism in Late Victorian England*. Chicago, 1989.

Parker, Barry and Unwin Raymond, *The Art of Building a Home: A Collection of Lectures and Illustrations by Barry Parker and Raymond Unwin*. London, 1901.

Parker, Joseph, *The City Temple: Sermons Preached in the Poultry Chapel, London, 1869–70*. London, 1870.

Parker, Joseph, *Ad Clerum: Advices to a Young Preacher*. London, 1873.

Parker, Joseph, *None Like It: A Plea for the Old Sword*. London, 1893.

Parker, Joseph, 'The Rebuilding of London', *The English Illustrated Magazine* May 1895.

Pearson, Lynn, F., 'Ideal Homes: Women and Cooperative Housing in Victorian Times', *Ekistics* 52, 310 (1985).

Pierce, Bessie Louise, *A History of Chicago: The Rise of the Modern City 1871–1893*. Chicago, 1957.

Podmore, Frank, *Modern Spiritualism: A History and a Criticism*. London, 1902.

Purdom, C.B., *The Perfect Master: Shri Meher Baba*. London, 1937.

Purdom, C.B., *Meher Baba by His Eastern and Western Disciples*. London, 1939.

Purdom, C.B., *The Building of Satellite Towns*. London, 1949.

Purdom, C.B., *Life Over Again: An Essay in Autobiography*. London, 1951.

Purdom, C.B., *Three Incredible Weeks with Meher Baba*. London, 1954.

Purdom, C.B., *God to Man and Man to God: The Discourses of Meher Baba*. London, 1955.

Purdom, C.B., *The Letchworth Achievement*. London, 1963.

Purdom, C.B., *The God-man: The Life, Journeys and Work of Meher Baba with an Interpretation of his Silence and Spiritual Teaching*. London, 1964.

Raven, Charles, *The Creator Spirit: A Survey of Christian Doctrine in the Light of Biology, Psychology and Mysticism*. Cambridge, 1927.

Readman, Paul, 'The Place of the Past in English Culture, *c.*1890–1914', *Past and Present* 186 (2005).

Richardson, Benjamin Ward, *Hygeia: A City of Health*. London, 1876.

Robbins, Keith, 'The Spiritual Pilgrimage of R.J. Campbell', *Journal of Ecclesiastical History* 30, 2 (1979).

Rouse, W.H.D., 'May-Day in Cheltenham', *Folklore* 4,1 (1893).

Shaw, George Bernard, *John Bull's Other Island*. London, 1904.

Shaw, Nellie, *Whiteway: A Colony in the Cotswolds*. London, 1935.

Spencer, Herbert, *Social Statics: Or, the Conditions Essential to Human Happiness Specified, and the First of Them Developed*. London, 1851.

Stetz, Margaret D., 'Publishing Industries and Practices', in Gail Marshall (ed), *The Cambridge Companion to the Fin de Siècle*. Cambridge, 2007.

Tappan, Cora, *Discourses Through the Mediumship of Mrs Cora L.V. Tappan – The New Science, Spiritual Ethics.* London, 1875.

Thacker, Joy, *Whiteway Colony: The Social History of a Tolstoyan Community.* London, 1993.

Thompson, David M. 'The Emergence of the Nonconformist Social Gospel in England', in Keith Robbins (ed), *Protestant Evangelicalism: Britain, Ireland, Germany and America c.1750–c.1950 Studies in Church History Subsidia 7.* Oxford, 1990.

Tidy, Josh, *Letchworth Garden City in Old Photographs.* Letchworth Garden City, 2016.

Tidy, Josh, *A–Z of Letchworth Garden City.* Stroud, 2018.

Tidy, Josh and Aimee Flack, *Arts and Crafts in Letchworth.* Letchworth Garden City, 2017.

Tizot, Jean-Yves, 'Radical Legacy or Intellectual Indelicacy? Ebenezer Howard's use of "the most admirable project of Thomas Spence" in the Garden City Concept', *MIRANDA* 13 (2016).

Unwin, Raymond, *Town Planning in Practice: An Introduction to the Art of Designing Cities and Suburbs.* Second edition London, 1911.

Walford, Edward, *Old and New London Volume 6.* London, 1878.

Walker, Nathaniel Robert, *Victorian Visions of Suburban Utopia: Abandoning Babylon* Oxford, 2020.

Watts, Michael R., *The Dissenters Volume III: The Crisis and Conscience of Nonconformity.* Oxford, 2015.

Yoshino, Ayako, *Pageant Fever: Local History and Consumerism in Edwardian England.* Tokyo, 2011.

Unpublished PhD thesis

Noble, David, 'Primitive Methodism in Hertfordshire from 1838 to 1932'. University of Hertfordshire, 2021.

Index

For the benefit of digital users, indexed terms that span two pages (e.g., 52–53) may often appear on only one of those pages.

Abercrombie, Patrick 2–3
Aberdeen, Lady (Ishbel Hamilton-Gordon, Marchioness of Aberdeen and Temair) 127–8, 130
Aberystwyth 157
Adams, Thomas 81–2, 85–7, 91, 101–3, 105–6, 118, 122–3, 143–5, 205–6
Addison, Christopher 178–9
Adelaide 78–9
Alden, Percy 85–6
Allon, Henry 21
Alpha Union 146–7, 156–61, 163–4, 167–8, 199–200
  Summer schools 157–60, 200–1
American Transcendentalists 24, 27–8, 91–2, 166–7
Anderson, Tempest 85–6
Anglicans 142–3
Arbor Day 24, 134–8
Arts and Crafts style 78–9, 91–2, 116–17, 124–7, 133–4, 154, 170
Automatic writing 14–15, 24–5, 198
Ayot St Lawrence 88, 196–7

Baba, Meher 149–51, 202–3
Baillie-Scott, M.H. 116–17
Baldock 114–15, 121–2, 142–3
Barnardo, Thomas 196
Barnett, Henrietta 51–2, 92–5, 122–3
Barnett, Samuel 51–2, 92–3, 114–15
Bebbington, David 2–3
Beevers, Robert 4–5, 7–8, 55, 63–4, 106, 122–3
Belgian refugees 173
Bellamy, Edward, *Looking Backward 2000–1887* 55–7, 66–7, 91–2, 123–4, 176
Benn, John Williams 58–9, 85–6
Bennett and Bidwell, architects 116–17, 154, 188

Berry, Sydney 143–5
Besant, Annie 159–61
Bhagavad Gita 163–4
Bible 162–4, 166–7, 201–2
Bible, parts of
  I Samuel 7–12, 25
  Isaiah 2:1–5 166–7
  Isaiah 55:2 66
  Matthew 15:8 166–7
  Luke 4:18–19 166–7
  Luke 6:46 165–6
  Luke 18:9–14 165–6
  Romans 14:1–13 165–6
  I Corinthians 15 43–4
  II Corinthians, 6:14 36–7
Bichener, Percy 152
Bills, Emma 11–12
Binfield, Clyde 6–7, 58–9
Birkenhead 193–4
Blake, William 195–6, 206
Boer War 81–2, 90
Boot, Jesse 184–5
Booth, Charles 58–9
Booth, William 60–2, 66–7, 73–4, 196
Borden, Iain 130
Bourne, Francis 171–2
Bournville 81–2, 86–8, 90–1, 106, 113–14, 117, 126–7, 141–2
Bracher, Samuel Veale 67–8
Branch, James 58–9, 67–8, 80–1, 84
British Humanist Association 3, 202
British Museum 178–9
Brooke, Stopfold 85–6
Brotherhood Church 80–1, 146–7, 152–4
Brotherhood Church, Croydon 67–8, 146–7
Brotherhood Church, Southgate 66–7, 146–7
Brotherhood Hall, Letchworth 152–4

Brotherhood movement (formerly Pleasant Sunday Afternoon movement) 152–4
Brotherhood newspaper 152–4, 157
Brown, Ford Madox 115–16
Buckingham, James Silk 72–3
Buder, Stanley 4–5
Burns, James 194–7, 205

Cadbury, Edward 100–3, 141–2, 175, 184–5
Cadbury, George 81–2, 85–7, 141–2, 175, 184–5
Callow, Alice 100–1
Cambridge 92–3, 138–9
Campbell, R.J. 23, 143–5, 157–9, 200–1
Canberra 2–3
Carnegie, Andrew 83–4
Carpenter, Edward 114–15
Catchpool, Egerton 196–7
Central School of Arts and Crafts, London 168–70
Chambers, Theodore 183–4, 186–7, 189–91, 205–6
Channing, William Ellery 43–4
Chatham 178–9
Cheap Cottages Exhibition 118
Chesterfield 115–16
Chesterton, G.K. 163–4
Chicago 26–32, 44–5, 54, 191–2, 198–9
Christian Social Union 91
Church of England 75, 147, 189–90, 200–1
City Temple (Congregational) 16, 23–5, 143–5, 157–8
Clairvoyance 23, 96–7
Clifford, John 60–1, 85–6
Cloisters, Letchworth 146–7, 154–6, 163–4, 167–8, 199–200
Cobb, W.F. 100–1
Cockburn, John 136–7
Cockerell, Douglas 168–72
Colby, Clara Bewick 159–60
Collyer, Robert Laird 29–30
Comte, August 22
Congregationalism 1, 13–23, 28–9, 58, 80–2, 94–5, 102, 141–2, 146–7, 152–4, 190
Congregational Union 50–3
Congregational Union Hall, Farringdon 67–8, 80–1, 89–90, 107–8

Cooperative housing 57–8, 123–30, 177–80
Cooperative movement 119–20
Corelli, Marie 85–6
Countryside, depletion of 61–2, 72
Cowell, Edith 171
Cowlishaw, W.H. 154–6
Crane, Walter 78–9, 85–6
Crickmer, Courtenay 116–17, 125–6, 168–70, 188
Crickmer, Mary 168–73

Daily Mail 82, 118, 120–1, 125–7, 129–31, 139, 173–5, 185–6, 189–92
Daily Mirror 82, 96–7
Daily News 102–3
Daily Telegraph 82, 85–6
Dale, R.W. 51–2
Darwin, Charles 163–6
    Descent of Man 27–8
Davidson, Samuel 21
Davies, C.M. 43–4
Dearmer, Percy 170
Derby Daily Telegraph 89–90
Desborough, First Baron Desborough 182–3
De Soissons, Louis 188
Dickens, Charles 78–9
Dickman, George 71–2
Digswell 180–3, 189–90
Draper, W.H., *Intellectual History of Europe* 27–8
Dublin 37–9, 62–3

Ebenezer Church, Howard County, Nebraska 25, 200–1
Ecumenism 145–9, 151–2, 171–2
Ede, William Moore 85–6
Edinburgh 101–2
Ely and Burnham, Chicago stenographers 27
Emerson, Ralph Waldo 27–9, 163–4, 166–7
Empire Day 134–5
Esperanto 138–9, 168–70, 191, 203
Evangelicals 143–7, 149–51, 167

Fabians 45–6, 56–7, 87–8, 126–7, 171–2
Fairbairn, A.M. 51–2
Farquharson, J.R. 183–4

Farrar, F.W. 72
Figgis, J.N. 159–60
Fin de siècle 2–3, 81–2, 90, 92–4, 114–15,
   141–2
First Garden City Company Ltd 103–6,
   121–2, 131–4
First World War 81–2, 130–1, 173,
   177–9, 190–1
  Conscientious objectors 173–4,
    185–6
Fishman, Robert 5–6
Fortescue, Adrian 148–9, 159–60,
   168–73
  The Greek Fathers 168–70
Freeman, Mark 166–7
Free thought 154–68
Furze, Michael 189–90

Garden Cities
  Acceptance of concept 81–7, 89–94,
    106, 131–2, 178–9
  And anxieties about the English
    race 81–2, 90, 107, 136–7
  And press coverage 81–6, 90–1,
    106–7, 120–1, 125–31, 139
  And women 80–2, 92–5, 130–1,
    163–4
  As described in *To-morrow* 72–5
  Howard's initial ideas about 33,
    49–50, 58–9, 62–6, 75
  Howard's later reflections on 75–6, 79
  Howard's slides and diagrams of 64,
    67–8, 73–5, 77–8
  Religion in 75, 141–73, 189–90
Garden Cities and Town Planning 138–9
Garden Cities and Town Planning
   Association 122–3, 139–40,
   178–83, 204–5
Garden Cities of To-morrow 2, 49–50, 67–8,
   78–9, 139, 163–4, 176
  See also *To-morrow: A Peaceful Path to
   Real Reform*
Garden City Adult School 146–7,
   149–51, 160–5, 167–8, 199–200
Garden City Association 80–91, 93–5,
   99, 101–8, 126–8, 131–2,
   138–40, 142–3, 200
Garden City Pioneer Company 89–90,
   102–4
Garden City Theosophical School 160–1

Garden Suburbs 137–9
  See also Hampstead Garden Suburb
Gaunt, W.H. 122–3
George, Henry 52–3, 56–7, 91–2
Gillie, R.C. 143–6
Gorst, John 72, 85–6
Grand, Sarah 85–6, 89–90
Grant, Annie 80–1
Grey, Fourth Earl, (Albert Henry George
   Grey) 86–7, 89–90, 107, 139–40
Griffen, Alonzo 27, 30–2, 91–2, 198–9
Gurney & Co, parliamentary
   stenographers 33–4

Haggard, Rider 136–7
Hall, Newman 15–16
Hall, Peter 5–6
Hampstead Garden Suburb 92–3, 122–3
Hardy, Dennis 5–6, 180
Hare, Harold 136–7
Harmsworth, Cecil 82, 85–6, 200, 205–6
Harrison family 14–15, 24–5
Hatfield 180–2
Hellerau 2–3
Helmsley, Marjorie, Vicountess 92–5
Hertfordshire County Council 185
Hignett, Cecil 116–17, 133–4
Hill, Octavia 92–3, 103–4
Hitchin 92–3, 104, 142–3, 149–51,
   168–70, 173
Hockley, Essex 67–8
Holborn Literary and Debating Society
   (the Zetetical Society) 1, 45–6,
   48–9, 164–5, 198–9
Holiday, Henry 85–6
Holland, Henry Scott 85–6
Holyoake, George Jacob 85–6
Homesgarth 58, 125–30, 177–8, 203
Homestead Act, 1862 25
Hooker, Stenton 96–7
Housing Act, 1919 186–7
Housing Act, 1921 185
Housing of the Working Class Act,
   1890 132–3
Howard, Ann, b.1818 (née Tow,
   mother) 10–13, 23–4, 57–8, 70–1
Howard, Annie, b.1847 (sister) 57, 109–10
Howard, Cecil, b.1883 (Arthur Cecil,
   son) 39–40, 109–10, 192–3,
   196–7, 204–5

Howard, Clara, b.1857 (née Bills, sister-in-law) 11–12, 34
Howard Cottage Society 125–6
Howard, Ebenezer senior b.1818 (father) 10–13, 15–16, 23–4, 40, 57–8, 70–1
Howard, Ebenezer b.1850
  Advice to biographers 3, 48–9, 203
  American influences 24–32, 41, 62–3, 91–2, 191–2
  Attitudes to First World War 173–9, 190–1
  Attitudes to landownership 25–6, 38, 49–50, 52–7, 65, 84, 198–9
  Attitudes to London 10, 55, 74–5
  Childhood 10–15
  Death and funeral 3, 194–6
  Education 6–7, 12–15
  Employment 15–24, 26–7, 33–4, 99–100, 102, 105–6, 138–9, 186–7
  Feminist sympathies 30–1, 49, 92–3, 126–7, 130–1
  Finances 37–41, 57, 89–90, 98, 102–3, 106, 110–12, 138–40, 192–5, 205–6
  Health 23–4, 26, 32, 193–5
  Historiography relating to 4–6
  Interest in Congregationalism 12–13, 15, 17–19, 29–30, 49–50, 198–9
  Interest in 'cooperation' 61–2, 65–6, 72, 103–4, 118–20, 123–4, 148, 164–5
  Interest in reincarnation 200
  Interest in Spiritualism 30–2, 42–50, 112–13, 158–9, 161–2, 176, 192–3, 198–200
  Interest in supernatural phenomena 14–15, 79
  Interest in 'unity' 29–30, 147–8, 164–5, 167, 177–8, 203–4
  Irish influences 37–9, 62–3
  Life in Letchworth 109–31, 134–9, 161–78
  Life in Welwyn 186–7, 192–3
  Marriage
    to Edith Hayward 110–12
    See also, Howard, Edith, b.1864
    to Lizzie Bills 34–41, 97–100
    See also Howard, Lizzie
  Posthumous reputation 203–6

  Religious life in summary 6–7, 161–2, 198–206
  Spiritual epiphanies 10, 48, 55, 75–7, 176, 180, 182–3
Howard, Edith, b.1864 (née Edith Annie Hayward, second wife of Ebenezer Howard) 110–12, 129, 174–5, 186–7, 192–7
Howard, Edith/Editha, b.1882 (Mrs Berry, daughter) 39–40, 49, 68, 98, 109–10
Howard, Elizabeth b.1848 (Mrs Harrison, sister) 12–13, 15, 23–5
Howard Hall (the Mrs Howard Memorial Hall) 112–13, 136–7, 146–7, 149–51, 159–66, 174–5, 177–8, 199–201
Howard, Harry b.1859 (brother) 12, 23–4, 57, 69–70, 101–2
Howard, Kathleen b.1881 (Mrs Rawlinson, daughter) 39–40, 49, 109–10, 186–7
Howard, Lizzie b.1853 (née Elizabeth Ann Bills, first wife of Ebenezer Howard)
  Courtship and wedding 34–7
  Death 100–1, 110–12, 199–200
  Early years of marriage 37–41
  Final years of marriage 96–100
  Health 36–7, 41, 68–9, 94–100
  Interest in Spiritualism 42–3, 49, 68–9, 96–8, 198–9
  Involvement with Garden City work 71–2, 92–7, 101–2
  Memorial (the Mrs Howard Hall) 112–13
  Public speaking 51–2, 58–9, 94–7, 101–2
  Religious views 34–7, 49, 97–8, 146–7, 151
  Tensions with husband 41, 95, 97–100, 106
Howard, Margery b.1890 (Doris Margorie, daughter) 39–40, 109–10
Howard, Muriel b.1886 (deceased infant daughter) 39–41
Howard, Tamar b.1856 (sister) 23–4
Howard, Thomas b.1855 (brother) 23–4, 34

Howardsgate, Welwyn Garden City 206
Howgills Friends Meeting House,
    Letchworth 154, 161–2
Hoxton Mission 95–6
Hughes, Hugh Price 51–2
Hughes, W. Ravenscroft 156–8
Hugo, Victor 78–9
Hunt, J.B. 189–90
Hunter, John 161–2
Hyndman, H.M., *The Nationalisation of
    Land in 1775 and 1882* 53–4

Ideal Village 185–6, 191
Idris, Thomas 84–6, 102–3
Intentional communities 43–4, 79
International Garden Cities
    Association 2–3, 138–9, 190–1
International Federation of Town and
    Country Planning and Garden
    Cities 191

Jackson, R.W. 145–6
Jefferson, Thomas 43–4
Jesus Christ 79, 95–6, 149–51, 165–6,
    201–2

Keeble, S.E. 159–60
Kenworthy, J.C. 67–8
Kerr, Alexander 195–6
King Edwardstown 137–8
King's Cross station 106–7, 109–10,
    180–3
Kitchin, George 85–6
Koran 163–4
Kropotkin, Peter 79

Labour Party, including Independent
    Labour Party 56–7, 174–5, 202
Lady's Pictorial 93–4
Lambeth, St Saviour (Church of
    England) 34, 36–7
Lamont, Peter 42–3
Land Nationalization Society 66–7,
    84, 156
Lander, H. Clapham 116–17,
    126–7, 188
Lawrence, Annie 146–7, 154–6, 160–1,
    163–4, 167–8, 199–200
Leakey, James 186–7, 203
Leng, John 80–2

Letchworth Brotherhood Literary and
    Debating Society 152–4
Letchworth estate 102–6, 113–14,
    131–2, 142–3, 149–51
Letchworth Garden City 105–6, 109–10,
    113–23
  Anglicans in 142–3, 147–9
  Baptists in 145–6, 148–9
  Business activities in 132–4, 148–9,
    167–8, 173
  Congregationalists in 143–6, 148–9
  Creation of 2–3, 80–1, 113–23
  Elim Pentecostals in 152
  Free Churches in 142–61
  Methodists in 145–6, 151–2, 167–8
  Mormons in 152
  Old Catholics in 160–1
  Plymouth Brethren in 152
  Quakers in 154, 163–4, 173
  Religion in 141–72
  Roman Catholics in 142–3, 148–51,
    168–72
  Salvation Army in 147, 152
  Shopping in 185–6
  Spiritualists in 160–1
  Theosophists in 142–3, 160–1, 163–4,
    183, 199–200
Letchworth Free Church 143–51,
    161–2, 195–6, 199–200
Letchworth Guild of Help 147–9, 171–2
Letchworth Men's Adult School 166–8
Letchworth, St Hugh (Roman
    Catholic) 170, 173
Letchworth, St Mary the Virgin (Church
    of England) 100–1, 142–3
Letchworth Trades Council 130–1,
    174–5
Lever, Elizabeth 94–5
Lever, William Hesketh 81–6, 89–90,
    100–4, 141–2, 184–5
Liberal Party 81–2, 131–2, 174–5
Liddon, Henry Parry 15–16
Lodge, Oliver 48–9
London, City of 10–12, 182–3
London, City of Westminster and
    environs 33, 74–5
London County Council 34, 58–9, 61–2,
    67–8, 80–1, 84–6
London housing conditions 50–2, 57–9,
    61–2, 95–6

London Housing Reform Union 118–19
London Spiritualist Alliance 75, 79
Longfellow, Henry 166–7
Lucas, Thomas Geoffry 116–17, 154
Luminiferous ether 46–8

McDonald, Ramsay 174–5, 184–5
MacFadyen, Dugald 4–5, 19–20, 146–7, 205
MacFadyen, Norman 173–4, 182–3
McNeill, John 90–1
Malgarth, Ellen 100–1
Manchester 101–2, 115–16, 122–3, 137–8
Manchester Courier 83–4
Mann, Tom 33, 66–7, 72
Mansion House 96–7
Marnham, Herbert 143–5
Marshall, Alfred 33, 66–7, 72–3, 79, 85–6
Marx, Karl 56–7, 64
May Day Revels 110–12, 134–6, 148–9
Meacham, Standish 5–6, 91–2
Meadow Way Green 58, 125–6, 130–1
Mearns, Andrew, and Preston, W.C., *The Bitter Cry of Outcast London* 50–2, 95–6
Medium and Daybreak 45–6
Methodist Conference 51–2
Meyer, F.B. 85–6, 143–5, 199–200
Midland Bank 183–4
Millthorpe 115–16
Mirfield, Community of the Resurrection 159–60
Monthly Missionary Herald 90–1
Montreux 157
More, Thomas, *Utopia* 56–7, 79
Morison, Herbert 173–4
Mormons 40
Morris, William 79, 114–16, 163–4
Moses 79
Moss-Eccardt, John 4–5
Mumford, Lewis 2–3, 149–51, 191–2, 202–4

National Council of Adult School Unions 162, 166–7
National Council of Evangelical Free Churches 145–6
National Garden Cities Committee 178–9

Nationalization of Labour Society 66–8
Nebraska 24–6, 122–3, 136–7, 200–1
Neville, Ralph 81–2, 84–90, 92–3, 101–6, 122–3, 205–6
New Earswick 117
New Towns Act, 1944 2–3
New York 40–1, 191–2
New York Times 191–2
Northcliffe, Viscount 82, 191
Northcroft, George 91, 99, 101–2
Norton village 110–12, 151, 166–7
  Norton, St Nicholas (Church of England) 142–3
  St Michael's, Norton Way (Church of England) 142–3

Osborn, Frederic 2–5, 29–30, 34–5, 39–40, 49, 98, 109–12, 149–51, 173–4, 178–87, 191–2, 194–7, 201–4
New Towns after the War 178–80
Ottewill, Roger 152–4

Pageants 134–5
Paine, Thomas, *Age of Reason* 30–1, 43–4
Panshanger 182–3
Parker, Barry 91–2, 105–6, 109–10, 113–17, 143–5, 188, 190–1
  The Art of Building a Home 114–15
Parker, Joseph 7, 16–25, 58–9, 68–9, 143–5, 157–9, 165–6, 198, 200–1
Paton, J.B. 51–2, 85–6
Paul 79
Paxton, Joseph 63–4
Pearsall, Howard 89–90, 98, 102–3, 129
Perceval, John 85–6
Phonoplayer 192–3, 196–7
Phrenology 18–19, 198
Plato 79, 120–1, 163–4
Pleasant Sunday Afternoon movement (*see* Brotherhood movement)
Podmore, Frank 43–4
Port Sunlight 102, 106, 117, 141–2
Poultry Chapel (Congregational) 7, 15–16, 24–5, 198
Preaching 15–19, 25, 163–7, 195–6, 200–1
Progressive League 157–8
Pryse, Gerald Spencer 139–40

Pullman, George 83–4
Purdom, Antonia 171
Purdom, Charles 110–12, 143–7,
        149–51, 161–2, 178–83, 186–8,
        190–1, 201–4
    Garden Cities After the War 178–9

Quakers (Society of Friends) 126–7,
        141–2, 146–7, 154, 159–60, 190
Queen Victoria 51–2

Raven, Charles 193–4, 200–1
Rea, Hope 160–1, 163–4
Reckitt, Juliet 154
Rectory Road Church (Congregational)
        Stoke Newington 49–50, 58–61,
        67–8, 70, 77, 94–5, 100–1, 143–5,
        198–9
Reeves, William 55
Regional Planning Association of
        America 191–2
Reichenbach, Karl von 46–7
Reiss, Richard 182–4
Remington typewriter company 1,
        39–41, 69–70, 109–10, 191
Richardson, Benjamin, *Hygeia: A City of
        Health* 31–2, 62–3
Richmond, Cora (also known as Cora
        Scott, Hatch, Daniels and
        Tappan) 1, 30–2, 43–5, 49, 71–2,
        91–2, 193–4, 198–9
    *Discourses through the Mediumship of Mrs
        Cora L.V. Tappan* 43–4
Ritzema, Thomas 102–3
Roman Catholic Church 75, 142–3, 147,
        168–73, 190
Rose, Lily 100–1
Rosebery, Fifth Earl of 72
Rothermere, First Viscount 82
Royal Commission on the Housing
        of the Poor 51–2
Royal Commission on Labour 33, 66–7
Ruskin, John 78–9, 114–15, 163–4

St Christopher's School,
        Letchworth 146–7
Salisbury, Fourth Marquess of 178–83,
        189–90
Salt, Titus 83–4
Salvation Army 60–2, 147

Savill, Norman 182–3
Science 14–15, 19–20, 42–8, 164–5, 167
Séances 44–5, 112–13, 193–4
Second Garden City Pioneer Company
        Ltd 183–4
    See also Welwyn Garden City Company
Shaw, George Bernard 1, 45–6, 87–8,
        175–6, 196–7, 204–5
    John Brown's Other Island 88
Sheffield 69–70, 101–2, 115–16
Sheffield Daily Telegraph 106–7
Sheffield Evening Telegraph 93–4
Sheppard, Dick 193–4, 200–1
Shorthand 15–16, 26–8, 33–4, 45–6, 68,
        112–13, 138–9, 178–9, 192–3
Sitte, Camillo 116
Small Dwellings Acquisition Act,
        1899 131–2
Social gospel 49–52, 58–62, 65
Society of the Golden Fleece 28–9
Spence, Thomas 53–4, 56–7, 65, 72–3
Spencer, Herbert, *Social Statics* 54–7, 65,
        72–3, 165–6
Spicer, Albert 81–2
Spirella factory 133–4, 186–7
Spiritualism 30–2, 42–9, 69–72, 96–8,
        100–1, 112–13, 142–3, 159–60,
        167, 195–6
Spurgeon, Charles Haddon 15–16
Stark, A.E. 146–7, 152–4
Stead, W.T. 50–1, 60–1, 198–9
Steere, F.W. 84
Stenography machines 39–40
Stoke Newington 11–12, 58
    See also Rectory Road Church
Strachey, John St Loe 118
Studdert Kennedy, G.A. 193–4, 200–1
Swing, David 28–9
Symons, Arthur 139–40

Talbot, Edward S. 85–6
Taylor, W.G. 178–9
Teetotalism 72, 180–1
Tennyson, Alfred 163–4
    The Idylls of the King 94–5
Theosophy 142–3, 146–7, 157, 160–1,
        167, 195–6, 199–200
The Times 44–5, 82, 86–7, 121–2
    Sunday Times 83–6
Thomasson, Franklin 102–3

Tillet, Ben 72
Tizot, Jean-Yves 53–4
Tolstoy, Leo 67–8, 79, 163–4
To-morrow: A Peaceful Path to Real Reform
        1–2, 7–8, 31, 78, 80–2, 95–6,
        107–8, 113–14, 118–19, 162
    See also *Garden Cities of To-morrow*
    Analysis of text 72–5
    Early drafts 62–3, 67–8, 75
    Howard's later reflections on 75–6
    Launch of 76–7, 176
    Publication of 71–2
Town Planning Act, 1909 131–2
Toynbee, Arnold 114–15
Treadwell, William 34, 39–40
Twiston-Davies, Ben 206
Tyndall, John 44–7, 164–6
Typewriters 39–41
    See also phonoplayer

Unionville 62–4
Unitarianism 146–7
Unwin, Raymond 2–3, 91–3, 105–6,
        109–10, 112–17, 122–5, 142–3,
        190–1
    The Art of Building a Home 114–15,
        124–5

Vasanta Hall, (Theosophist/Spiritualist)
        Letchworth 160–1
Vegetarianism 142–3, 158–9,
        177–8, 203

Wakefield, Edward Gibbon 72–3
Wallace, Alfred Russel 84–6

Wallace, J. Bruce 66–8, 80–1, 85–6,
        99–100, 109–10, 123–4, 146–7,
        152–4, 156–64, 167, 198–200
Ward, Colin 5–6
Warwick, Daisy (Frances, Countess of
        Warwick) 85–6, 89–90, 92–3
Webb, Sidney 1, 45–6, 171–2
Wells, H.G. 85–6, 120–1, 125–6, 128,
        132–3, 175
Welwyn Free Church 190, 195–6
Welwyn Friends Meeting House 190
Welwyn Garden City
    Creation of 2–3, 180, 183–6
    Development of 187–9
    Religion in 189–90
Welwyn Garden City Company 192–3
    See also Second Garden City Pioneer
        Company Ltd
Welwyn, St Francis of Assisi (Church of
        England) 189–90
Welwyn Stores 187–8
Whiteway Community 67–8
Whitley, J.H. 81–2
Whitman, Walt 91–2, 163–4
Whittier, John Greenleaf 98
Wickstead, Philip 171–2
Williams, Aneurin 56, 122–3, 139–40
Williams, Charles Fleming 58–9, 61–2,
        67–8, 77, 84–6, 146–7, 198–9
Williams, Clifford Fleming 146–7
Willian, All Saints (Church of
        England) 142–3
Winnington-Ingram, A.F. 85–6
Wolfson Economics Prize 5–6
Women's Liberal Federation 92–3

Titles in the series include

Walter Lippmann
American Skeptic, American Pastor
Mark Thomas Edwards

Mark Twain
Preacher, Prophet, and Social Philosopher
Gary Scott Smith

Benjamin Franklin
Cultural Protestant
D. G. Hart

Arthur Sullivan
A Life of Divine Emollient
Ian Bradley

Queen Victoria
This Thorny Crown
Michael Ledger-Lomas

Theodore Roosevelt
Preaching from the Bully Pulpit
Benjamin J. Wetzel

Margaret Mead
A Twentieth-Century Faith
Elesha J. Coffman

W. T. Stead
Nonconformist and Newspaper Prophet
Stewart J. Brown

Leonard Woolf
Bloomsbury Socialist
Fred Leventhal and Peter Stansky

John Stuart Mill
A Secular Life
Timothy Larsen

Christina Rossetti
Poetry, Ecology, Faith
Emma Mason

Woodrow Wilson
Ruling Elder, Spiritual President
Barry Hankins